THE RATHER BORING LIFE OF THOMAS H.

TOM WATSON

ISBN: 978-1-922788-79-5
Published by Vivid Publishing
A division of Fontaine Publishing Group
P.O. Box 948, Fremantle
Western Australia 6959
www.vividpublishing.com.au

A catalogue record for this
book is available from the
National Library of Australia

1 MILLNESS

One morning some time ago I awoke in a lovely house, with perfect parents, two sisters and blonde curly hair. The eyes of a child are fickle as I clearly remember just a few years later that everyone lived in a better house, everyone had better parents, brothers and straight brown hair.

The house I woke in that morning was 3 Millness Row a council house in Millness. Millness is a hamlet in the county of Westmorland, England. Millness Row was a group of four council houses that were built in the early fifties for low-income families. There were more council houses like this dotted around South Westmorland in hamlets and villages all built to the same design and in hamlets in groups of four and it would appear in villages in groups of up to twenty. They were built, of course, to fulfil a housing shortage in a booming Britain. On reflection, I'd say these houses were foisted on any village or hamlet with a flat field that was easy to build on.

Britain was going through a population explosion, although there was not yet the sexual freedom I was to see in my lifetime, there was a lot of it going on. Contraception was crude, condoms unreliable, the Crawford's method was both noisy and subject to operator error and young men made promises they were unable to keep. Marriage guidance was different then, and often given in a firearm-related manner. I'm quite sure my parents married for love because they were much older than those of my peers and were, of course, loving parents.

The people of Millness Row were all different, very different. At number one were the Blairs, Mr and Mrs Blair and their son Ian, a couple of years older than me. Mr Blair was very tall, about six feet I'm guessing and never seemed to wear a hat. Probably because it would interfere with the weather, him being so tall. Another thing about Mr Blair was his hair was always straight and flat, I thought perhaps because his head was always rubbing on ceilings and things. Mr Blair had an important job with the Ministry of Agriculture and a black car that he kept in a garage where his front lawn should have been. I don't remember Mrs Blair, but I do so hope she had red curly hair as her son Ian did and it didn't come from Mr Blair. If Mr Blair had an important job with the Ministry of Agriculture, why was he living in a council house?

At number two were the Haytons, Mr and Mrs and children Susan and Keith, Mrs Hayton was 'hot' I remember her and I liked Susan and Keith, who were younger than me. I liked them not so much as playmates but because the Haytons had a television and I liked television. Mr Hayton, Dick worked for Marley Tiles and had a Marley Tiles van which was parked at varying angles on the road outside number two. Dick frequented the *Gatebeck* Working Mens' Institute in Endmoor most evenings hence the parking angles. The Haytons were designed for council houses.

Number three housed the Watsons, Tom and Mabel Watson were a couple in their forties with young children, I called them Mum and Dad. Tom was a farmworker who worked on his father's farm 'Cox Bank' some two miles away. The Watsons didn't have a car and Tom cycled to and from work every day. Tom smoked a pipe and wore a trilby hat whenever he went outside, even then his hair wouldn't flatten like Mr Blair's but he wasn't as tall.

Mabel was homely, not only in appearance but in demeanour, she could create something out of nothing in the kitchen so hunger was never a problem at number three. Marion the eldest child by four years was always rather studious and good at school, she was a nice girl. Thomas, the middle child had had the miss fortune to be Baptised with two

Christian names, Thomas Hodgson, with a name like that one would have at least thought it could have been Americanised and become Thomas Hodgson Watson the Third but no, he'd been lumbered good and proper. I think I would have preferred 'Sue'. At secondary school one class teacher always referred to me as Thomas H. I rather liked that, it would have done me. Thomas was a boy and as such did not like girls much, he had blonde curly hair and with it became noticeable on the lanes of Millness. Thomas would often look unkempt and carried it with aplomb into being scruffy, he wasn't a nice kid. Barbara, the youngest child by about eighteen months was a moody little bitch or at least seemed that way to the casual observer. She was in fact, quite nice and understood boys and could play with them and I assure you mix it with them, she kicked a mean shin. Council houses were designed for people like the Watsons.

Number four Millness Row housed the Duffs, Mr and Mrs Duff and their daughter Ellen, I don't remember Ellen she was much older than us, grown-up I think. Mr and Mrs Duff were old, like really old, in their fifties I'd guess and poor. The Watsons at number three were poor but the Duffs were poorer, much poorer. From memory, Mr Duff was in the army, the Salvation Army and probably not paid very much but what the Duffs lacked in wealth they sure made up with kindness, they were very kind. I clearly remember Mr Duff giving me some broad bean seeds, I planted them and have been hooked on gardening ever since.

Every Sunday we'd see Mr and Mrs Duff walk to the bus to play in the Salvation Army band in Kendal. Mr Duff with his rather tarnished big silver thing you blew in to make a noise, I think it may have been a euphonium and Mrs Duff with her handbag. I'm sure Mrs Duff would have played the tambourine or the triangle, yes I could see Mrs Duff playing the triangle, but I'm sure Mrs Duff would have been a triangular virtuoso. The Duffs didn't belong in Millness.

The rest of the people of Millness lived across the road, there were eight more houses, a mill and a farm.

2 WHAT MILLNESS HELD

The most important thing Millness had was water or to be more pacific watercourses, four of them to be exact, two man-made and two natural. There is nothing quite like a watercourse to get the blood of a young boy up because, we all know, that water is an essential ingredient in mud which in its wild state and far enough away from soap, is fun.

The closest watercourse was the 'mill race' a concrete-lined stream that was designed to drive the watermill which in my time was never used as a mill. This stream ran quite fast and as it was concrete-lined not very good for making mud. This watercourse was however ideal for 'boat races' where it went under the road. A 'boat race' is when you and your friend throw a stick each into the water at one side of the culvert in this case and see which one comes out first, there cannot be a draw. As the mill race ran quite fast this exercise sharpened up your reflexes and your speed across the road.

There was a natural stream which ran into the river Bela and this had mud aplenty and hours of my time were spent there. The river Bela was most times way too big for a little kid like me but it somehow formed an island where there was a u-bend in the river and sometimes in early autumn when the water was very low the three Watson kids would wade across the river onto the island guided by big sister Marion. This expedition was, I thought a great adventure but it was for financial gain and serious business. The island, out of bounds most of the year harboured a great bounty, rosehips, we Watson kids picked rosehips, the fruit of the wild rose and sold them at school for threepence a pound. If we'd worked as a team we would have been champions but we were selfish little buggers and kept our threepences to ourselves. The rosehips were used to make rosehip syrup which was full of vitamin 'c' and good for babies we were told.

The watercourse which brought the most adventure, mystique and fear was the canal, which of course, wasn't a watercourse at all but just a long, stagnant pond, albeit a very long one. The Lancaster-Kendal canal hadn't been used for over a hundred years but was still maintained to a degree, the towpath was mown every year.

The canal harboured swans that could break your legs with their wings or even peck you. It had water you couldn't see through but you would surely drown in if you fell in it. It had ice sometimes in winter which would break and you would drown in the coldest water when you fell through it, why wouldn't a kid spend half his life there?

It seems there was one redeeming feature of the canal, fish, course water fish, perch, roach and pike. I think I caught one of these fish once or more likely acquired one, a perch reputedly the best eating of the three, it was bloody awful.

Once or twice a year my canal was invaded by fishermen (No women.) they arrived on a coach and walked slowly over the bridge and down the steps to the towpath, all the time in single file and picked their spot on the bank of the canal. These men were uniform in their attire and their equipment, they all wore flat caps and tweedy sort of jackets and carried a cane fishing basket and a fishing rod in a long canvas bag, but none of them wore a smile. They were silent and once setup motionless unless they caught a fish.

Brave as I was around older people there was no way I was going to tread on that towpath while those psychopaths were stationed there. I always had visions of being hurled into the canal by one of these weirdos for daring to make an utterance that may scare the fish. Having tasted one of these fish, it had my little brain confused as to why you would travel on a coach to catch the bloody things, it was obvious they didn't enjoy the process. I've never quite embraced fishing.

There were no children my age in Millness so I had to be friends with kids either older or younger. The Hayton kids next door had a television but the closest to my age was Susan and she was a girl so it was rather hard to mix with them even though the television made hard things easier. There was Neil Watson(No relation.) in the bungalow across the road, two years older than me, a biggish lad with straight blonde hair (Why did everyone have straight hair?) Neil was nice enough and would take me on adventures and tell me how exciting they'd been and the miles we'd travelled and none of it was true. Neil was something of a bullshit artist and at number three Millness Row honesty took pride of place so I found my relationship with Neil difficult.

The other boy I could be friends with was Max Falkner who lived in one of the Mill Cottages and then at the mill when his father became the manager. Max was also older than me and dull and didn't do adventure, the only thing Max had going for him was the mill. The mill was no longer a mill but a stockfeed outlet for J.Pye and Co and as such had the most beautiful smell which was engrained in the wooden floorboards, I can't describe it, it was well, a mill smell and I loved it. It was addictive and poor Max was my drug dealer, I imagine as close to crime as Max would ever get.

My very best friend in Millness was Dick Bainbridge, Dick wasn't a child he was around thirty I'd say and had a wife and lots of little kids, much too young to be played with. Dick had a cowshed (shippon) full of cows which he milked night and morning. I can't remember which milking I attended, probably both as I was besotted. I, all two foot six of me helped Dick with the milking, I imagine most of this help was in a supervisory capacity. I must have spent hours mesmerised by the milking of cows and being Dick's friend.

What was it that drew me to the milking of cows? Was it the swaying of the cows' udders, I don't think so, as I never really became a tits-man in my adult years. It sure as hell wasn't the smell of warm fresh milk as I've always found that rather repulsive, it must have been the hypnotic pulsing click of the milking machines. Having a friend like Dick was great, there were no expectations from me and as long as Dick turned up for milking I was happy. These were days of innocence.

One day Dick and his cows disappeared, I don't know where they went but in one day they were gone. I was shattered and ran home in tears to be consoled by my loving mother. Mum, I'm sure would have explained what had happened to Dick and I'm sure it was nothing dreadful but to this day it remains a mystery to me. That day must have started the decline of my innocence and led me to be less trusting of others, especially adults.

3   COX BANK

I'm not sure how often but from time to time Mum would walk my younger sister Barbara and me to Cox Bank, my grandfather's farm some two miles away. Big sister Marion never seemed to do this trip with us, I'm thinking she would have been at school. This was a long walk for a little kid and little sister Barbara had the luxury of a push-chair for which I was too big. The most eventful part of this journey was the walk through the yard at Preston Patrick Hall, I'd say you could call Preston Patrick Hall the manor farm and the owner Kenneth Pumphrey the lord of the manor, he certainly had that air about him. In saying that he wasn't all-conquering and above the level of the common man but almost nurturing of the farmers surrounding his large farm, a man before his time, a Quaker.

Preston Patrick Hall smelled of silage, a rare smell in those days, Mr Pumphrey was a pioneer of silage-making in the area. The yard of the Hall was surrounded by large buildings totally out of canter with the usual farm buildings of the day, it was an exciting place with tractors, livestock and activity most times we passed through. You walked through one gate to enter the yard and through another to leave and although the gates were almost always open (It was a thoroughfare.) you always had this feeling of entering and leaving. After we had left the yard there was a field with a pond in it and a gaggle of Chinese geese or at least that's what we called them, exotic to a simple child.

We walked on to 'Hall Wood', the track became goatworthy and there were trees and a deep ghyll with a stream gurgling along its bottom on one side and a high hedge on the other, quite eerie for a little kid but I braved it out. We left the wood and within a few moments, Cox Bank came into sight those simple buildings on the side of the hill meant the world to me. They also meant 'Dad time', as dad worked on the farm we didn't see that much of him as the hours were long. Here at Cox Bank, I could spend hours with Dad and I did, just trailing along behind him like a dog, absorbing his every move and worshipping the ground he walked on. My favourite thing was sitting between Dad's legs on the seat of the Ferguson tractor, I was grown-up then.

I remember taking the sheep to Camsgill to be dipped because Camsgill had a 'state-of-the-art' dipping facility if there could be such a thing. This tradition was to go on for many years after the Watsons left Cox Bank. My time with Dad was precious.

I think that I lived in a time when grandparents in general were old and didn't much like or understand their grandchildren, my relationship with my grandparents was distant. I liked Grandad Watson, he was nice enough and rather dapper and he didn't seem to wear work clothes like dad. Granny Watson was a large lady, not in height but in girth, Mum was what in the day was called stout but Granny Watson would make two of her. By my estimations, Granny Watson was almost as wide as she was high. I worried about her because even with my limited knowledge of physics I knew that if she fell over there was no way she could get up again and living on the side of a hill as she did she could easily roll away never to be seen again. If something like the aforementioned was to befall Granny Watson I would never again taste her bread and butter.

Now Mum could make bread, good bread but not like Granny Watson's bread. Granny Watson made the best bread, it was never really fresh but it was great, rather firm and then the Granny Watson touch, the slicing, Granny Watson could slice her bread about half the thickness of modern-day sliced bread. And then she carefully smeared it with her bright yellow butter and a limited amount of raspberry jam and why wouldn't you worry about her having an accident? Again,

Mum could make butter, usually when there was a surplus of milk and in a bottling jar that was shaken for what seemed like days but it was pale anaemic stuff not like Granny Watson's.

The kitchen at Cox Bank was not like the modern one at three Millness Row, it had a wood stove not electric like ours and it had ham and bacon hanging from the ceiling, it was always cool and there were paraffin lamps also hanging from the ceiling and a smell. It was the kind of place a young boy could sit at a giant wooden table and be mesmerised and I often was as we enjoyed our afternoon tea before heading home to Millness.

Cox Bank had its downside, only one, actually there was more than one and they were called guinea fowl. These bloody things I believe are related to peacocks but possess no tail and very little brain and strongly dislike little boys. Why these monstrosities were tolerated at Cox Bank I'll never know but sadly they were. I saw no use for these birds as they never seemed to get eaten and laid small spotted eggs which no doubt my mother snook into the odd cake without my knowledge. The sole purpose these things existed seemed to be to fly across the yard at Cox Bank and scare the living daylights out of me. I think they may have been classed as exotic but I lived in fear of these awful creatures.

There was a mystery at Cox Bank, at least for me, in the form of Cyril, Cyril was around twenty I guess, educated at Heversham Grammar School, he drove grandad's car, wasn't their son and worked on the farm. He was a relation, but I didn't know how? He was nice enough and I thought he was rather cool and always kind to me. I'm sure I would have asked how Cyril was related to us but I must have gotten one of those answers which wasn't an answer that my parents were rather good at. It was a mystery to me for years and my lack of knowledge never really hurt me and did Cyril's image no harm at all. He was, I discovered much later, my cousin, the illegitimate son of my Post Mistress Aunty Margaret and raised by my grandparents. I presume my parents couldn't explain the 'illegitimate' bit of the story or preferred not to.

All good things come to an end and that was the journey home, little boys get tired and this little boy was no exception, the goat track through Hall Wood was tough on little legs, even though it was downhill and dusk would be around making the wood darker. It always felt like forever before we reached Preston Patrick Hall where the road got smoother and the knowledge that home was getting closer brightened my spirits. What did brighten my spirit was again entering the yard at Preston Patrick Hall and there was a new activity in the air, it was milking time. The place still smelled of silage but the air was electric literally. Preston Patrick Hall had electricity, powered by a water-driven generator on the Bela river.

Mr Pumphrey was very much before his time. This electricity meant the whole place was lit up like a Christmas tree and buzzing with the hypnotic pulsing of the milking machines and men rushing back and forth. I could have just stood there forever soaking up the (At least to me.) excitement in the air. Mum doesn't share my delirium and hurries me up and we head home for our evening meal. Those were the days I cherished the days I spent at Cox Bank and the excitement of Preston Patrick Hall, life was simple then.

4 THE END OF LIFE EXPERIENCE

Life in Millness was perfect for the happy-go-lucky Watson kid, although he didn't have friends his age he had made friends with himself and that was to hold him in good stead in the tumultuous years ahead. The day was to come when all this easy life was to end and according to the adults around him things were going to be wonderful. Adults don't understand kids or kids wouldn't have to cry. That day when my life was forced to change was 25th February 1954, the day I turn five and had to go to school.

Now, I'd been told this experience would be wonderful and I'd make new friends my age, I'd learn to read and write and I'd enjoy it. This, of course, was a load of bollocks dreamt up by adults who know nothing about kids.

Endmoor Church of England Primary School was about a mile and a half up the road and we got there by bus - we being my big sister Marion and I - I liked bus rides. I don't remember my first day at school, I imagine the horror of it erased all memory. I do remember the school seemed to be divided into three groups of children, girls, village kids and country kids. Well, the girls were girls, the village kids lived in Endmoor and already knew each other so didn't mix with my leftover bunch of country kids.

Regardless of the huge divide we were all put in the same class, even at five years of age, I could see this stupid social experiment wasn't going to work, regardless the teachers persevered with this experiment. For the first time in my life, I had to live to a timetable, I had to do what every other kid did.

Our school day started with assembly ably led by the headmistress Mrs Bryers who was dreaded by every child in the school, even me who'd never met her before. We sang a hymn and said a prayer and it was off to our respective classes. My class was for the new kids I'm guessing we all turned up on our fifth birthday as I had but on reflection, there must have been a time when all the kids born that year started school, I presume it was after the Easter holidays if they had a later birthday.

At lunchtime, I had to hold the hand of a girl and walk the couple of hundred yards to the canteen and eat beetroot. I didn't like beetroot. I must admit that school meals were generally good, except for beetroot, they were designed with our health in mind, stewed rhubarb and custard, stewed figs and custard, one or the other each week to keep our bowels moving. I didn't need these bowel openers in my already healthy diet and the addition of these foods (Which I liked.) caused me to lose control of my bowels during class, I was a 'pants shitter'. I think it could be said I was a 'serial pants shitter', although this was embarrassing and it shames me to admit it. It did have an upside, girls weren't queuing to walk hand in hand to the canteen for lunch and teachers didn't ask you to stand up in front of the class to read aloud (Something I dreaded.).

I wasn't the most popular child in school but in return, school wasn't too popular with me. The regimentation was hard for a kid who loved to wander, the learning wasn't too hard but at times seemed pointless, who gave a toss what Dick and Dora did, they had the most boring lives. Spelling was a waste of time because the teachers never spelt words how they sounded or how I would spell them. Sums, arithmetic, now that was my field, it was black and white straight forward and I could do sums without writing them down.

I must have been a lazy child as I never really warmed to writing, I could write alright and reasonably neat but I just didn't like doing it, I didn't like doing most things at school. Of course, I wasn't the only child with a chip on his shoulder about school I'd say most of the country kids had problems adapting to the system and socialising in this new world but we eventually started talking to each other and becoming friends.

I think the thing I learned best in my first few years at school was avoidance, how to avoid being the best or the worst in the class because being best meant you usually had to show off your work in front of the whole class and that meant standing up to read what you'd done. If you were the worst the teachers thought ridicule would be a great motivator and drive you on to better things, of course, this never worked and would be frowned upon today.

The social experiment I disliked so much drove me to mediocrity and a love of school holidays when I could again wander and go to Cox Bank. I felt for the first time my parents had let me down, they had told me I'd enjoy school and learn and be clever and all I'd learnt so far was how to avoid reality. I disliked school with a passion and adults weren't fairing too well in the equation either.

5　BATH NIGHT

Now school had been inflicted on my life all I had was weekends and holidays and perhaps the odd day when I could pull off a serious dose of hypochondria. Weekends were now a mixed bag, good and evil – and I mean serious evil. Saturday started well enough with my usual wander and search for dirt but I had to be home in the afternoon as every Saturday afternoon the Watson kids got a white paper bag filled with sweets. A quarter of a pound of the sweetest sweets ever made, we never knew what we were to get just that they were sweet and we had spent seven days deprived of sugar.

This bag of sweets lasted all of thirty minutes unless they were hard ones and had to be sucked for an eternity and then it could take an hour to dispose of the bag's contents. Where these sweets were bought I don't know, all I do know was they turned up each Saturday in good times and bad, the one constant in our lives. We never got pocket money like other kids but we always got our quarter pound of sweets every Saturday.

Saturday night was bath night at three Millness Row as I believe at every other house across Britain in those days and probably now. Now everyone knows water runs downhill so when you see a tub of it upstairs in a council house you know something is wrong, it's unnatural for water to be upstairs, it's out of its natural environment and it shouldn't be there. But it was and we had to be cleaned in it. We, my younger sister Barbara and me.

The one thing I learned from this unnatural exercise was that girls seem to have a design flaw, no 'willy'. Not only did they wear stupid clothes they are, because, of this design flaw, forced to squat or sit to do a wee and must wear knickers to stop their insides from falling out. Perhaps I'm being a little harsh on the other species and should be more understanding of their dilemma, after all, I had a willy and could wee standing up and not worry about my insides falling out.

My mother was the kindest most gentlewoman ever to take oxygen but on bath night she turned into a monster. Mum kindly guided us into the bath and we sat facing each other - me wondering how I can fix my little sister's design flaw - when mum takes up the - rather carelessly named - soap. It was in reality, a small brick of granite, infused with some noxious chemical that makes your eyes sting beyond belief and has twelve razor-sharp edges which would cut all but the toughest kid in Millness to shreds.

This carelessly named piece of soap takes time and vigorous rubbing against a delicate child's skin to lather and to adult eyes isn't working unless it lathers. Yes, my gentle kind mother has in a few seconds turned into a monster, vigorously rubbing every part of my body (Even parts as a five-year-old I didn't want a woman rubbing.) with that razor-edged granite brick that was now diffusing its noxious chemical infusion. This granite brick was also used to wash my hair and of course, the noxious chemical flooded my eyes and no amount of tears seemed to clear this blinding chemical nor soften my mother's resolve to cleanse me. We seemed to survive this weekly torture and even forgave Mum. Torturous as the bath was it didn't seem to stop me from getting dirty, but that had to wait until Monday as the Sabbath had to be celebrated.

Some Sundays we went to Church. Now, I'm not sure what the rules were here but it was from time to time. We were the only people in Millness Row who went to Church, the Blairs never went, the Haytons most certainly didn't and the Duffs were playing in the Salvation Army Band - little did I know that that counted as Church in the eyes of God. At least four other people in Millness went to Church every Sunday. Albert and Ruby Falkner and Ruby's mother and father Mr and Mrs Coates. Albert and Ruby went twice every Sunday as Albert was a Churchwarden and Ruby was the organist. This means that Max, the Falkner's son must have gone too but I have no memory of it.

When it was raining we didn't go to Church but the Falkners did. Rain, hail or shine the Falkners went to Church twice every Sunday, rain or hail they walked, shine they took the car. Albert was a car polisher and didn't take his car out in the rain, this was a great source of amusement for Dad who didn't have very high regard for Albert. I presume this is why we referred to them as Albert and Ruby, respected members of the community always had first names like Mister or Missis.

Dad never went to Church, he was too busy in the garden or had something else to do so we three kids went with Mum. I was never quite sure why we went to Church, it was not the least bit exciting, in reality, it was boring and the worst thing was putting money in the collection, we'd only just got the money the moment before we left the house and now we had to part with it, not fair.

The Church was a large building on the top of a hill, less than half a mile away. I liked the building and I liked the single bell which rang out from its tower as we walked to Church, most likely rung by Albert. I didn't mind the hymns but was often confused as to when to stand, sit or kneel. The Vicar seemed to ramble on a bit and the whole thing was something I couldn't understand, it made me curious as to why people went to Church and Dad didn't.

Sunday lunch was always a roast, the scrag end of some dead animal or other which was all we could afford from our butcher, my uncle Chris, Mum's brother. Roast potatoes or new potatoes in season and whatever vegetable was ready in the garden. After lunch, with the washing-up done we all took off for a walk. I loved walks, it was time with Mum and Dad and it was a wander, which as a wanderer, took me further than my wanders took me, it was the best. Of course, these walks were mystery tours, would it be Watery Lane? The lanes of Milton? Or would it rain and stuff the whole thing up and I'd have to sit at home and play with my hand-me-down toys?

Weather permitting, the walk would always happen and we kids would search the hedgerows for food. Wild strawberries were a favourite, blackberries, Mum would have brought a tin for us to put them in, wild raspberries and even wild gooseberries, they were a touch sour, sloes and crab apples also left a sour taste but if they were there we'd find them. Foraging was second nature to the Watson kids and Mrs Watson could jam or preserve almost anything. On reflection, I think Sunday was a day to keep clean after Saturday's bath and walking down country lanes with Mum and Dad seemed a good way to keep fairly clean.

6 CONFLICT

I would have been seven years old when the conflict between adult and child took a stronger hold. It would seem I had been gifted with parents who had no understanding of children at all and although my mother made all the right noises or tried to I was not convinced. Mum was the one left to do the communicating, Dad just made the decisions and Mum passed the inevitably bad news to us or so it seemed to me. I still loved to trail around after Dad, ride on the tractor with him at Cox Bank and generally worship the ground he walked on. Perhaps this was because it was Mum who gave us all the bad news.

One day out of the blue Mum announced that Granny and Grandad Watson were to retire and they had started to build a bungalow at Gatebeck Lane-End. Before Mum had finished her little story I was elated. This meant that Dad would take over as the farmer at Cox Bank and we would go to live there and I would leave school and help Dad on the farm. Seems I hadn't quite got it right and all my dreams and aspirations were killed off with Mum's next line. "Cox Bank will have to be sold and Dad will have to look for another job." Mum quietly related to us.

I knew this was rubbish as the eldest son always takes over the farm and his eldest son leaves school to help on the farm and I could say goodbye to school forever. I didn't buy Mum's story and told her she was wrong and Dad had to take over at Cox Bank, tears ensued. Mum did her best with what she had and tried to explain to a distraught child that Granny and Grandad weren't rich like other farmers and that the money from the sale of Cox Bank would be needed for their new bungalow.

I now realise in the wisdom inherited from my loving parents that Dad probably never wanted to inherit Cox Bank and was only too glad to see the back of the place. Dad had seen his father battle for years as a tenant farmer and it was only in the later years that he had had the opportunity to buy Cox Bank and most likely still owed money on it.

It all came to pass and Cox Bank was sold to a farmer from Barrow for his son Jack Beck, who had a young wife and son, it was loudly proclaimed (By my grandmother.) that their son had been conceived out of wedlock. My grandmother was bitterly jealous of the new owners of Cox Bank and spent many hours at her new home, a mile and a half away, watching them through binoculars. Mum was greatly amused by this and rather liked the young man who had taken over at Cox Bank as he never passed her on the road, he always stopped and gave her a lift. Much as I disliked the demise of the Watsons at Cox Bank and the fact I still had to go to school, I too rather liked this young man.

Well, life went on and as a result of Granny and Grandad leaving Cox Bank, we seemed to get a couple more uncles and aunts. Two of Dad's brothers lived quite a long way away, Uncle Jack lived in Yorkshire somewhere and Uncle Dick lived near Preston in Lancashire.

When my uncles and aunties visited Granny and Grandad at Cox Bank their whole time was taken up there as it had been my uncles' home too. Now Cox Bank was gone we got to share their visits, even though it stuffed up our Sunday walks it was pleasant enough and for some reason, children seem to like relatives.

Uncle Jack had a motorbike and sidecar which for a little boy is a package of excitement. Uncle Jack rode the motorbike with authority and Aunty Agnes rode in the sidecar, cocooned in her glass-topped box. Uncle Jack was next in age to Dad and they seemed to get on well, I liked the sound of his motorbike. Aunty Agnes always seemed to be wearing a lot of clothes so you couldn't get very close to her, I suppose the clothes were to keep her warm in the (I'm just guessing.) rather draughty sidecar. They didn't have any kids so were always kind to us, I liked their visits, they were a byproduct of the demise of Cox Bank, so perhaps my parents weren't that bad.

Uncle Dick was Dad's youngest brother, a small dapper chap with a small dapper car and I liked him. He worked for a large building company in Preston and had a smallholding where he reared poultry. He had been in the war and Mum told us he'd been a prisoner of war and escaped in a laundry basket, which made him extra exciting. He never spoke of his war service back then but opened up about it in later years.

Uncle Dick's wife Aunty Margaret was a smallish woman with a degree of roundness, she wasn't fat just round and follically challenged. She had hair but not a lot and on Saturday before she visited us, she must have visited the hairdresser and had what little hair she had coloured, teased and spread over her head to make her look glamorous. The trip to the hairdresser and the money spent was wasted.

Aunty Margaret had a strong Lancashire accent and wasn't afraid to use it, she could breathe in through her nose and still blow out of her mouth. She would have been a master with the didjeridoo. I bet there were times when Uncle Dick wished he had a motorbike and sidecar like Uncle Jack.

The Watsons from Preston did cause a little confusion for my lazy brain as I already had an Aunty Margaret and she was the Post Mistress in Endmoor. Mum simplified it for me by making Aunty Margaret from Preston, Aunty Margaret from Preston and Aunty Margaret the Post Mistress, Aunty Margaret from the Post Office.

The confusion continued as the Watsons from Preston had two children, Norman who was older than my sister Marion and Marion who was my age. I already had a sister Marion but this was much easier as in England, all children have a prefix to their name, it's 'our' or in the case of someone else's child 'your'. If you are speaking in the absence of a parent it is of course 'their'. So it was simple to define which Marion you were talking about if it was our Marion, we'd say 'Our Marion' if in the presence of Uncle Dick and Aunty Margaret and talking about their Marion we'd say 'Your Marion' and in the absence of Uncle Dick and Aunty Margaret and talking about their daughter it would be 'Their Marion'. I didn't much like 'Their Marion', she had inherited her mother's strong Lancashire accent and her didjeridoo playing skill and she was a girl.

These extra relatives were nice in small doses and unlike my parents didn't bombard me with bad news. I don't remember seeing them much around birthdays and Christmas, they probably were much too busy around that time of year.

7 MY DISCOVERY TIME

My years of mediocrity at school were to come to an end. Because of my generation, our school had to change. There were too many of us kids born in nineteen forty-nine and there wasn't enough room for all of us in the original school building. This was remedied by making another classroom in the canteen just for our year. This classroom was to be called the 'annexe', now I had no idea what an annexe was but it did sound exotic, I'm sure we just carried on calling it the canteen.

This had upsides galore, no more having to walk hand in hand with a girl, to and from the canteen, we only had to walk one way each morning after assembly. We were at the canteen and could smell what we were to have for lunch - it would seem that beetroot doesn't have a smell. We had the playground to ourselves on breaks, we didn't have to share it with big bullying kids or small annoying kids. Uncle Chris was the school butcher so I got to see him, albeit, from a distance. He was also Mrs Foss' butcher so took her order when he delivered the school's meat.

The real upside of this move was having Mrs Foss as a teacher. Mrs Foss was in her late thirties, tall and seemed to wear a lot of hound's tooth-checked suits, with dignity I should add. She was childless, which was a mystery to me because all married women of that age had children. For some dumb reason, I rather liked Mrs Foss, it was hard for a boy who disliked school with a passion to actually like a teacher.

It must have taken Mrs Foss all of ten minutes to spot my mediocrity, and she pounced on me like a seagull on a chip, I was done for. I didn't become the teacher's pet, I became the teacher's pet project, she seemed driven to extract me from my mediocrity and reach my full potential. It didn't take her long, in no time I was up with the best of them: Colin Redmayne, David Metcalf, Tony Mason, but I couldn't reach my nemesis, Gwen Clarke.

Gwen was a year younger than the rest of us, her mother was president of the Women's Institute and a J.P. don't tell anyone, but I was secretly in love with Gwen. Gwen was best at everything scholastic, but may have lacked in the sporting department but was drop-dead gorgeous, she always looked immaculate and had what drives eight-year-old boys into a sexual frenzy, long black plaits. Not that I knew what a sexual frenzy was or had any ability to exercise it, I was just secretly besotted.

The very best thing Mrs Foss did for me, was introduce me to Mole and Ratty. Yes, for about fifteen minutes before we left school for home, each day Mrs Foss read 'Wind in the Willows' to us. I was entranced by the lives of the mole and the water rat, so much like the life I wanted to live, and was making every effort to live. I couldn't wait for the next chapter to be read, while that book was being read to us I couldn't even catch hypochondria, I just had to be at school for the next reading. I was becoming seriously close to enjoying school. This enforced social experiment that I thought was fraught with disaster a couple of years earlier was, it seemed, starting to work.

On the home front, something was going on and I wasn't privy to it. There had been a family meeting of the Hodgsons, Mum's family and Dad had attended. Dad didn't usually get involved with Mum's family, so something was afoot. It wasn't long before I found out what was afoot, a foot my arse, it was a mile and a half.

Mum had elected herself as my Grandad Hodgson's carer and we were to go and live at Ivy Garth, my grandparents' home. Added to this catastrophic news was the fact that Dad had refused to live at Ivy Garth unless Mum and Dad had ownership of the place, and let's face it my parents weren't very financial. Added to the debt my parents had put themselves in, was the fact that when Grandad died we couldn't cut and run, we were lumbered with this place. Without the encumbrance, our stay could have been brief as Grandad Hodgson had been in no sort of health in my eight years.

As usual, my parents had stuffed up, Ivy Garth, as the real estate people would say; 'Was inconveniently located in the historic hamlet of Goose Green.' Historic, as nobody under the age of ninety, lived there and inconvenient as it was miles off a bus route. And then there was the matter of Granny and Grandad Hodgson, two of Goose Green's younger residents and they were old.

I don't think I'd spoken to either of my Hodgson grandparents, Grandad Hodgson was always sick and we never seemed to have any conversations. Granny Hodgson was stone deaf so there was no point talking to her.

The house, Ivy Garth was dark, damp and miserable, it was old with bulging walls, not new and modern like 3 Millness Row. Yes, my parents had got themselves into debt beyond their wildest nightmares (There was no vendor finance.) and we three kids were being dragged along into a life of poverty and misery, living with our least loved grandparents. In hindsight, of course, my father had made a very sound decision and freed himself from a lifetime of rental accommodation, I was only eight, so I didn't have much hindsight.

My life seemed doomed, I was happy in Millness, let's face it, I would have become Lord Mayor of Millness in the next couple of years, such was my fame there. Now I had to move a mile and a half up the road to Goose Green and reclaim some semblance of authority in a new hamlet.

There seemed to be very little foot-dragging going on and things seemed to get swiftly done. No sooner had I found out about this disastrous move than it was on. A truck, which during the week carried livestock, and was owned by a distant cousin of Dad's arrived at 3 Millness Row was loaded with our modest furniture, and driven the mile and a half to Ivy Garth.

Of course, our furniture and Granny and Grandad's furniture

wouldn't fit into Ivy Garth so some of it was stored in the farm-style building adjoining the house. I had forgotten in my disgust and horror at having to move to Ivy Garth, that it had extra buildings and three acres of land. There was also a large garden, raspberries, blackcurrants, rhubarb, an apple tree and a driveway and a gate with a metal plaque saying 'Ivy Garth'. Not only had I lacked hindsight in my exuberant youth, but I'd also lacked foresight, and what looked like the end of the world was only just the beginning.

I got a bedroom to myself, Marion and Barbara shared the larger bedroom and now I'm confused as to where Mum and Dad and Granny and Grandad slept. I have a feeling Granny and Grandad slept downstairs away from the upstairs bathroom as there was a 'guzunder' emptying every morning. I had been right about the house being a hell-hole, for a few moments each morning it was a smelly hell-hole, and our lives were being turned upside down.

We had to learn how to communicate with a deaf grandmother, we had to write on a piece of paper what we wanted to say, but would have been pointless saying. You couldn't overuse the paper or old messages could be construed as new messages, so much paper was used. Mum was forever thinking of ways of saving paper, pencils and rubbers would have seemed to be the easiest solution.

Mum settled on a device which you could write on with a sharp instrument and after being read just lift the surface and you were left with a blank sheet, a sort of reverse carbon paper. We only had one of these things so a lot of paper was still used as my grandmother was not the most patient of people and refuse to attempt lipreading. Grandad spent most of his time in bed so we never really communicated with him. Life in the house was as I'd expected, it was not a happy household.

8 DISCOVERING GOOSE GREEN

Goose Green consisted of three smallholdings, two small rows of houses, three in one row and four in the other, a large house and a bungalow in which my aunt and uncle lived. Ivy Garth was one of the smallholdings and my grandfather had built many walls on his small-holding. Separating the landholding and farm-like buildings and the house, they seemed to be drystone topped with cement with pinnacles of limestone set in the cement around six inches apart giving the walls a fortress-like appearance. Fortunately, these weren't the boundary walls or we would have really felt trapped.

Next to the house was a low wall - at least on our side - again topped with cement but flat and easy to sit on, it had a 'through' (A stone or in this case a flagstone that holds the two sides of a drystone wall together.) about half the way up, again on our side. This flat top made a perfect seat for sister Barbara and me the moment we escaped from the house, we'd discovered this seat previously on our rather infrequent visits to Ivy Garth and rather liked it. The other side of the wall was twice as high and there the through stone was about three-quarters of the way up the wall, if we were ever to go over the other side, we would have to clamber back using the through stone for leverage.

It must have been our first day living at Ivy Garth that we took to the seat and suddenly, we hear a rather boisterous voice call out, "Hail, Watson children."

My God, we had never been called 'Watson children' before and surely hail was something that fell from the sky. The boisterous voice was that of what we would come to know as Mr Fletcher, Tommy Fletcher was an enigma of a man, he was unlike any other man in the district.

Mr Fletcher was the same age as the century, fifty-seven, he was solidly built and had an eternal smile. He had farmed Challon Hall, a farm that surrounded Goose Green and retired when I was born, unheard of in those days, the retirement age was sixty-five. He seemed to play golf all week, mess around on his smallholding, go to bowls one evening a week and to football on Saturday afternoon, he liked sport.

Barbara and I took the huge leap down to the other side of the wall and shyly wandered over to Mr Fletcher, he looked down at us and said, "You must be the famous Thomas Watson, and this is?"

"Barbara." Barbara meekly replied.

"Bar-Bar-a, that's a fine name Bar-Bar-a." Announced Mr Fletcher.

"You must come and meet the ladies, you haven't met the ladies yet have you?"

So off we went to meet the ladies, "This is Winnie and this is Hilary." Mr Fletcher introduced us. "And this, ladies is Thomas and Bar-Bar-a Watson from Pelter Paddock."

We looked quizzically at each other 'where the hell is Pelter Paddock?' we were both thinking. (Pelter Paddock was the previous name for Ivy Garth before my grandfather changed it.)

These ladies had been named with their characters aforethought, Winnie was the most gentle-looking thing I'd ever seen, she had the loveliest eyes, a small fleck of black crept over her nose and her horns curled gently down her face. Her udder hung low between her legs and she had short stumpy teats which, when she got to know me better allowed me to squeeze and draw milk.

Hilary, on the other hand, was I presume, named after Sir Edmund who had climbed Mount Everest. She was much darker than Winnie, not only in colour but in character, her horns reached for the sky like those on a Viking helmet and she had a much finer composition than Winnie with neater formed udder but big black ugly teats. When we,

Hilary and I got to know each other better she too allowed me to squeeze her teats but squeeze as I might I could never draw milk. I think the only reason Hilary allowed me to squeeze her teats was that she was bitterly jealous of Winnie.

God put Tommy Fletcher on this earth so that he could be my hero. It wasn't long before I was worshipping the ground he walked on and I'm sure he knew it and did things for my benefit, he wasn't afraid to show off from time to time.

Most of my time at Ivy Garth was spent at Springfield, Mr Fletcher's smallholding or at least in the early years. Winnie and Hilary were milked by hand, something I'd never seen done before, Mr Fletcher was a brilliant milker and had milk flowing freely from even Hilary's teats. Looking back I never remember either Winnie or Hilary ever having a calf, yet I know cows for milk production need to have calves annually to keep producing milk and Winnie and Hilary were milked forever and never had a calf, could there be something I didn't know?

Mr Fletcher kept hens for egg production and got most annoyed when one of them got 'broody,' that is the desire to sit on eggs rather than lay eggs. His cure for this was to take the hen by the legs and swing it in a circular motion three times rapidly around and on the fourth circuit release it. The hen would fly helplessly for a while and eventually land disorientated and confused. I'm not altogether convinced this worked but he didn't have many broody hens.

When Mr Fletcher wasn't playing golf, he would often be practising in his fields. He did this by having tyres placed in his upper field and hitting the balls from his lower field, the idea of this was to hit the balls into the tyres, but I don't think he ever did. Perhaps this was one time he tried to show off and failed, well it was a lot more than one time as he did the same thing most weeks and still no golf balls in the tyres.

One year Mr Fletcher made hay for Winnie and Hilary using only a horse and manpower. This was unheard of in the late fifties and what an experience for me. I think the grass may have been cut with the aid of a tractor but the rest was horse and man. He borrowed a horse

(Long retired.) from his cousin up the road and a couple of haymaking pieces of horse-drawn machinery and a cart to bring the hay in. The hay was successfully made and stacked in his barn by one man and his horse, was there anything this man couldn't do? Get a golf ball in a tyre perhaps.

There was some mystique around my hero, he grew tobacco and dried it, yet I never saw him smoke. He seemed to go missing on Sundays but he never went to Church. I followed him everywhere but never entered his house. He never came close to Ivy Garth but lived only fifty yards away. Little things I can ponder now but still not fathom. His relationship with Mrs Fletcher was none existent to me, as she never seems to talk to him nor him to her, he seemed to be delighted to have us around, yet Mrs Fletcher loathed us.

My life at Ivy Garth centred around Tommy Fletcher and his mystique only made the relationship stronger.

9 THE REST OF GOOSE GREEN AND LOSING GRANDADS

Apart from Tommy Fletcher, Goose Green was all I'd expected of it, terrible. The Watsons had increased the population of Goose Green by twenty-five per cent, there we were a household of seven living in a hamlet where the average household was below two, before our arrival. As I've already said, Goose Green had three smallholdings, the third was Fern Bank, the home of the only other child. Yes, Fern Bank housed the Wadsworths, a deeply Methodist family, Mr and Mrs Wadsworth and their son Thomas.

It would seem that Thomas only shared my name, he was a year younger than me and everything being equal should have made an ideal playmate for me. He didn't. Thomas Wadsworth didn't really do play, he was much too serious for that. We attended the same school until I was fifteen and I never remember him at school, perhaps he was unspectacular, well he was.

The Wadsworths however, had the most productive smallholding in Goose Green and kept loads of hens which they bred for chickens. They took everything very seriously, especially money and religion and I think would have slept with one of their chooks to keep it alive.

I remember one day Mrs Wadsworth operated on one of her beloved hens. Her diagnosis was that this particular hen had swallowed a blade of grass and the grass had become entangled in its 'crop', a sort of hen stomach where the hen grinds grain before it goes into the stomach proper. Please note that this may be a load of bollocks, as I know nothing about the inner working of a chook but it is what I saw on the day.

Mrs Wadsworth gently removed a few feathers from below the hen's neck and revealed a lump under the hen's skin. As I'm revealing this to you I'm presuming that the hen was being restrained by little Thomas. I was all eyes as Mrs Wadsworth took a knife and cut the rather calm chook open. She then, with a light squeeze exposed the hen's crop, a sort of semi-transparent bag and sure enough, there was a dark strand in the crop. Then she cut into the crop and removed the strand which was, in fact, a blade of grass. Correct diagnosis Mrs Wadsworth. Everything was neatly sewn up and the hen was put in a cage to recuperate. There was an amazing lack of blood throughout this process. The most exciting thing ever to happen at Fern Bank.

The rest of the people in Goose Green lived in ones and twos. In the Springfield Cottages were Mr and Mrs Fletcher who lived at number one. At number two lived the Crossleys, Mrs and Isabel. I don't recall ever seeing Mrs Crossley and I only briefly sighted Isabel her daughter who wasn't young and could safely be called a spinster. At number three were the Masons, Mr and Mrs who by Goose Green standards could be classed as normal but like so many people in Goose Green rarely left their house.

Number four Springfield housed the Armers, Mrs and Ted her son. Mrs Armer could have been buried in the garden for all I know as I never saw her. Ted, on the other hand, was something to lighten our Sundays. Most days you never saw Ted, he was I think in his forties. Every Sunday morning Ted took off on his bike to the Punch Bowl, a pub in Barrows Green a few miles away, there were closer drinking holes but the Punch Bowl was his haunt.

Every Sunday afternoon Ted returned on or perhaps off his bike in varying states of repair. If he was on his bike it was only just and would be swerving from side to side, other times when he wasn't on his bike he'd be slumped over the crossbar of his bike staggering helplessly along the road. Nobody ever went to his aid, one had to presume he liked a drink on Sundays, it never happened any other day.

Down in Goose Green Cottages lived three single people, number one housed a bachelor builder called Shan Mason who I rarely saw (Goose Green harboured many shy people.) he owned a Jowett Javelin car which he garaged over the road. The car was as shy as its owner and I never saw it on the road. Mrs Jackson lived at number two and was out of place in Goose Green, she was something of a gossip and would watch out for my mother or any other unsuspecting passer-by to gossip with. At number three was old Mrs Collinson who practised witchcraft and was just a little reclusive, she would have been quite a catch in her day with so much mystique.

Next to the Goose Green Cottages was a large whitewashed house containing yet another woman of mystery, Miss Wignall. Miss Wignall was, to me at least, of mysterious age and was from time to time visited by a Mr Knibbs of Milton who was old and nasty.

The first or last house in Goose Green depending on which direction you came was The Bungalow. This was the home of my Aunty Bell and Uncle Wilf. This was the best house, it had an immaculate garden with a manicured lawn and a stream running through the garden. There was a retaining wall holding the whole lot in and a tiny privet hedge along the top of the wall. Uncle Wilf and Aunty Bell didn't have kids so we were half welcome there, but we couldn't make a mess and in all honesty, we couldn't, not make a mess. Aunty Bell was Mum's sister and spent a lot of time at Ivy Garth unlike me who was only too glad to be out of the place. She would have, in those times rated as our favourite aunt but circumstances were to change.

Somewhere around now as we were settling into Goose Green with its rather sombre residents I was to lose my Grandad Watson, not lose him in the sense of not being able to find him but in the sense, that he died. This was most inconvenient as I was just getting to know him now he'd retired and I always admired the way he had terraced his front garden at their new bungalow. It didn't seem fair that the grandfather I could speak to should die so early in his retirement. Tommy Fletcher had been retired for years and he was never going to die.

We weren't, of course, allowed to go to the cremation, which I thought would be quite exciting. Watching the coffin on the fire rather appealed to me but I had a long wait for my first funeral and then wished I'd waited longer. Not a good experience.

Death was to haunt us around then, next to go was Grandad Hodgson. This was not so sad, it was exciting. Grandad Hodgson had been rehearsing death for as long as I'd known him, I don't think I'd seen him upright or at least not unassisted. Of late he'd seemed quite chipper and this Saturday afternoon he had been manoeuvred into the living room and propped on the lounge. He had very much been a party to this manoeuvre as Uncle Chris the butcher and his only son would be delivering our weekly meat and he was keen for him to see him semi-upright. Well, the best-laid plans of Grandad Hodgson were destined to fail.

All lay in wait for Uncle Chris, Grandad Hodgson, Aunty Bell, Granny Hodgson and Mum with us kids outside avoiding the excitement. Poor Grandad surrounded by three women must have felt a little frustrated and found a reason to shout at my stone-deaf grandmother. It was that one Saturday afternoon shout that tipped the scales, and Grandad fell silent and dead.

A couple of seconds later, I burst into the house for no particular reason, and there on the lounge, eyes bulging and mouth open lay Grandad Hodgson. I'd never seen a dead man before and in Grandad Hodgson's case, it wasn't that different from the living version. Mum quickly ushered me out saying, "Grandad's died, you go off and play." The most exciting thing ever to happen in Goose Green and I was supposed to 'go off and play'. What sort of parents did I have?

This was some event but nobody knew what to do, they could have gone off and played because there was nothing they could do for Grandad. No idea where Dad was, no phone, and Tommy Fletcher was playing golf, nothing for it but to wait for Uncle Chris, he did have a bit of experience with dead bodies.

The one Saturday that Uncle Chris was late had arrived. No sooner had Uncle Chris arrived than he was being rushed into the house, he was there a while. We were off playing, you must be joking, we were watching every move around that front door from our observation post. It was sometime later Uncle Chris emerged from the house looking calm and composed and much later, that we were allowed back in the house.

By now Grandad had disappeared, I wasn't going to ask where. Lots had been going on and it was three or four days later Dad took me aside, and Dad never took me aside. This time it was serious stuff, "Come and see tha Grandad lad." he said, I followed him into the sitting room, which had been Granny and Grandad's bedroom and there by the window was the coffin.

"Go on take a look." Said Dad, I looked and Grandad looked in better shape than the last time I'd seen him.

"Touch him," Dad said.

"Where?" I queried.

"Anywhere." Replied Dad.

I touched Grandad's cheek and to my amazement, his stubble had grown since Saturday.

The first, the only and hopefully the last time I touch a dead body. We didn't get to that funeral either, seems kids aren't welcome at funerals.

10 A FATE WORSE THAN DEATH

Just as I was starting to enjoy learning at school and Mrs Foss is going to have a baby. This viewed from my sheltered eyes, was not possible, women of Mrs Foss' age didn't have babies, she was in her late thirties. I, of course, didn't remember that my mother was in her late thirties when I was born but of course, school teachers are different from real people. I didn't like this news one bit and after the summer holidays I would be going into Mrs Bryers' class, a fate worse than death. I just had to make the best of these summer holidays.

It was two days into the summer holidays and the population of Goose Green increased by two, or one if you take into account the death of Grandad Hodgson. Naturally, this increase wasn't due to births but to the arrival of two little boys from Sheffield. Mr Fletcher's grandsons John and Michael, both had straight blonde hair (Was I the only kid in the world who had blonde curly hair?). John was a little younger than me and Michael had been born when his parents thought they were on a 'roll'. About a year and ten seconds later. These boys were the perfect playmates for me, as for one, they were Mr Fletcher's grandsons and being younger couldn't bully me.

The Fletcher boys loved cricket, to me it was a game and I'd play it. Mr Fletcher had prepared a perfect pitch for the boys, it was slightly downhill for the bowler and fell away a little to the off-side for the batsman if he was righthanded. I'm sure poor little Michael was lefthanded so had a bit of trouble with this quirk of the pitch. This all meant nothing to me and I was pretty happy to have a couple of playmates and there was no chance of injury. We had a tennis ball, balled underarm, you couldn't get out on the first ball and hit a six and you were out. Hours were spent trying to perfect this game but it was futile, it already was perfect. I believe adults have stuffed it up completely and some have been killed playing what to us, was a simple game.

The Fletcher boys' other favourite pursuit was fishing, and this is where these 'city kids' showed up this country kid. Yes, I was a gatherer, I could find and pick berries in places that no one else could but I wasn't into this hunting caper. I didn't like fish and my experience with the fishermen of Millness was still fresh in my memory. The Fletcher boys weren't into fishing with rods they had somehow learned to fish with their hands, something a country boy like me should have found second nature. After all, I did spend most of my time around water playing in the natural stream which ran through Goose Green.

Well, I rather enjoyed watching the brown trout bask in the sun and I knew which places to find them, but catch them, what for? John and Michael really could catch these fish and they took them back to their grandparents' home and Mrs Fletcher cooked them and I'm told they were very nice. I acted as a scout for these avid fishers. The last thing I wanted to do was to put my hand into a slimy crevice on the bank of a stream and spend the rest of the day smelling of fish, but I was only nine. I did however once catch one of these brown trout, I think it was dying, it didn't put up much of a fight and it wasn't very big and yes it had to be eaten. I much preferred smoked cod.

The summer holidays spent with the Fletcher boys were great fun until we had that inevitable dispute. I can never remember what we fought about or why we fought but every summer we did and so I went about a week with no playmates. Just as I don't remember what we fought about I don't remember how we made friends again. I think Mr Fletcher had something to do with 'making-up' but for those last few days before their return to Sheffield we were best of mates but the next school holidays were never discussed.

It was now time to return to school, I was terrified, I was to be in

Mrs Bryers' class and she was an awful woman. We'd all seen her beat Tommy Collinson to within an inch of his life, to his credit Tommy turned up the next day. And here I was to be exposed to this horror and my parents, as usual, didn't care. Other kids had been sent to school in Kendal so they didn't have to face this dreadful woman.

I refused to go to school, well that didn't work. Mum dragged me to school or at least most of the way. Mum didn't often get worked up over what I did but that day was the 'bitter end' as she would have said. That afternoon Mum was waiting for me outside the school and if that wasn't bad enough she whisked me off to the doctor's surgery.

Mum told my tale of woe to the doctor who looked sort of understanding, perhaps he'd heard this tale of woe before as Mrs Bryers had one hell of a reputation. I had to take one little blue tablet every morning. Dad had a few stern words for me when he came home from work. This whole day's exercise, whatever you choose to call it, was a total waste.

Mum dragging me to school was what tipped the scales, I'd proudly taken the last few steps unaided but the other kids could see my mother had brought me to school.

"Why did your mum bring you to school today?"

That question from a thousand kids was to ring in my ears all day. Dad's stern words more or less inferred I was a wus and that first day in Mrs Bryers' class was uneventful, I even learnt something, and hell I was to learn more.

11 FINDING GOD

The twin parishes of Preston Patrick and Preston Richard got a new vicar and we lived within those parishes. The vicars of Preston Patrick and Preston Richard had, in the past, always been rather pedestrian, not in that they walked, but rather that they were bland and could put the most alert parishioner to sleep with their sermons. This new bloke was not in their mould, he, it seemed, came out of a huge round mould, and I do mean huge, and I do mean round.

Dr Smart, the new vicar, was a rotund fellow with a cheerful disposition, he didn't seem to be able to speak without smiling. He was the shape of a tennis ball and seemed to have the same bounce, at least, in his voice. If I'd been younger, I would have thought the Church was trying to get rid of him by placing him in a parish with a Church on a steep hill because this bloke was built to roll and out of sight. Of course, in my maturity, I knew his arms and legs would have saved him.

No sooner had we got back to school than we get a visit from Dr Smart, at school, it is a Church of England school after all. I think the other vicars visited the school but tried not to have any interaction with the students, we were a snotty-nosed bunch of urchins. Dr Smart wanted to address our class, which had never been done before, but we are happy to be out of Mrs Bryers' glare for a while.

Dr Smart tells us that he and Mrs Smart would like to start, or a least revive the choir at the Church. It seems this new vicar with his rotunda and beaming smile is a veritable 'Pied Piper' because when he asked who wanted to be in this new choir, almost every hand in the class went up, boys and girls. And of course, mine was there, not knowing what I was putting myself in for but won over by this man's charisma.

The next Sunday we presented at Church, not all the hands that had gone up at school were in attendance but most were there. Some may have been headed off at the pass by their parents who weren't too sure about this new vicar or even Church. But here we, the faithful are, ready to be kitted out in our cassocks and surplice. Suddenly, I discovered I'd been going to school with a bunch of crossdressers because not one of them seemed to mind being dressed up in a frock.

The girls didn't have to wear pants but we had to wear a frock, it seemed the girls already had nice Sunday frocks. There was one small flaw with the boys in frocks, the scruffy dog-eared collars of their shabby shirts were exposed above the neckline of the cassocks. It wasn't long before Dr Smart had this remedied and we were to wear a ruff around our necks. God, I looked cute, can I say the cutest?

I rather liked this newfound Christianity which had flowed over me, others were not quite as Godly as I and attendance in the choir were fading at times. Again Dr Smart came up with the idea of rewarding the best attending choirboys with a medallion which they would wear on a ribbon around their necks over their frocks on Sundays. I found myself at the Church twice every Sunday and I attended Sunday school at the vicarage most Sundays too.

I perhaps should now confess that my enthusiasm for things Christian, wasn't due to a devotion to God but more, a curiosity about God. Rather than being a neophyte, I was a hypocrite trying to find what others had discovered in Christianity. This curiosity was tinged with fascination and that was at a climax at the vicarage, a huge building housing Dr and Mrs Smart where we had Sunday school in the kitchen.

We went to the front door and rang the bell, well we pulled the bell, this was great fun. We had Sunday school as I said in the kitchen taken by Mrs Smart. Mrs Smart didn't have the charisma of Dr Smart, it's true to say, Mrs Smart had no charisma, but she had an impressive row of bells high on the kitchen wall. One for each room in the house, this place dated back to when vicars had paid servants. Pulling the bell was so much fun we soon had to enter through the back door but we'd still gaze at the bells in the kitchen and pay no attention to what Mrs Smart was trying to teach us. Sunday school didn't last very long.

12 BREAKING THE LAW

To say I was having trouble at school would have been an understatement. I was torn apart, I was by law supposed to be terrified of Mrs Bryers but I wasn't. I was by my very nature supposed to dislike school with a passion, but I didn't. I didn't want to learn anything as I didn't want to pass my eleven-plus examination, but I was learning a lot and enjoying learning. Torn I was, between what I expected of myself and what was happening.

Mrs Bryers filled every day with education, not just reading writing and arithmetic but with poetry, music, geography, history, colour and light. Sadly all this education had to be done without fun but I loved it and was a sponge mopping up every bit I could. Poetry had me transfixed, Wordsworth and Masefield (The reigning Poet Laureate.) were my favourites;

'For oft when on my couch I lie, in vacant or in pensive mood.'

Or, 'Dirty British coaster with its salt-caked smoke stack.'

Not that I knew what a vacant or pensive mood was, even though I spent lots of my time in both and I'd never seen a dirty British coaster nor knew what one was.

We went on an excursion to see Wordsworth's daffodils by Ullswater and to his house 'Dove Cottage'. For history, we went to Chester to see what had been an old Roman city with its walls. Mrs Bryers often holidayed in Holland so we learned of tulip fields and canals and Dutch auctions and Edam and Gouda and yes, these lessons were illustrated with slides, colour and light. How could this ogre of a woman teach so fervently and yet show no emotion towards her students? How could everybody dislike her so much when she taught so much? I can question these things now but then it was the law to dislike the woman so I was like the others and had to dislike the teacher who was the teacher who taught us so much.

At Church, there were two choirboys of note who wore the medallions for Church attendance with pride. Tony Mason, a sober soul with the voice of an angel, Tony was lucky to be born when he was, a few centuries earlier and he would have been 'gelded' for sure. Tony could stay still for great lengths of time, up to five minutes was not beyond him, and read flawlessly from the Bible. He was almost the perfect choirboy. All Tony lacked was that flash of blonde hair.

The other choirboy of note was yours truly, this was one of the miracles often mentioned in the Bible. Through the back door of the vestry, a scruffy little urchin entered, into the Church a cherub strode, side by side with Tony Mason the medallioned pair led their motley crews to the choir stalls, cassocked, surpliced and ruffed. I was perfection personified as a choirboy because I had that dash of curly blonde hair. If I'd been born centuries earlier I would have escaped the gelder's knife as I couldn't sing, I was merely cosmetic. I couldn't stay still in a concrete suit and wasn't able to read from the Bible without tripping on some word or phrase.

My attendance in Church was to study Christianity, not to read from the Bible and sing, although I didn't mind the singing bit, it wasn't that good for those close to me. One of the first prayers at the beginning of the morning service was 'The Absolution' we had to recite this prayer along with the vicar and it wasn't an easy prayer, it didn't flow like the 'Lord's Prayer'. The difficulty of the Absolution caused me to study it to get on top of its complexity. It seems this prayer wipes the slate clean, absolves your sins and puts you on track for the next week.

But what if you haven't sinned? That sparked something in the urchin/choirboy, I may have sinned but I didn't get caught, did that count? It was, of course, my duty to sin or this whole prayer was a waste of time. The sinning was only minor stuff, the loose button on the cassock found its way into the collection plate, and constant fiddling and talking during the sermon, it didn't matter as all my sins would be absolved by next Sunday. Strangely enough, the buttons in the collection plate stayed with me for fifty years so the Absolution wasn't as good as it claimed to be.

Being a choirboy and not disliking Mrs Bryers as much as I should, didn't do much for my credibility with the village boys at school, I guess Tony suffered the same fate even though he was a village boy. Between us, we needed to lift our credibility.

At home, we had acquired a pig of the female persuasion from my Uncle Chris. This huge sow had just given up its latest offering of piglets and needed to be 'serviced' by a boar pig. This meant she had to be walked the mile or so to the 'Kennels' where the servicing boar was in attendance. This got one curious little growing mind working overtime as to how. Where? What? Well, I was a country boy and was learning about bits and pieces by observation and cobbled together what I thought happened. As it happened I wasn't that far off the mark.

At school, on Monday I mentioned my suspicions to Tony. Now, I failed to mention that Tony is a 'pantsman' and has been seen kissing girls. Seems Tony has not only kissed girls he has spoken to them too. One little girl who lives close to Tony has a bigger sister and her mother has told the bigger sister a bit about what goes on and how terrible it is. This goes on to say boys are evil and bigger boys are even eviler and some of the things they do are disgusting. Needless to say, this woman doesn't have a husband and is warning her girls of what's in store if they stray.

When push comes to shove the information Tony has backs up my theories and we have the information at our fingertips that will give us that much-needed street credibility. At last, I'd discovered that what I thought was a design flaw in girls was in reality, somewhere to put babies.

Armed with our superior knowledge, Tony and I dispensed it liberally amongst the other boys, some of whom were a year older than us. This didn't go over as well as it should have, we weren't believed, well where the hell did they think babies come from? It seemed that the boys I went to school with were dumb and some even dumber.

After being given knowledge beyond their years these - you can only call them morons - went home and asked their parents if what Tony and I had told them was true, their parents for goodness sake. I can only presume the answers they got varied from a sort of mumbled, "Well sort of." to a "That's absolute rubbish don't you ever talk to those boys again." It would seem our credibility was still in doubt but most of the boys gradually saw the light, but I don't think we got that much-needed credibility. This knowledge I'd acquired was one of the most useless pieces of knowledge I would acquire at school, for many years it was to remain hand in hand with logarithms.

13 ENVY

My older sister Marion was thirteen or fourteen when I became envious of what she had, so much more than me and all the things I desired. Marion had a school uniform, not something I desperately desired but it was rather smart. She had a bike, something I coveted with a passion and had a job, albeit a small part-time job, it was employment. This was something I really desired and my whole life revolved around gaining employment even though I was much too young to have a job.

And the other thing Marion had was a swimming certificate saying she could swim across the swimming pool at Kendal Baths. It's fair to say, I too would have liked a swimming certificate but it certainly ran a miserable third to the bike and the job. She had a tennis racket too, I'm not sure what I would have done with a tennis racket but it would have been nice to have one.

Marion's job was in a grocery store in Kendal, I think Mum may have had something to do with its procurement. Mum rarely went shopping, her shopping was ordered from a man who called every Tuesday and took an order and it was delivered on Thursday. We also had a lady from the Co-op call every week and do the same thing but she didn't get as good an order as the man from Cooper's got. The man from Cooper's also got a cup of tea and a piece of cake and in turn, Marion found herself with a job. I knew I would get a job one day, I just had to wait, first, the bicycle had to be conquered.

Swimming and riding a bicycle are things you don't learn, it's a case of mind over matter and confidence is king. It was part of our duty as school children to attend swimming lessons. This was done in our case by transporting us on a bus to the Kendal Baths, the only swimming pool in the area.

Much as I disliked school, I disliked swimming lessons even more. Yes, I loved the water, but in its natural state and at a depth of about twelve inches so my pants didn't get wet. The water at Kendal Baths was not in 'its natural state,' a little water had been added to the chlorine and the smell was horrendous, you didn't have to have a religious-sounding name to walk on this stuff. It was also three feet deep at the shallow end, I was told it went to six feet at the deep end, no way would I be measuring that. Kendal Baths was an echo chamber that gave me the creeps, I've since discovered all indoor pools are like that.

It would seem that athletically gifted children find swimming quite easy, even academically gifted children master swimming reasonably easily. Devotees of commonsense like Thomas Watson and a couple of other like-minded children weren't going to drown in chlorine and found swimming impossible. First of all, we were handicapped by our swimming costume, largish woollen underpants, woven from the coarsest wool available. Did the designers of these garments know how much water wool can absorb?

When we all got in the pool the level of the water dropped, it seemed we had suddenly been given a five-pound weight belt to restrict our ability to float in this rather floatatious chlorine. I think the first act we had to perform was to put our heads under the chlorine and get our eyes stung, what a good idea. This torture continued for years and my desire to gain my swimming certificate lessened with each year. Needless to say, my swimming certificate never made it from the printers.

The next mind-over-matter job was, of course, bicycle riding, this was in the hands of parents not teachers. In my case in the hands of Dad, Dad didn't have much time for me anymore so it was up mostly to me. I had to steal my sister's bike and try to ride it down our sensible driveway. I usually managed to crash into the gate at the bottom of the driveway before I mounted the bike. This was so much more important than swimming when you lived miles from anywhere, bike riding was an essential skill.

I had to master this balancing act and at least I was left to my own devices and didn't have to dunk my head in a bucket of chlorine with every lesson. After many gate crashes, I eventually mastered the balancing of my sister's bike and made those essential turns of the pedals. I was elated but bikeless, it was all very well to steal your sister's bike to learn on but taking it out of the gate was another matter, it couldn't be done. I needed a new bike and this was impossible as my parents couldn't afford a new bike.

It seems my father had more than one bike so perhaps I could have one of his old ones, this was facilitated. Dad dragged out an old bike, lowered the saddle as low as it would go, oiled the chain, blew up the tyres and proudly announced, "There tha is lad." Wow, my own bike, this isn't really what I'd envisaged. It was as tall as me and weighed as much as ten pairs of wet swimming trunks. It had rod brakes and my hands barely reached down to the brake levers and my feet barely reached the petals on the downstroke, it was alright if I left the seat, I could just manage. This was one of the benefits of having poor parents, it was character-building.

All the other kids I knew had bikes that were the right size for them, not their fathers. Most of the other bikes I'd seen had cable brakes, not those old-fashioned rod things I had on my bike. I had to learn to ride a bike for the second time as this one had a crossbar, unlike my sister's, a girls' bike. I've never worked out why boys' (In my case, men's) bikes have crossbars. I'd just discovered I had reproductive organs and here I was riding a bicycle that seemed intent on damaging the aforementioned. This was just like learning not to swim, it made your eyes water.

It didn't take me too long to adapt to my unique riding style, hooking my leg over the crossbar when I came to a stop and anchoring myself to the ground with the other foot. Reaching down to grab the brake lever and then I slipped my thumb over the handlebars. The bike and my strange riding style gave me mobility, I could now ride to Church to conduct my choral duties on Sundays and just ride places. In all honesty, I think sometimes it would have been easier to walk than ride as there was lots of hard pedalling and getting off to walk up what were no more than inclines but downhills were, wow!

Most of the other boys were proud of their bikes, well let's face it they had cable brakes, were suitably sized, had three-speed gears and some even had drop handlebars. I got around on my bike and could hide it almost anywhere, not so that it didn't get stolen, but so it didn't get seen.

14 THE GREAT DIVIDE

At home, in the house at Ivy Garth things seemed more, 'at home'. After Grandad Hodgson's death, we'd still had to put up with Granny Hodgson and her deafness and have Aunty Bell visiting most days. I'm sure without meaning to Dad managed to get rid of both of them, he objected to having his slippers warmed (I think it was supposed to cause chilblains.) by a thoughtful Aunty Bell and she took off in a huff never to return. I rather liked her.

Getting rid of Granny Hodgson was not quite as simple, Ivy Garth was after all her home, even though we Watsons held a degree of ownership, along with the bank. Granny Hodgson eventually moved out to live with Mum's sister Aunty Edith and Uncle Alec in Burton.

Now, at last, the Watsons had their own home like they had at 3 Millness Row, just the five of us to play happy families. Of course, life wasn't meant to be easy and it wasn't, especially for Mum and Dad. First Dad got sick, with an ulcer, which was pretty sick back in those days. After being sick for some time Dad also became unemployed.

A caring and understanding son I wasn't, I couldn't get sick enough to get a day off school, how could my Dad get sick enough to not be able to work? And the unemployment, had me stumped, how could anybody not want to employ my Dad? My respect for Dad was starting to break down. I must have been a selfish brat, my parents were battling with finances and in turn with emotions which flow on and I cared about myself.

My parents were caring about me too and were bracing themselves to be able to afford to send another child off to grammar school, my older sister was there already. Our education was top of my parent's list of priorities and the chance of me passing my eleven-plus examination was pretty high.

Back at school, we were all being primed for the long-awaited eleven-plus examination, the exam we all sat in those days, that in the eyes of our teachers, decided our future. Most of us at Endmoor Primary should have been pretty safe in the knowledge that we'd had the best teaching available and had every chance of passing this life-changing exam. Little did I know how life-changing this exam was, it wasn't so much life-changing in the way adults thought it was, but the social change it would inflict on innocent eleven-year-olds was immense.

I was favoured to pass my eleven-plus examination, I was well up with the smartest kids and most times topped the class with arithmetic, my one flaw was I wrote rather slowly. The dreaded day came, the day of the eleven-plus exam. We didn't know what to expect, we hadn't done a practice run and we'd never had an exam before. I'm sure it was a Saturday, I know it was at Kendal Grammar School and the air was full of strangers, squillions of kids I'd never seen before and teachers I'd never seen before.

Lambs to the slaughter, herded into rooms we'd never been in before, issued with exam papers we'd never seen before and given our instructions. I'm sure there were two of these sessions with a break in between. We had all, I'm sure been told how important this exam was, one slip of the pencil and you had failed.

I'm sure most of the kids were nervous, but I, being of a nervous disposition for some reason wasn't nervous. Well, the reason I wasn't nervous was that I didn't want to pass this stupid exam, I didn't want to go to a grammar school and be a smart grammar schoolboy with his nice blazer, I wanted to be a scruffy secondary schoolboy with his shirt continually hanging out.

With the eleven-plus behind us, it was back to school and back to learning, Mrs Bryers had lots more to teach us and if we were to go to grammar school we had to be prepared. I think the teaching got more intense and I know I enjoyed it. In arithmetic (We would call it mathematics in our next school.) we started to learn algebra, wow, sums with letters, it looked impossible at first but I got the hang of it and loved it.

Still, there was poetry and music and a whole lot you needed to learn if you are to succeed at grammar school Thomas. Yes, in the eyes of Mrs Bryers I was going to grammar school but the results of the exam weren't in yet.

It would have been June or July when the eleven-plus results arrived at Endmoor Primary School, all but one of the smart kids were on the edge of their seats. Of course, the results came out in alphabetical order so I was second last, Linda Westbury came after me and we knew she'd failed, as had I. I felt a pang of disappointment, for my parents who would have been so proud of me if I'd passed and for Mrs Bryers who had taught me so much. I didn't dare show any disappointment and we failures rejoiced in our failure.

I wasn't quite ready for what came next, the playground split, those who had passed and those who had failed. Nothing was said but we grouped off into our new school groups; the Kendal Grammar School boys; the Kirkby Grammar School boys and girls (Where I would have been going.) and the Longlands School for Boys where I was going. There were only four of us I think, but we were already learning how to scoff at grammar schoolboys.

There was a social divide that teachers and parents couldn't see, it divided children who had until the age of eleven been the closest of friends. Children who had learned the same things and learned where babies came from. These children had been thrust together when they were five and now by the same silly system were to be forced apart.

Most of the summer school holidays seemed to be spent getting me rigged out for my new school. There was a uniform to be purchased and it was just as flash, if not flashier than the one the grammar school boys and girls wore. I was going to a brand new school, which had been built just for us, the boys (There was one for the girls too.) of the booming generation. Here I was thinking I'd be saving my parents' money going to a 'secondary modern' school rather than a grammar school, where I would be able to go to school scruffy and we could all live a little better.

It seemed to me that this new school was going to cost my parents squillions. A nice black blazer with a badge on the pocket, a grey, red and black tie, grey pants and socks to match, oh, and new shoes. This was worse than any grammar school uniform and then there was the sports gear, black shorts and a white singlet and football boots and plimsolls, and there must have been socks to go with these too. Even with the Watson's tight budget, no shortcuts or economies were allowed, I think there was one, the satchel for my books, perhaps a hand-me-down from my sister or secondhand. A new satchel, for my books, would have been money well wasted.

15 LONGLANDS SCHOOL FOR BOYS

The day had come and I was off to secondary school. Arrangements had been made for me, I didn't think that necessary for a grown lad like me, but I was easy going on that front, as I would have made no arrangements. Our milkman, John Fletcher, a relation of my hero Tommy Fletcher had recently married a widow from Old Hutton, a village a few miles away. His new wife had two sons, one my age and he was going to Longlands School for Boys too. It had been organised that I would meet this new lad at the bottom of his road and we would ride our bikes to Granny Watson's at Gatebeck Lane End, leave our bikes there and catch the bus into Kendal and school.

We met as arranged, it could be said, I didn't like this lad from the moment I saw him but that would be unfair. The poor lad looked like someone had put his head in a vice and it hadn't recovered, he was to get the nickname 'Egghead'. We were kind children in those days, his real name was David Thompson. Of course, he had a bike that suited his size, unlike my oversized effort, but it was just a bit daggy, with pannier bags, Sturmy Archer gears, chain guard and the like. This kid knew everything, he was the original 'know-all', at least till we got to school. This travel to our bus stop was to continue for the next four years, but we never became close friends.

We had a pass for the bus which we called a 'contract' for some reason and we kept it in a plastic wallet and had to show it every time we got on the bus. We had all been kitted out in our new school uniforms, no exceptions, as this was a brand new school with a brand new uniform and you had to conform. We should have all looked immaculate but I just didn't have that way of looking as I should, crooked tie, shirttail out was more my persona.

This was a new school, the newest in the county and probably the Northwest of England. We were to experience a new level of secondary education the likes of which had never been seen before. Everything at this school was new, the building, the desks, the books and my year of pupils, the older boys had attended the old Stramongate secondary school.

The first thing to happen when we got to school was, that we were divided into our classes, I presume this was done after analysis of our eleven-plus results. I was in 1A the top class and David Thompson was in 1B the second class, backing up my theory on his knowledge level.

I'd never been in a building this new, it sparkled and had windows right down one side of every classroom. This was a great advantage to me because I was to become an avid window gazer. The heart of the school had three storeys and our room was on the third storey, top marks for putting me in such a prime viewing position.

We had sparkling toilets with porcelain urinals, at Endmoor we'd had a wall a gutter and a drain. There was a giant hall with a stage for assemblies and a dining room, where we ate lunch, a library with heaps of books, two woodwork rooms a metalwork room and a gymnasium with change rooms and showers. I, we and others had never seen anything like this. Outside there were football pitches and tennis courts and acres of tarmac playground, no dirt and rocks like we'd had at Endmoor.

Every new lesson was a new experience with a new teacher for each subject, unlike having Mrs Bryers for every lesson. I only knew two boys in 1A, Dennis Atkinson, who had been at Endmoor but for the last two years gone to school in Kendal to avoid Mrs Bryers. Stephen Hunter was the other boy I knew, a tall skinny kid with a dash of blonde hair and we'd been at Endmoor together since starting school, we sat together when classes were in our homeroom. All the other boys were from other places in the surrounding area and stuck to their own, the Kendal boys were the strongest contingent.

One of our first lessons was maths and our class teacher Mr

Richardson took us for maths, as teachers go he was alright but he wasn't teaching me anything new. English was to come next, I was rather looking forward to English as we hadn't had many straight English lessons with Mrs Bryers.

I was sadly disappointed, Mr Turner came into the room and said, "Write a composition on…" Well, it didn't matter, he just wrote the topic he'd chosen on the board and left us to it. At the end of that memorable lesson, a gigantic book was dumped on our desks, it was 'Great Expectations,' by Charles Dickens. "Read it." I think, were the words Mr Turner uttered. A whole one-hour English lesson and seven words had been spoken. I read half the first page of Great Expectations and never looked at it again. This was the new level of secondary education we were to experience for the next four years. I'd disliked school before, but it was soon to take on a new level of dislike and I became a little inattentive.

Gym, physical education, sport, whatever you chose to call it was also a new experience for most of us who had attended small country schools where P.E. was a few exercises in the playground. The equipment in the gym was mind-boggling and in the case of medicine balls eye-watering. There was all manner of things to jump over, onto or in my case fall on. My sporting prowess was picked up by my classmates pretty early on and I was the last one picked on any team. If I was the only one left the teacher would add me to the stronger team as a handicap.

The great eye-opener - for us country boys at least - was in the change rooms and showers; mass male nudity, albeit prepubescent mass male nudity. It was our first experience of mass male nudity. In the cold of deepest darkest Westmorland nudity was not common and probably bath night was the only time it happened and then in the privacy of your own home and now out of the sight of your sisters.

I imagine that due to a lack of prepubescent nudity before secondary school, there was a degree of curiosity and it was eyes down, left and right. Nothing much different to see there, but there was, I was different, only a tiny bit different but different. I had been circumcised, I had no idea what circumcision was and I don't doubt any of the other boys did either, as they hadn't been.

Even as boys we could be gentlemen and nothing was said. Nothing was said about the boy who only had one testicle either so there was great discretion amongst our motley crew. I took my circumcision well as I didn't know it had happened and just thought I was different. I'd known I was different before I noticed my difference and seeing it with my own eyes reassured me, that I could continue my life being different, confident and strong in the knowledge that I was different. My parents had done me a favour I didn't even know they'd done.

16 BEING GIVEN RESPONSIBILITY

Now doing penance by attending school, I lived for the weekends when I could be free and do what I wanted to do. My parents had other ideas and found a couple of things I could do which weren't chores but duties. The first of these was going to Endmoor to my Uncle Chris' butcher's shop to get the meat.

So every Saturday morning off I went to get the meat from my Uncle Chris, I liked this job as I liked my Uncle Chris, he had an aura about him, he was a businessman. I don't know why I got this job, because Uncle Chris came round to deliver meat every Saturday afternoon. Was this some ruse to get me out of the house?

As I look back, I ponder this but it was something to do and it never did me any harm. It did teach me that Uncle Chris was not only a butcher of note but also a magician. He had a shop attached to his house and there was no meat in it. I'd follow him into his coolroom and there was no meat in that either and I'd go home with a bag of meat, where did it come from? To this day I don't know, what I do know, is that some Saturday mornings he sent me home with sausages, he may well have been a butcher of note and a magician, but he made the world's worst sausages, they were awful.

The rest of my Saturday morning was mine, I could mess in my garden, yes, I'd been given a useless piece of the garden out the back of the house which rarely saw the sun and I was free to grow whatever I wanted. I think there was a proviso that I kept the hell away from Dad's patch, I loved gardening and when I grew up I wanted to be a gardener.

Perhaps my desire to be a gardener was aided by the fact no one else on the earth wanted to be one and I knew I was different.

The one thing which could get me out of the garden and into the house was our wireless, I loved the radio. This of course came from my parents who were avid fans of 'The Archers'. 'The Archers' was, and I believe still is, a radio serial broadcast across Britain at quarter to seven every weekday evening. It was so real to us, the characters, the sound effects, the storylines and they even published a newspaper about once a year which Mum bought, 'The Borchester Echo'.

The pictures I could see on the radio when there was no television entranced me, it was all real. The Navy Lark, Round the Horn, Take it from Here and there were detective series too, all real to me canned laughter and all.

I was growing up, well I thought I was and I wanted more grownup stuff. And there it was waiting for me every Saturday morning between ten and twelve on the Light program, 'Saturday Club'. Amazingly, the British Broadcasting Corporation was producing a music program for young people, jazz, skiffle, blues, rock and pop were just starting to reach the airwaves. This was pre-Beatles, pre-Stones, this was me and this was real, my love of radio had just shot up a notch and for two hours every Saturday morning, I was glued to the wireless, listening to this new music. I had no musical talent but I loved the sounds, I must have as it dragged me into the house, no transistor radios then only the valve radio on the sideboard.

Mum and Dad had another duty for me to perform on Saturday afternoons. When I first heard about this brilliant idea I was not very happy, I was to go to Granny Watson's and keep her company. I must have made myself pretty obvious and Mum moved in, to sugarcoat the idea; "You'll be able to watch the wrestling on the telly with Granny, she gets very excited and even jumps up and down."

Now, the magic word here was 'telly', Granny Watson had a television and she wasn't afraid to watch it. The idea of Granny Watson jumping up and down scared the life out of me because she was one rotund woman but the idea of watching anything on television, and in the afternoon got me in.

Apart from Granny jumping, which I thought was impossible and scary, what was I going to say to her? Having a conversation wasn't my strong suit and conversation with grandparents wasn't something I'd had much experience with. Off I went expecting the worst, Granny was expecting me and little needed to be said, the television was on, 'Ironside' a detective in a wheelchair. This seemed a little strange to me but it was television, did it matter, I was hypnotized by the flicker of the screen and I rather liked Ironside.

Afternoon tea, Granny's cakes, enough said. Then the wrestling came on and my eyes were on Granny, 'come on jump' I thought, but no, she was motionless, transfixed by the action on the screen. It started slowly and quietly, the encouragement of the good guy, warning him when the bad guy was about to swoop and there was no jumping, there was concentration, concern and excitement. This was Granny Watson as I'd never seen her before, the hypnotic flicker of the screen was forgotten by me, I was watching Granny it was much more fun than the wrestling.

My parents weren't so bad after all, how had they known that I'd love my afternoons with Granny? Granny and I got on famously, I watched Ironside and she watched the wrestling and sometimes we spoke to each other, she was a lovely lady and loved the wrestling on television, I wonder if she ever realised it wasn't real?

My Sundays were pretty much absorbed by Church, I wasn't a very devout Christian but I was a loyal choirboy, albeit one who couldn't sing. I liked Church, I don't know why I liked Church but it gave me a purpose in life. Could it be that looking angelic for a couple of hours a week was good for the soul? Or was I just a show-off who realised he looked good in this kit? I tend to think it was the latter.

I was by now pretty high up in choirboy land, I got jobs like lighting the altar candles, perhaps I was just pyromaniac and just liked lighting fires, it was a cool job and you could practice your bowing to the altar and making all the right moves. Of course, they had to be extinguished and this was done with the candle lighter too but using a cone on the shaft, more bowing but in an empty Church.

My main task at Church was not one normally undertaken by a choirboy but one I greatly enjoyed, people-watching. That was what drew me to Church in the first place. Why did all these people go to Church? And under Dr Smart's leadership, there were good congregations so lots of people were there to be watched and have their devotion questioned by Thomas Watson.

Albert and Ruby Falkner from Millness, never missed a service, Albert was the Churchwarden and sort of organised the sidesmen and such, he was very important in the scheme of things, not hard to see why he needed his place in Church, to feel important. Ruby was the organist, always out of sight of the congregation but never silent when her fingers touched the keys of that organ. Ruby played the organ with gusto, her body rocking and rolling like Ray Charles, the congregation didn't know how Ruby played but I did, I watched her from the choir stalls. Ruby's motivation, to me, was simple, she loved playing the organ.

Mr Knibbs, that evil old man from Milton who visited Miss Wignall from time to time, what drove him to Church? I could simplify that by answering himself because he did, was there a Mrs Knibbs? Did she know he visited Miss Wignall? I'm sure there was a Mrs Knibbs. Mr Knibbs was in the adult choir and may have been the Church treasurer, he disliked me and often found buttons from my cassock in the collection. There was nothing Christian about this man, why on earth would he go to Church? Perhaps to search for buttons in the collection.

I worked my way through the congregation, pew by pew, why did some people sit in the same place every Sunday? And people would move if they sat in their seats. It was becoming obvious to me that the most important reason for going to church was to be seen, after all, it was why I was going, to be seen in my nice kit and to show off in my pretty boy frock.

The weekends in my life had become predictable but for the most part enjoyable, far more enjoyable than the torture of school, my distaste for school could only intensify as they more and more failed to teach. I'd be back there on Monday because at eleven it's impossible to fake illness with any conviction.

17   BLOODY POSER

Being twelve must be the hardest time in a man's life. The first hard thing that comes to mind is the fact that you aren't a man, but you want to be. You're small and you want to be big, your brain is exploding with things you want to be but your age and the rules of society will not allow you to be. You're in short pants and you want to wear long pants, life simply isn't fair when you're twelve. Some may say these frustrations of a twelve-year-old are prepubescent driven. This was not the case with me, I was so far away from puberty that I believed the boy with one testicle had more chance than me.

My brain was big but my body was small, I had a serious case of 'little man syndrome.' In the adult form, this creates a need to own big cars, big boats and of course, big-breasted women. In the twelve-year-old boy, it creates a desire to be noticed, you become a 'show-off', which of course I became.

Step one in becoming a show-off is you (If you're a scruffy little urchin like me.) have to smarten yourself up and be cool. For this, you needed long pants and I was still in short pants. Mum had to hear how much I needed long pants every day and how I was now the only boy at school who still wore short pants, along with numerous other mothers I imagine.

All I could do in the smartening-up department was to learn how to tie my tie in a 'Windsor' knot because I wasn't going to get long pants any time soon. I'm not sure who taught me how to tie a Windsor knot but I should, because it made me just that little bit cool. It wasn't any of the older boys who, if they were anywhere near cool, wore their tie with a Windsor knot, they couldn't possibly divulge such information to someone younger. It must have been a classmate who'd learnt from his older brother in the secrecy of their own home. School lessons would have been held in the toilets.

With the Windsor knot now in place, I was on track for adult life but no one else thought the same way. The only place where a twelve-year-old was to be treated as more grown-up was Church. At Church twice every Sunday I was dressed up as a girl, but at least they wanted me to be more grown-up. At Church, it was time to be 'confirmed,' lessons were required for this procedure, which I felt was a little like school and it got under my sensitive skin. Could the rot be starting to set in, in my relationship with Church? If it was, I wasn't letting it show as at least they were accepting you into adulthood and from your confirmation, you'd be able to drink alcohol, albeit a sip at communion.

Drinking alcohol appealed to the little 'show pony'. I romped through the confirmation lessons without hearing a word, after eighteen months at secondary school and not learning anything I was well-practised in the art of inattention. Just like at school you were never tested, did they care? I couldn't wait to get my first taste of communion wine, couldn't wait for the Bishop to lay his hands on my now beautifully coiffeured hair. I'm sure I'd now had my first haircut at the barber, Dad's efforts were behind me and I needed to look good for my confirmation.

I didn't wait for that first taste of communion wine. I was a trusted choirboy, I knew the vestry like the back of my hand, I knew where everything was kept and I was often the first to Church on Sunday mornings. There was no point in me waiting for the Bishop's sweaty hands to mess up my hair.

The communion wine was kept in the cupboard below where Dr Smart's vestments were kept, just like the vestry, the cupboard wasn't locked, at least not on Sundays. The temptation was too much for the little boy who had for years now, dressed up in a frock and looked angelic. I was ready early one temptation Sunday, to sin, dressed up in my frock, I opened the cupboard, took the bottle of communion wine out, removed the cork, silently and took that first swig. Wow, it was kind of rich and sweet and warm, and the smell. The smell was so strong, that I couldn't possibly get away with this mortal sin. I fumbled the cork back in the bottle and placed it back in the cupboard exactly where I'd found it and closed the cupboard. I imagined my breath must have reeked of this, not unpleasant fluid.

I was done for, not only had I committed a horrendous sin, the least punishment would be my expulsion from the choir and the worst, my parents would be told about it. I had to get this smell off my breath and fast. I left the vestry, a sinner reeking of communion wine and ran and ran around the Churchyard until I was sure the smell of wine had cleared my system. I must have raised some suspicion in the mind of Mr Knibbs at least, as my behaviour that Sunday was exemplary. No fidgeting during the sermon, no buttons in the collection and no elbowing the other boys as we paraded into Church.

This was my secret, I was never found out or even suspected to my knowledge. On reflection, not being caught was not all that good, if I'd been caught the news of Thomas Watson swigging communion wine would have spread through the community like wildfire and I would have had forever a bad boy reputation without too much effort. As it was, I now had to work on building that image. Not much later I gave up being a choirboy, dressing in a frock didn't suit the new image I needed and perhaps the guilt of that swig of wine got the better of me. I still had to go to Church my parents insisted, but now it was only once every Sunday.

Being bad or at least mischievous wasn't a hard task to undertake, especially when you're twelve. To get acclaim in the field of mischief isn't easy when you're surrounded by peers because they won't boast for you. They may admire your feats of bravery when you've pulled off a 'dare' but they won't go and tell girls and adults about it.

A true gutsy twelve-year-old needs an audience, the only audience I could find was on the bus to school and the bus home; girls and adults, I had them captured inside the bus. They may not have wanted to watch my performance but when the right bus conductor was on the bus, they got it. The right bus conductor is the one who insists you behave on 'their' bus, yes, they are the ones who believe it's their bus when all along it's, my bus and it's my right to perform and I did.

I did manage to get acclaim, but it was at a cost, the odd caning and a few miles of walking. I don't think I beat the bus conductors as the canings were for my efforts on the way to school, they made sure I got to school for the caning. The miles of walking were on the way home when they didn't care how you got home as long as it wasn't on their bus.

18 BECOMING A TEENAGER

1962 saw Britain, I think unbeknown to its population, on the cusp of a wave of greatness. A little 848cc motor car first made in 1959 was in that year to be marketed as the Mini, previously it had been sold as the Morris Mini-Minor or the Austin 7. This little car was to go on to become one of the great marques of the twentieth century.

That same year a little-known band manager by the name of Brian Epstein was knocking an equally little-known band from Liverpool into some kind of shape. He was getting them to dress better, in uniform almost and also finding them a new drummer, their long-time drummer Pete Best just wasn't fitting in. Enter Ringo Starr, this group of musicians were to be renamed the Beatles and go on to be a great British phenomenon.

Just as the year I was born, Britain was starting to boom again and I was to become a teenager. What better time to become a teenager? I entered my teenage badly equipped, I was very prepubescent, had a cumbersome bicycle and my parents were desperately poor. My older sister had at thirteen, got a job and joined Preston Patrick Young Farmers Club and seemed to me to be so grown-up, that of course had been four years earlier when I was so less grown-up.

On the twenty-fifth of February 1962, I had two goals in my life, those my sister had attained when she became a teenager. A job and to join Preston Patrick Young Farmers Club. To join the young farmers you needed money as there was a membership fee and as my parents were poor I needed a job to get money, no pocket money for the Watson kids.

Since early childhood, I'd wanted to be a gardener when I 'grew up.' I was now pretty close, in my eyes at least, and at thirteen in Britain you could have a part-time job, I think there were tight restrictions but they were the least of my worries. There was only one commercial gardening enterprise within bike riding distance of Goose Green and that was the 'Greenhouses' as we called it. It was called Woodlands Nursery but not by any of the locals.

I'm not sure how long after my thirteenth birthday, but I am sure, not long, I took my cumbersome yet trusty bicycle and rode off one evening to the Greenhouses. The house there was large and not unlike the vicarage, the driveway showed that the front door was no longer used and there was an obvious track to the back door. I timidly dropped my bike and walked up to the back porch and tapped on the door. My tap was answered by a loud barking of what sounded like two ferocious gigantic dogs, they were large but not ferocious and they were being held by a curious thirty-something woman.

An older man had answered the door, cigar in mouth and not looking too happy at being disturbed from his television viewing. I bravely asked if I could have a job, I think it went something like this; "Hello, I'm Thomas Watson and I was wondering if I could have a job."

I'd thought this out pretty well, I thought. The reply was not what I'd expected, in a strong Lancashire accent, which I disliked, the man said; "No we haven't got any jobs going." And the door closed, I thought, on my life.

The bike ride to the Greenhouses had been easy, mostly downhill or level going, the ride home was far from easy, even the level lengths of the road seemed to have an uphill feel about them. I didn't cry, but it wouldn't have been hard. I got home totally dejected and told my parents that I hadn't got a job, they tried to pacify me but my teenage was in tatters. The only job I wanted was not to be, strangely enough, my life went on just like it did when I was twelve. Getting the meat from Uncle Chris on Saturday morning, listening to Saturday Club on the radio and then going to Granny Watson's and watching television on Saturday afternoon, was that all I was good for?

It was some weeks after that fateful day, that I was returning from getting the meat from Uncle Chris and outside our front gate there was an aqua-coloured Morris Minor estate car parked, the one with the wood trim. No one ever visits the Watson's on Saturday morning as they know Mum hasn't done the baking yet and we don't know anyone who owns an aqua Morris Minor estate car.

I tentatively approach my own home, wondering who the hell could be visiting us. As I reached the steps up to the front door our visitor turned to face me, it was the old bloke from the Greenhouses, what the hell did he want? He'd done his dash with me, he didn't have a job for me, he'd made that obvious in a few brief words weeks ago. Mum broke the silence.

"This is Mr Sanderson, Thomas and he'd like you to go and work for him at the Greenhouses."

"Eh, you can work, school holidays and Saturday morning for a start and see how you go." Piped up Mr Sanderson in that awful Lancashire accent.

"Can tha start on Monday?"

It was the Easter holidays, of course, I could, and I'll even put up with your awful Lancashire accent. I was at a loss for words, I think all this had been organised for me and I didn't need words. I was taken aback that I'd got this dream job, how on earth had this man found me, I'd briefly given my name but he didn't know who the Watsons were or where they lived, I sure as hell wasn't going to question any of this, I was starting work on Monday.

Monday came, after two of the longest days of my life and my first job was cleaning out stinking rabbit cages. This wasn't what I'd signed up for, I didn't know this man kept rabbits, I thought he grew tomatoes. My second job was weeding carnations, this bloke grew flowers, not tomatoes. Could this dream job be a nightmare? It was a job, I didn't much care, I had a job.

It was the first afternoon I discovered how Mr Sanderson had found me. Rolling up for work on her trusty bicycle was Ruby Falkner, the organist from Church and Millness dweller, she, of course, knew me from my time living in Millness and my time in the Church choir. The curious thirty-something woman I had seen that evening I went for the job turned out to be Mr Sanderson's housekeeper and worker in the greenhouses, Rene Fell.

These two ladies liked a chat and I can imagine the conversation which found me after my predecessor had left Mr Sanderson's employ, he was my friend in Millness, what seemed like a lifetime earlier, Neil Watson.

"Tha was lile lad came round other night looking for a job." Rene would have started.

"And he were nobbert small wi' big bike and blonde curly hair."

Ruby would have replied with her chest pushed out. "Ee-i." Ee-i is more a breathing exercise than an utterance, used when someone from south Westmorland has some superior knowledge they wish to impart.

"That would ha' bin Thomas Watson no relation to Neil he's a nice lad is Thomas used to live in Millness council houses and knock around with our Max and they moved to Goose Green to look after her fatha and he got sick and was out of work and big sister Marion she's clever at school and such and Thomas was int' choir at Church use to put buttons int' collection little beggar. He were a nice lad were Thomas." Fortunately, 'were' can be used in both past and present tense when spoken in south Westmorland so I found myself still alive and employed.

Woodlands Nursery consisted of around half an acre of glasshouses which looked a little dilapidated on the outside and stunk on the inside, the smells were new to me, mostly I think they were fungal, some were decidedly toxic as strong chemicals were used to keep pests at bay. It was always warm, I loved that and the ground was littered with Manakin cigar tins. Mr Sanderson was the first person I'd ever met who chain-smoked cigars. The smell of smoke was ever-present as Rene almost chain-smoked Woodbine cigarettes. This was a whole new world to me, it was only two miles from Goose Green but it seemed a million miles away. Most of all I had attained one of my teenage goals.

19 BACK TO SCHOOL

Having a holiday job at thirteen was to me at least, worldly, but you need the right equipment. Mum sorted this out for me without the need to buy anything, one of Mum's specialities. I needed a lunchbox, a thermos flask and a shoulder bag, this was easy as Dad was out of work and I could use his for the time being. Not sure how Dad felt when his son had gotten a job when he was out of work. Somehow or other I managed to get this bag over my shoulder and clamber onto my bike, I must have looked the clumsiest sight.

Each day at work was more exciting than the last as I watched Mr Sanderson building new rabbit cages. He was using tools I'd never seen before. He had an electric drill that was converted into a circular saw and was cutting up sheets of asbestos, which must have been good for our lungs. It seemed he burnt out the motors on these drills at an alarming rate and of course, they were still under warranty, so of course, had to be replaced.

Then I saw mass plantings being watered for the first time. We had pot plants and Mum gave them an odd drink from a jug from time to time. Mr Sanderson had a one-inch hose with a length of copper pipe on the end which had been bent to just the right shape to allow him to water between his rows of carnations. The water came straight out of the pipe no rose to interfere with the flow. There were huge bottles of blue liquid connected to the hoses and this delivered liquid fertilizer into the water and so to the plants.

Huge pipes were going everywhere in the greenhouses, it seemed in winter these were to heat the greenhouses carrying hot water. From time to time these pipes would develop a leaky joint and Mr Sanderson would fix it, there seemed no end to this man's talents. It was all done with a cigar in his mouth and a trilby hat on his head and wearing the same three-piece suit and work boots. It was a year or so later I leant that when the three-piece suit was deemed dirty enough and worn enough it was dispensed with and replaced. Most people would have had their clothes cleaned at some stage, Tom Sanderson got a new suit.

My first three weeks (My Easter school holidays.) at Woodlands Nursery seemed to fly by and I was so wide-eyed, following Mr Sanderson's every move. Even with his awful Lancashire accent, he was fast becoming my new hero, he was the only person I worked with, the ladies, Rene and Ruby just worked with the flowers.

At the beginning of the third week, a new face appeared, it was Alan Inman who lived on the farm across the road and it appeared to me as if he had come to steal my job. Alan was to work at Woodlands, I was sure it was to replace me. I wasn't very happy about this situation but I did like Alan, he was in his early twenties, newly married and we got on well, and he told a good story. It was good to work with a younger person but I wasn't confident that my job was safe.

It wasn't until Saturday morning when Alan didn't work that I found out I was still required. It was the first day that week that I had worked with Mr Sanderson and as midday drew close, Mr Sanderson went through the payment ritual, the shuffling in his pockets and the removal of two pounds ten shillings, as if it were his last. He handed over the money and said, "We'll see you next Saturday then". My job was safe.

I returned to school the following Monday, a grown-up who earned money and was no longer the poorest kid in school. Well in my eyes I did, in reality, I just went back to school and was the same horrible child. None of my classmates were the least bit interested in my new job, none of them had jobs and if they did it was only a paper round or some such, not a proper job like mine.

I went back to school because it was the law and my parents would be in trouble if I didn't. The standard of education wasn't improving as we got older but we were this term going to learn logarithms. Well, you don't learn logarithms, you are given a logarithm table, a booklet full of numbers that enable you to add two logarithm numbers together and get another logarithm number and find it's easier than long multiplication. I believe that's the theory. What you are supposed to learn is that the logarithm is the square root of the number you wish to multiply or some such. No self-respecting numbers person would be seen out without a logarithms table. Maths was the only subject at school I had a real grip on and now I'd lost that.

I now had to achieve my other teenage goal, that of joining the Preston Patrick Young Farmers Club. That didn't throw up too many challenges except they were now coming into their summer recess to allow for haytime, I'd have to wait.

During the wait, I had now worked through the summer school holidays and thanks to Alan got a dog and a new bike. The dog was free but I'd paid some trifling sum for the bike. I was on the road to cool, almost without the Young Farmers. My dog was a puppy, Fly, Dad decided to call her, Wine had been my first choice as it was all she did for a couple of days. I was to be fully responsible for her, walks, food, training and the lot, she was a beautiful dog and she kept me to my side of the bargain without any doubt.

The bike was a bit of a wreck in that it had no mudguards and looked scruffy. It did have straight handlebars and cable brakes and potential and weighed a good bit less than the God-awful thing I'd been riding the last few years. The first time it rained I realised it needed mudguards, I made these from a strip of aluminium I scrounged from Mr Sanderson. I turned the handlebars around and they then became a sort of semi-drop handlebar, I had a bike, oil flowed freely from every moving part and the pilot could make this thing fly.

By September 1962 I'd joined Preston Patrick Young Farmers Club, along with a couple of classmates from school and to my displeasure some boys younger than me. At the time, Preston Patrick was the premier club in the county and drew members from far and wide. With this goal achieved, you could join in the fun, sadly there wasn't much of that for us younger ones, as fun was going out drinking, going to dances and having girlfriends. We got to hang out with the big boys though and that was cool enough for us, little did we know you were expected to be involved in activities of the club.

These activities included cattle judging, public speaking, acting in plays and one day becoming the secretary or treasurer, what had I signed up for? None of this stuff sounded like fun, more of a learning exercise like school was supposed to be. I wondered if I was going to need my logarithm tables to truly embrace this club.

20 BEST OF THE FAILURES

For my last two years at school, I must have been a monster, not only to my supervisors (Calling them teachers is too long a bow for me to draw.) and to my classmates. I was, in my eyes at least a man, albeit trapped in the body of a child. I had no interest in Biggles or adventure stories, I had no interest in girls and girls seemed to fascinate some of the boys. My body hadn't grown as fast as the other boys and the things they did with girls didn't sound that nice, anyway I'd learnt about that sort of thing years ago. I had so little in common with my fellow students, they seemed a tad childish to me.

It was in those last two years the educational powers that be woke up, that we weren't getting the education we'd been promised and took steps to remedy the situation. Too little, too late is how I can see it now, at the time I didn't care and had long since given up on the system. We were to spend many hours deliberating on our future, or rather our supervisors were. 'What are you going to do when you leave school?' Was the question posed to us, this question was answered in some cases by blank looks and silence. Of course, I was quick to answer, "Work at Woodlands Nursery sir." Yes, you always had to lob in the obligatory 'sir', which you had now learnt to do with a touch of sarcasm.

The supervisors loved the blank-look answer but just put me down as a waste of time, which I was. The blank look gave them the chance to bang on about getting a better education and the chance to get a better job and join a class of elite students that they planned to put together. As there were no elite students at Longlands School for Boys (We'd all failed our eleven-plus exam.) it defied logic that this could be done.

An elite class was formed and we were yet again driven apart by this wonderful education system, I was to now learn alongside the boys who had been deemed dumber than me. Well, of course, learning was against school policy so I just gained some new classmates, fortunately, some of these boys took schooling as seriously as I did and we got on quite well.

Just to show that we were getting a superior education to our predecessors we all had to sit this new exam called 'The Northern Counties Examination'. If we passed this exam we would have a piece of paper to say we had passed this exam no one had heard of, whoopee! There was a catch with this exam, to get the certificate, you had to pass both Maths and English. English was not my strong suit and as I hadn't had an English lesson in my time at Longlands I failed English, so no certificate. I did, however, gain fame and notoriety, it was announced at the presentation of the certificates that Thomas Watson was the best of the failures.

Being 'the best of the failures' was not the only time my name got an airing in the assembly hall in those last two years. Somewhere out of nowhere the man who presented himself in our English time-space, (Lesson was not a word you could use for this wasted hour.) announced that we were to enter a story writing competition and the best two stories from each class would win a book. He told us he wouldn't be judging the stories, which to me seemed pretty obvious, as surely the people running the competition would be judging them.

Turns out he got some woman, I think from the girls' school to judge the stories, and mine was one of the two which were sent in. I knew this wasn't the idea and that all the stories should have been forwarded to the competition, and judged by their judge as to who had written the best two stories in the class. I really shouldn't complain as I'd got a free ride and won a book. At this time of my life, books were something of a foreign object, even though I'd just read one, 'Shane', a cowboy book by Jack Schaefer, it had been a class book like Great Expectations but this one we all read. I think the other winner chose a book which showed a little class and it was announced at the presentation quite clearly, and then me. "The other winner is Thomas Watson and he has chosen, (There's a drop in volume here.) The Stirling Moss Book of Motor Racing". My one school trophy and the headmaster frowned on it, fair to say, I frown on his school.

I entered my last year at school knowing it was not going to be quite that long, you could leave school when you were fifteen. In my case, it would be the following February, I was counting the days. And then it happened, was it a rule change? Or perhaps a misunderstanding on my part, but it was deemed that we couldn't leave school till the end of the school year.

Four months had just been taken off my life, no time off for mis-behaviour, nothing could change this rotten, stinking rule. It was as if they knew, the worst thing they could do to you was make you stay at school. Yes, they knew alright, some of the staff had been at school for over fifty years and they still had a few years to go, no wonder they smoked so much.

I don't remember my last day at school, I imagine we did nothing so it wasn't very different from any other day, and my first day at full-time work was just like any other, it was the next day. This was the day my life was to start properly, my destiny was in my hands, I was to pay Mum board, I was to make my own decisions and my own mistakes and I was a working man. I'd waited so long for this day and it was just like any other.

21 BEING A YOUNG FARMER

I was now a working man earning five quid a week, albeit retaining most of my boyish features. The social life I'd had at school was behind me, but it hadn't been very social anyway. I now had the Preston Patrick Young Farmers Club as my social life and these were all after-work activities. I joined in wherever I could, there was cattle judging, public speaking, the annual play and carving a chicken. I was equally useless at most things but participation was the name of the game. I was dragged into the chicken carving because none of the girls wanted to do it, the public speaking was the same, I was a failure at both so didn't get selected again. And how often have I mentioned I learned nothing at school? That was one trick I'd picked up.

Cattle judging was something we did on balmy summer nights, making it a good excuse to get out. I was, of course, no good at it but for some reason persisted. We visited various farms and 'judged' four cows that were tied up in the cowshed (We called it a shippon.). I was a gardener and rabbit cage cleaner so didn't know much about cows. The only cows I'd had much to do with were Winnie and Hilary, Tommy Fletcher next door's cows, they had characters and horns so they were easy to judge and their horns related very much to their characters.

The cows we had to judge had no horns, it was now 1964 and most cows were dehorned by that time. I was lost, these cows were feature-less. The main part of this exercise was the speaking part, you had to stand in front of the main judge and explain why you'd judged the cows in the order you had. Excitement was at its highest level. The most exciting part of this exercise was when one of the cows urinated, and one always did. I don't know how often cows urinate but guess it must be about once a week because it's big. There's a warning, the cow arches her back and lifts her tail high in the air and lets loose, what can only be called, a torrent of bright yellow liquid. This liquid stinks beyond belief and splashes over an immeasurable area, no one escapes this flow and we all arrive home smelling of cow piss.

I get selected to perform in the annual play, an honour as we are pitted against the rest of the clubs in the county. Rehearsals for the play are held at Overthwaite, a large farm miles away owned by the Parsons family, their children, Moira and Bernard are highly thought of at the club as they are stinking rich. The fact that they're stinking rich means they don't have to be involved in club activities but can look good by hosting play rehearsals.

Riding my bike all the way to Overthwaite would have been a big ask so sympathy is offered (It was winter.) I was to ride my bike to Farleton and the Atkinson girls would give me a lift the rest of the way. The Atkinson girls, Isabel and Mary, weren't girls in my eyes as they were in their early twenties. Unlike the Parsons siblings, the Atkinson girls are involved with most things at the club and gave freely of their time. They even gave this horrible kid a lift to play rehearsals.

The part I play in the play is huge, I play an Irish Priest, I walk on, say one line and walk off. I got this part it seemed, because I had the best Irish accent, not because I had the physique of an Irish Priest. For this role, I had to find a suitable costume, a cassock and a dog collar. Shouldn't be a problem for an ex-choirboy like me. It was hard, I had to go to the vicarage and ask the vicar if I could borrow a couple of cassocks and dog collars (I had an offsider who had no lines.).

Dr Smart was really good seeing as I'd deserted his Church and choir a couple of years earlier. I soon realised how big Dr Smart was, the old dog collars he gave me would have fitted around my waist never mind my neck. Somehow we struggled through and the play was a failure, due in no small part to my being miss cast as the Irish Priest.

The Atkinson girls and other like-minded young ladies at the Young Farmers Club were, it would seem sick of having to buy new shoes after every young farmer's dance. I presume this as they, for no other reason than self-preservation, could have put themselves to the sword as they did.

They decided to hold dancing lessons for us younger boys, I think their story was that it would increase attendance at dances. Girls our age were included, but I don't remember them much, there were certainly no male teachers. Well, I for one was up for this, my attitude to girls was changing for obvious reasons and if I could go to dances and dance, who knows what might happen?

The dancing lessons were done on a no-cost basis in the Preston Patrick Memorial Hall, where we would later dance the night away with the girl of our dreams, dreams indeed. Isabel and Mary were running the show and giving most of the instructions. A girl called Lesley Evans from Barrows Green brought her record player and the music. It was the music that most interested me, as that was owned by a girl called Kathleen Howson, who also hailed from Barrows Green. She had what I thought at the time, was a fantastic collection of records. Beatles, Stones and anything, that was hot at the time.

Kathleen didn't do much, just dug out the records and watched us make fools of ourselves. She didn't get involved in the teaching and was very quiet and unbelievably lovely. We boys were not the best students but we stumbled through and I presume learnt the basic steps as I danced on for years.

After the serious lessons, we had a free for all with hot records blaring from Lesley's record player and our choice of partners. It was now time for my past to haunt me, these girls had memories. None of the girls that attended the classes wanted to dance with Thomas Watson, the pants shitter from Endmoor Primary School, his father doesn't own a farm and you should have seen the trouble he got into on the bus to school. Apart from the very odd one, I didn't want to dance with them, with their plaits and braces.

I had bigger fish to fry, she was two years older than them and me too, had reddish hair with a natural curl and didn't know about my accidents at primary school and owned the world's best record collection. Kathleen Howson was mine, genuinely she was mine, she asked me to dance at the end of the lessons every night. I was in love, I was in fact, so much in love that I was dumb-struck and just didn't know what to say to her. It was not unrequited love, as she too didn't know what to say to me, we smiled a lot. I, at least, lived for the next dance lesson and to dance with Kathleen.

I would have crawled all the way (About four miles.) to Barrows Green over broken glass to lick dog shit off Kathleen Howson's shoe. Kathleen, of course, was too much of a lady to step in doggy doos so I was never called upon to perform my gentlemanly duties, our relationship went no further and my dancing never improved much either.

22 LEARNING PROPER STUFF

Most of my life in 1964 centred around work. When I first started work at Woodlands Nursery all Mr Sanderson seemed to grow was carnations, his other project was, of course, his rabbits. The rabbits were even smellier than the carnations but at least the rabbits had an excuse. During my time at Woodlands, things were beginning to change. Some of the changes involved me, as I helped with the work and learned new skills.

No tradesmen were ever employed at Woodlands, Mr Sanderson could turn his hand to anything. New boilers were fitted, glazing on the greenhouses was upgraded and a new range of flowers was grown. This was all very interesting for me and I was learning so much, I'm sure Mr Sanderson taught me one big lesson, if someone else can do something, there's a good chance you can too.

The fitting of the new boilers to heat the greenhouses in winter involved me as the old boilers had to be removed and it was hard work, so hence, it involved the worker. It was not uncommon for me to arrive home requiring a bath, and by English standards, that's bloody dirty, soot and dust were heavily coated on a white body.

Seeing the boilers being fitted together was intriguing, giant u-shaped, hollow, cast iron pieces bolted together and sealed with asbestos rope, they then formed a tunnel of water to be heated by fire. Fire bricks and fire cement for the base and a hopper for coal, a worm to feed the coal to the fire and a fan to force the fire. It all seemed to happen effortlessly under Mr Sanderson's supervision and my fellow worker Alan's, strong hands. I was kept clear as if one of these boiler pieces had fallen on me, I would have been no more.

The upgrading on the greenhouse glazing was a messy job, it involved running an extremely sticky tape over the timber and edge of the glass, this would once have been done using putty but Mr Sanderson had discovered this new tape called Slyglas. It was the dirtiest job of all time and yet I didn't get it. Slyglas was a cloth tape covered with the stickiest light brown substance, which was waterproof and hence unable to be washed out of clothes.

Mr Sanderson employed prisoners from the local 'open' prison for this job. I guess these men were close to the end of their time and putting Slyglas tape on greenhouses was part of their rehabilitation. I'm not sure who washed their clothes but they didn't get Slyglas out of them. I wasn't overly exposed to these prisoners, but shared lunch hours with them and heard their stories of greatness in Gordy or Scouse accents. I watched with fascination as they rolled the thinnest cigarettes. Their lunch hours weren't very long as they had to wash the Slyglas off their hands before they could eat and this was no fast process and involved paraffin and then soap and water.

I didn't envy the prisoners their means of transport, they had the same un-cool bicycle I'd had a few years earlier and it was painted red, everyone knew they were prisoners as they rode to and from their jobs. In the case of Mr Sanderson's men, they were also covered in a light brown sticky substance.

Carnations were still the primary crop grown at Woodlands and had a three-year rotation over three of the largest greenhouses. In their first year, the carnations established themselves and produced a light crop of flowers and grew through supports of wire and string. The carnations were the domain of the ladies, Rene and Ruby who strung, disbudded and picked them.

It was my job at the end of the third year to rip them out, a hard and stinky job that left me smelling mouldy. I then had to fertilise the cleared ground with, you guessed it, rabbit dung and cultivate it into the grown with a rotary hoe. I was then responsible for planting the newly purchased plants in the spots carefully marked out by Mr Sanderson. The marking for these spots was made by what appeared to be a giant rake with tynes just the right distance apart, drawn first along the beds and then across, X of course, marked the spot.

Flowers were the name of the game, and out of nowhere, Mr Sanderson came up with new ones to grow, gladioli, freesias, anthuriums, sweetpeas, stocks and chrysanthemums. These flowers were pretty much run-of-the-mill, common or garden, but not in the hands of Tom Sanderson and grown in glasshouses. The sweet peas grew about ten feet tall and were picked from a stepladder. The gladioli were not the large clumsy things thrown by Dame Edna but a delicate pretty version.

The stocks were the ones that fascinated me the most, as stocks come in both single and double form, the singles are worthless as a cut flower but the doubles are much prized. The stocks Tom Sanderson grew were all doubles, this was achieved by some sort of genetic manipulation, the double seedlings had pale green leaves and the singles had dark green leaves. This must have been cutting-edge in 1964.

It seemed that chrysanthemums were grown for me to learn about because I was responsible for most of their care or should I say manipulation. They were planted in beds much like the carnations, by me. The first job was to nip the centre bud out of the plant as soon as it got growing. My fingers were getting greener daily as chrysanthemums have dark green foliage which passes to the fingers with ease.

Once the plants had developed side shoots, I was required to reduce these to three per plant. This was rather delicate work and my nimble fingers were required, if any plant had more or less than three side shoots after being given my treatment, it was pointed out to me in no uncertain terms. The plants grew and grew through the same wire and string supports used for the carnations. Once flower buds formed, (This was around the beginning of November as chrysanthemums are very seasonal and were being grown for the Christmas trade.) my nimble fingers were once again called into action.

I was given full responsibility for the disbudding of all the chrysanthemums, and there was a lot. The disbudding entailed removing all but the central flower bud. This was done by rubbing the side buds out using your thumbs, yes both thumbs, it had been explained to me very early in my horticultural career how many hands I owned. Before Christmas, I not only had green fingers but green thumbs.

And my first storm came, my first storm in the greenhouses. It was raining, a little windy and cold, outside that is. In the greenhouses, it was warm and calm and weeding wasn't such a bad job after all. As the wind built up outside so did the sounds inside, the creaking of the greenhouse framework, the rain on the glass and then the bang, and the sound of glass breaking over there. How soon would it be before the glass was landing over here?

There were random bangs and rattles of broken glass, it became unsafe and I was soon called out to work in the rabbit shed, with more rabbit droppings to move. Nothing could be done to save the random panes of glass as they fell to earth, work for another day. Now I was working full-time I had to witness a storm sooner or later, in the years I'd been working in my school holidays the storms only came when I wasn't there.

Tomorrow came and I was now to repair all the missing panes of glass. The weather was bleak but calm and I was to have my first stab at glazing. This was done from a ladder laid on the roof of the glasshouse, the base in the gutter and the top on the ridge of the glasshouse, just a little precarious for a first-time glazer. Each pane of glass was expertly cut to size by Mr Sanderson and I was given instructions as to how the glass should be fitted. "The top fits under the pane above, two pins on either side and then one under the bottom of the pane on either side, off tha goes." No hammer to tap the pins in, just a one-and-a-half-inch mortise chisel, surely an expert like Mr Sanderson would have the proper tools for the job, after all, there was around half an acre of glass at Woodlands.

I did question Tom, but the reply was less than satisfying, "It's best thing fo' t' job." 'Bollocks' I thought, 'I made a tack hammer at school and it would do the job like an expert.' The next day there was still more glass to replace, I turned up with my tack hammer and showed Mr Sanderson, "I'll tell thi, it won't work." After breaking a couple of panes of glass, merely by showing them my tack hammer, I had to yield to greater wisdom. There was very little this silly old fool didn't know.

23 AUTHORITY AND ME

Authority had stolen my fifteenth birthday or at least any chance I had, had of enjoying it. Authority had made me stay at school until the end of the school year when I thought, that I should be able to leave the day I turned fifteen. This strengthened my resolve that no one was going to mess with my sixteenth birthday, least of all, authority. I was now my authority, I made the decisions in my life, I earned a wage, I paid my way at home and I spent my money how I liked. I must confess, how I spent my money was not always as my parents would have liked me to do but they did no more than 'told me so'.

Since entering the workforce at thirteen I'd turned up at home with quite a collection of, shall we say, dubious acquisitions. Rabbits, bantams, fantail pigeons, hens which laid dark brown eggs and glass panels with which I made a cold frame and never grew anything in. I believed that my bike and my dog were worthwhile and couldn't be persuaded otherwise.

A lot of my Saturday afternoons were spent wandering around Kendal and making the odd purchase with my freshly acquired wages, I felt that winkle-picker shoes and drainpipe pants were essential for a young man of my standing. Obviously so, as my parents didn't tell me otherwise, they just looked at me strangely. I didn't tell them about the time I spent half a crown for a peach in Mark's and Spencer's and just stood there and ate it, I'm sure they would have thought it was a flagrant waste. It was worth every minute of the two hours it took me to earn the money.

As now a young adult, (In my eyes at least.) I was encouraged to save but there was no compulsion. I spent as I wished and still maintained my fiances in reasonable shape and never sought my parents' counsel when making mistakes with my money.

I had my sixteenth birthday, not much fanfare as my parents probably knew that I was going to do something stupid and thought it best to let the event slide past. Going to Kendal on Saturday afternoon as a sixteen-year-old was a lot different than going in as a fifteen-year-old. No more standing out the front of O'Loughlin's Motorcycle shop dreaming of turning sixteen and owning one of these gleaming machines.

I was in O'Loughlin's Motorcycle shop trying to find which of these machines I could afford. The choice was easy, there was only one I could afford, it didn't gleam and it looked rather daggy, but it was a motorbike and I bought it. I became the owner of a B.S.A. Bantam 125cc motorcycle, a bit of paperwork, money handed over and yes they'd deliver it to Ivy Garth that afternoon.

Forty quid lighter, the bus and bike ride home seemed to last forever. Forever and I couldn't wait to give my parents the good news. Seems the news wasn't as good as I'd thought, both Mum and Dad thought I'd made a rash and stupid decision.

My older sister Marion had a motorbike I pointed out, (It was a Honda fifty and didn't count as a motorbike in the real world.) and it was my money, I was sixteen and it will be here any minute. I'm sure they were now thinking 'We should have made him stay on at school, made him try harder with his eleven plus'.

Just as I was happy to own a motorbike, there was a strong belief in the community of Preston Patrick and Preston Richard that motorcycle ownership brought only two things, death, or even worse, debauchery. I wasn't much interested in death, the idea of debauchery was probably what drew me to motorcycle ownership. Mum at least wasn't very keen on me succumbing to either, Dad, of course, knew I was bound to succumb to debauchery sooner or later but wasn't keen on the death part, he knew it was a messy business.

The motorbike arrived at Ivy Garth, duly unloaded, the nice gentleman gave me instructions on how to operate the machine and I was home and hosed. We had fields at Ivy Garth so I could practice there, I found the gears a little tricky at first but mastered them. I got the beast into top gear and was flying towards a wall, I had to stop and soon. It's easy on a bike you just think to stop and apply both brakes, not so on a motorbike, when you apply the same two brakes you discover one of them is the clutch and the other is the front brake which when travelling on grass, doesn't stop the motorbike. Soft landing, damaged pride.

Arriving at work on Monday morning on my motorbike, I felt so proud, Mr Sanderson was also happy for me. I thought Mr Sanderson was going to take possession of my pride and joy and take it for a test ride but he just admired it and was the only person who thought I'd made a good choice. Yes, of course, he'd owned a motorbike as a lad and had happy memories of his motorcycling youth.

Rene, his housekeeper/worker was not so impressed as I was getting all the attention that day and Mr Sanderson was going to bore her with his motorcycling stories which she'd probably heard before. Couldn't help thinking they had a rather strange relationship, nothing going on there, as she was much younger than him.

With my motorbike came newfound freedom. My travel history was very limited, apart from primary school excursions I'd never travelled much more than six miles from home. My first Saturday afternoon on the motorbike took me to places far and wide, down roads I'd never travelled to places I'd never heard of. I went to one place where all the streets seemed to have the same name 'culdesac' and to my amazement, the streets went nowhere. On arriving home, I explained this to my parents who immediately burst out laughing and explained that a culdesac is a dead-end street. With a motorbike under me, I could see that my world was going to be so much bigger.

My first real adventure on my motorbike wasn't a travel adventure, but more of a life adventure. I decided to attend the Whittington races. I had a preconceived idea that horse racing was glamorous and exciting and that it would be very grown-up and it would fit in very well with my new grown-up status. The Whittington races were a steeplechase, not racing as in everyday horse racing.

I knew almost as much about horseracing or steeplechases as I knew about culdesacs a few weeks earlier, I didn't even know how to get to Whittington, never mind the race track and it wasn't far away. My grandparents Hodgson had once lived in Whittington so there was a natural connection, once I found Whittington and the race track this was going to be the most exciting day of my life.

I found the race track and was somewhat underwhelmed, there were a few cars parked in a field and a couple of 'huts', I think that's the best way to describe the toilets and betting facilities, and pretty much nothing else. There were spectators but they looked less than glamorous and the race track was, what seemed miles away. We, the spectators, were on a hillside and the horses ran and jumped around a badly marked track, on the flat land below, at some stages of the race the horses were barely visible.

I was now to place my first-ever bet, with my in-depth knowledge of horseflesh, I just picked a horse with a nice-sounding name. Five shillings seemed a sensible amount to wager, yet those around me were betting with notes, not coins. After the race had finished I returned to the betting booth, ticket in hand and handed it through the grill, only, to be told it was no good as the horse didn't win. I persisted with this for another hour or so and won nothing and was rapidly getting rid of this week's wages.

It was a cloudy dismal day and I'd wasted more money than I would dare to tell my parents. I didn't enjoy watching a few horses running and jumping around a field and had come here on my own to get a taste of glamour. I couldn't wait to get back to my motorbike and fire it up and head for home. My parents were so happy to hear I'd had an awful time, it was almost sickening. This had been a bitter pill to swallow but it cured the itch that I'd had, no more would I feel the desire to go to the races or believe anyone who told me gambling was fun.

24 FRIENDS BEING FOUND FOR ME

The Young Farmers was now my social outlet. In my almost three years as a member, I had proved myself to be pretty useless as a participant in their activities but I was fairly sociable. I was, however, something of an oddball, as I didn't attend meetings smelling of silage and cow shit and I owned a motorbike. Only one other member, to my knowledge, had owned a motorbike, that was Arthur Barnes and he was dead. Sadly, for the parents of Preston Patrick and surrounds, Arthur had not died riding his motorbike but had been electrocuted while fixing something electrical while standing in water. I missed Arty with his eternal smile and his A.J.S. 250.

Before meetings we lads had a meeting of our own in the men's cloakroom, telling dirty jokes and stories of carting muck. It was at one of these pre-meeting meetings that I was searched out by none other than Bernard Parsons, the stinking rich farmer's son from Overthwaite. This had only happened once before when he'd wanted to introduce me to one of his father's workers who, although he'd brought him along, couldn't be seen mixing with.

For some reason, he could let this labourer loose on me and we'd get on fine, we didn't. It seems this was another of those occasions and I was introduced to an older-looking lad called Richard. Bernard hadn't brought this lad along, he'd got there under his own steam, on his motorbike. It was a little threatening for another member of the Young Farmers to have a motorbike, I rather liked being the only one.

This lad also had an accent, not a strong one but an accent nonetheless, somewhere north of Kendal was my guess. He also had an infuriating habit of adding 'like' to the end of all his sentences, "It were grand tha knows, like." when I picked him up on this he was less than happy. Like Bernard's other underling, I could see I wasn't going to get on with this bloke either. Nobody who was a true native of Preston Patrick had an accent, newcomers were easy to detect and always treated with suspicion.

This Richard bloke had a motorbike, so like me, was something of an outcast amongst these conservative farmer's sons and after our original mistrust of each other, we got on quite well. Richard didn't take the death side of motorcycle ownership as seriously as he should have and it wasn't long before he met a car. The stupid car driver was going the wrong way when Richard collided with him and Richard took to the air and landed in a rather bad shape. Exit my newfound friend, for a few weeks at least, life had to go on and the social side of the Young Farmers was just starting to kick in. Dances, excursions and my parents rather encouraged me to go to whist drives which they told me were fun even if they had nothing to do with the Young Farmers.

I dragged myself along to my first whist drive for an evening of fun. A whist drive is a little like a flirtation barn dance, what seems like hundreds of people sit at long trestle tables and play the artful game of whist (A card game it seems, invented for people who enjoy being unhappy.) at the end of each hand the players move to the left, the people on the other side of the trestle table did the same, hence you change partners after each hand.

It's really fun, I can tell you, you meet so many unhappy people with a fierce desire to win. It's a form of gambling as there are prizes to be won so I can't see why my parents steered me down that path. Mum and Dad loved whist drives, was there a generation gap? I'm not sure but I only ever attended one whist drive.

With my motorbike and the dancing lessons, I'd had, courtesy of the Young Farmers girls. I was well equipped for Young Farmers dances which were held at the Preston Patrick Memorial Hall, ironically the whist drives were held there too. I may have jumped in too early with the dances, I arrived on time, which was too early and I was stone-cold sober, which was also too early and as the night wore on I was the youngest attendee. I found myself terrified of the 'older woman' and there were no girls my age there. I got the odd 'pity dance' but that's all it was.

I did, however, get to dance the flirtation barn dance, well the 'older woman' I'd asked to dance, would be out of my grasp in seconds so she was happy to accept. This it seemed was my forte, with my simplistic one-liners and youthful charm I was in my element, this was fun, proper grown-up. I rode my motorbike home around one o'clock, pretending I'd enjoyed myself, I had briefly.

A Young Farmers excursion to see the Blackpool illuminations sounded exciting, I hadn't been on an excursion since primary school and they were always fun. Motorbike to the Memorial Hall and onto the Stainton's bus, my motorbike wasn't taking me very far but I had something no other member had (Richard didn't count as he wasn't around.). The fact that I owned a motorbike and disbudded chrysan-themums made it a little hard to mix with some of the muck carters I was travelling with. There were also some members of the Kent Estuary Young Farmers Club on this excursion, young girls who didn't know I used to shit my pants at Endmoor Primary School, I could do alright on the romantic trip home.

Blackpool illuminations drew people from every corner of the British Isles, I was led to believe. I can't understand why, in the words of a great philosopher of the time, Thomas Hodgson Watson, "It were nowt." The Stainton's coach arrived in Blackpool around nine and drove at a snail's pace along the waterfront. We strained our necks to get a look, out of the windows to see these famous illuminations, had the tide been in we may have seen the reflection of the lights on the water, but it wasn't.

We finally came to a stop, just below the famous Blackpool Tower, the climax of the light show. We all piled off the bus like a mob of school kids, which some of us had been not much earlier in our lives. There weren't many oos and aahs and it was not the most exciting excursion I'd been on I thought. We'd been allotted a time to be back at the bus so I had to stay pretty close to someone who owned a watch, I didn't.

The bus driver had I'm sure, taken off to a local pub to relieve himself and grab a couple of pints to help him with the boring drive home. Oh how I wished I could have a drink of beer too, that would make me a man. Lots of boys my age were getting the odd drink, of course, they looked older than me, sadly I had kept my youthful good looks. It was, I found rather detrimental to my desire to drink and passion for the girl of my dreams. Most girls went for the more mature-looking lads.

At the allotted time we all returned to the bus, the lucky older ones had probably found a pub to slake their thirst just like I presumed the driver did, they had partners too, lucky bastards. There wasn't the same enthusiasm to get on the bus as there had been to get off, we younger ones headed for the back and slithered into seats, any seats. I was sitting next to a girl from the Kent Estuary Young Farmers, this was our first meeting.

I must commend the girls from Preston Patrick for their discretion, it was obvious they hadn't mentioned to this lovely girl that I used to shit my pants in primary school. There is something about a Stainton's coach and darkness that raises the hormonal levels in young people and it was evident in the seat I had chosen. I went in for my first 'pash', wow, so that's what it's like?

There were a few girls on this bus who would have killed for this. They didn't know what they'd been missing and nor did I, till now. It got rather heated, did this girl's parents know that their daughter was pashing the hell out of a motorbike owner, did they care? There was a whip-round for the driver but when the collector got to sweetness and me, he claimed we were asleep. Was he just being polite and didn't want to 'spoil the moment' or was he embarrassed by what he was witnessing? Either way, it saved me a few coins. It was some way into the journey when I discovered this girl's parents (At least her mother.) did care. She had been fitted with, what was in its day one of the best contraceptive devices available. I must confess it had me flummoxed and it was some time before I learnt that it was called 'pantyhose'. I offered her a ride home on my motorbike but she was with friends.

25 MOVING ON

I squandered my time as the only sixteen-year-old in Preston Patrick with a motorbike. I could have been 'King of the Road', a rebel without a cause, the main man. I was none of these, I was just a kid with a motorbike who rode it to work every day. And just as I was that nothing, that bloke who worked at Overthwaite returned to the scene with an accident record and a brighter, shinier motorbike than mine.

Richard Berrie, that chubby bloke from Troutbeck who worked for the Parsons' had returned to steal the thunder I'd failed to put together in his absence. It was probably his chubbiness that saved his miserable life (Softening the fall.) and now he'd returned to my Preston Patrick to be the blain of my life. Amazingly, we got on well and started going to motorbike scrambles (It would later become motocross.) and anything that related to motorbikes.

It was at these motorbike-related sporting fixtures that I discovered two things that would have a profound effect on my life. The first of these things was Castrol 'R', a vegetable oil especially refined for use in two-stroke racing or performance engines, it was illegal to use it on the road. So what was so special about Castrol 'R'? It was, of course, the smell, it was a fantastic smell, verging on addictive, it was like something that had been cooked and not quite burnt, a perfect smell.

The second thing I discovered was my sporting prowess, my true sporting prowess. I was to discover, that I was one of the world's greatest spectators. I could watch these men ride their motorbikes at neck-break speed, perform jumps, have crashes, get covered in mud and sustain a fatal injury, and I felt nothing. To me, this was what sport was all about, the thrill and excitement and no pain or exertion. Not like that awful stuff they'd forced on us at school. Richard, on the other hand, was a little sporty and played rugby union, a sport I couldn't understand and made no effort to do so, I failed as a spectator at that.

Richard and I soon became great mates and if Richard and I were going somewhere, we went on his motorbike, which was a touch more reliable than mine. I was starting to realise I'd bought a dud motorbike, it was daggy, not very fast (That could have been a plus.) and was terrible to start. The traditional kick-start wasn't working for me and I took to 'bump starting' it. This is done by slipping the bike into first gear, drawing in the clutch, pushing the motorbike along the road till you get up a good speed and then jumping onto the seat and releasing the clutch.

I became quite adept at this practice but it was embarrassing if I failed the first time and was running out of the downhill road. The crunch came when I was to go for my motorbike licence, I couldn't start the test with a 'bump start', regardless of how proficient I was. Richard lent me his motorbike and I passed the test, I also learnt how easy it was to start a Japanese motorbike compared to the British bike I owned. The examiner complimented me on what a nice bike I had, little did he know.

As my friendship with Richard flourished and my desire to smell Castrol 'R' grew stronger, my fragile relationship with my father was becoming seriously fraught. We spoke rarely, and in-depth never, Dad's words would run to something like, 'I telt thi so.' Or 'Nowt good'll come of it.' In return, I found it easier to say nothing or just utter a couple of words as I left the house, conversation was non-existent.

So one morning when Dad started talking to me in a normal manner, without a hint of negativity, I was rather taken aback. "I was talking to Trefor Jones tuther day and he ses he's looking for a lad to work for him, 'cos John Booth is leaving to go to work with his fatha on't new place in Yorkshire." Dad starts. 'What the hell are you telling me this for Dad.' I'm thinking but listened on. "Ih it'd be a grand job for you, tha knows, he's a nice chap is Trefor, looks after his lads." Dad continues. Here's my father suggesting I should give up the job of my dreams to become a 'muck carter' a lowly farmhand, didn't being a farmhand get him where he is today, a dust-man with South Westmorland County Council? 'I'm sixteen, I had a job when you didn't Dad, I'm supposed to take career advice from you, I've heard you but I'm not listening.' Are the words going through my head but are left unuttered. "Tha'll be on better money than tha's on now tha knows." These were the last words Dad uttered as he left for work.

The idea of me becoming a farmhand left me cold, I was becoming a gardener and learning all the skills associated with gardening, what I'd always wanted to do. I was earning five quid a week and now my lifestyle was using that up with ease. My friend Richard was a lowly farmhand and always seemed to have plenty of money, he'd just changed jobs and was earning a bit more now.

My mind wasn't on the work at hand that day and Mr Sanderson calling out "Get thi mind on't job." Jerked me back to reality but those final words from Dad echoed through my brain, "Tha'll be on better money than tha's on now tha knows." It was obvious that Dad wanted me to apply for this job with Trefor Jones. That in itself told me I shouldn't do it, doing what Dad wanted me to do went against the grain, had he told me not to apply I'd have been there in a shot. "Tha'll be on better money." "Tha'll be on better money." Those words wouldn't go away.

My dog walk that Saturday afternoon was longer than usual, up to Cox Bank and across the top and down the track I'd trod with Dad years ago taking the sheep from Cox Bank to be dipped at Camsgill. Camsgill was Trefor Jones' farm where Dad thought I should apply for a job, heaven forbid that I would have told Dad of my planned route or that I'd knocked on Trefor's door when I got to Camsgill. It was very much against my better judgement that I did knock on Trefor's door.

My second job application, "Yes?" Trefor says as he answers the door.

"My Dad says you are looking for someone to work for you." I meekly reply, "Who's your Dad?" Trefor asks with a blank face, seemingly having no idea who I am.

"Tom Watson" I reply expecting instant recognition.

"Tom Watson?" Trefor queries.

'This isn't going as well as it should.' I'm thinking.

"From Cox Bank," I answer.

"Oh, Watson." Trefor comes out with as if my father is some subspecies, Trefor is rather posh for a South Westmorland farmer.

"Well actually, I am looking for someone, and you'd be interested?" Trefor continues.

'What do you think I'm doing here?' I thought, "Yes." I replied.

The interview continued, did I have a job? Where? etc: 'For Christ's sake Trefor everybody knows where I work, everybody it seems but you, knows I'm a good worker, why the third degree?' I'm asking this question in my mind. It was rather casual but I found it formal, perhaps that was Trefor's posh manner.

I was to call back next week and we could work out some sort of training schedule and the timing for me to start the job, would I be able to work a few Saturday afternoons to ease me into the job? I was going to be a muck carter, how much training does that need?

I wandered home, wondering whether I'd done the right thing, I had hadn't I? I at least answered the question in the affirmative, I would become the best farmworker in South Westmorland and I'd be earning much more than the other muck carters, I may one day have a farm of my own. Dreams are two a penny when you're walking your dog. Reality hit when I got home and told my parents.

"Tha's done right thing." Said, Dad.

I knew then I hadn't because it was against everything I knew to be in agreeance with Dad. Mum the ever-practical one said, "You'll have to tell Mr Sanderson what's going on."

'I can't do that just yet as I'm not sure what is going on.' I thought to myself. 'How was I going to tell the man who gave me my first job and backed that wimpy kid in, all those years ago, that I had found another job and was leaving in favour of someone who had done nothing for me?' It wasn't going to be easy.

26 BECOMING A 'MUCK CARTER'

My next three weeks at Woodlands Nursery were pretty much like the three years previous. Mr Sanderson wandering around, cigar in mouth and his housekeeper/worker Rene, smoking her way through another few packets of Woodbines. It was a reflective time for me, as I knew I wasn't going to be here much longer and this place had become a part of my life. It was very different from life elsewhere in the closeted area I'd grown up in.

Smoking to the extreme was not normal in Preston Patrick and Mr Sanderson's chain-smoking of cigars was weird. He also wore that damned suit every day with work boots. Mr Sanderson was also, what locals liked to call a 'latecomer', someone who wasn't born in the area, this was obvious from his strong Lancashire accent. This is strange coming from me because I'm sure he'd lived in the area longer than me.

As I did my case study on my boss and his housekeeper/worker, I was also trying to work out how I was going to break the news of my impending departure. I think I worked harder and quieter than usual, so anyone with knowledge of my character would have smelt a rat. I was led to believe there was a Mrs Sanderson, I think my parents had said something one day, she was never sighted. There was a son who visited twice a year or thereabouts, so there had been a Mrs Sanderson. Yes, Mr Sanderson was a 'latecomer', a man of mystery.

Rene, Mr Sanderson's housekeeper/worker was a local girl, or she had been twenty-five or so years earlier. If Mr Sanderson's chain-smoking cigars was weird, Rene's relationship with him was even weirder. Rene made it very clear she didn't like the man and made fun of him at most opportunities. The fact that Mr Sanderson was a Freemason gave Rene every chance to laugh about it, she referred to Masonic robes as pyjamas and was quick to pick up on visits from his Masonic friends.

In turn, Mr Sanderson was very kind to Rene and allowed her to keep two Labrador dogs, had they both been Golden Labradors they could have been cloned from Rene. One was golden and the other black, they, like Rene were a touch overweight and had a Rene-like walk or should that be waddle? Being a local, Rene could pass herself off as normal but she wasn't what I'd call normal.

Like Mr Sanderson wore his suit every day, Rene wore a cotton dress, she did at least change it every day, unlike Mr Sanderson's suit, the style always remained the same and perhaps a size smaller than would have been comfortable. Rene did her own hair which was a golden colour (Not sure if it was natural or not.) in saying she did her own hair, I mean curled it, around the edges at least. There was a patch on the top of her head which was just flat, it was quite nice from the front but when she turned round it looked hideous. Added to her hair she also had one golden hand from the Woodbines.

Every Saturday morning Mr Sanderson took Rene home to her mother's place in Milnthorpe, a couple of miles away. For this Saturday ritual, Rene tarted herself up and I promise you I've used the right term. The dress was 'the usual,' but sparkling clean, the hair freshly curled, heels were worn, makeup applied and I mean applied and led by the brightest red lipstick and she stunk of the cheapest perfume available, it even overpowered the Woodbines.

Over my three and a half years at Woodlands I learnt that Rene was a virgin with vast sexual experience because from time to time when Mr Sanderson was out for the afternoon, Rene would tell me of her vast sexual experience. Even for a sixteen-year-old innocent, these experiences bearly rated, boys at school had done better than Rene. For a sixteen-year-old with high testosterone levels, words that contained letters like 'E' or 'X' or 'S' uttered by a woman caused great discomfort. Even with her limited experience Rene, obviously knew this, as when

I left the realm of discomfort and reached the point of agony, she returned to the house to do some housework. Yes, I'd made the right decision, I'd be much better off away from this madhouse.

The first of my three Saturday afternoons of training began. I finished work at Woodlands and headed home to Ivy Garth, wolfed down some lunch and off to Camsgill for a one o'clock start. I wasn't the least bit nervous or apprehensive about my forthcoming training as I was only going to be a muck carter after all, and I'd grown up surrounded by farms and farm animals, what was to learn?

My tutor was John Booth, a local lad whose father had a farm. I knew John, I'd been in the same class as his sister at primary school and he had been my fellow Priest when I made my acting debut, John had the non-speaking part. My first lesson was starting the tractor, how many people need lessons in starting a tractor? It's obvious, I did, as the tractor had to be heated before it would start, and then there was the driving of the tractor, I'd never driven a tractor. Fortunately, I picked these things up without too much trouble, next I had to learn how to reverse the said tractor with a muck spreader on the back.

An accomplished muck carter could do this blindfolded, I had difficulty but John was a patient tutor and we got there. I'd come to Camsgill safe in the knowledge that John Booth wasn't the sharpest knife in the drawer. Within two hours he had made me look completely useless, I was beginning to wonder if I'd made the right decision after all.

Afternoon tea, in the house - I'd worked at Woodlands for three and a half years and never set foot in the house. I meet Mrs Jones who is a dour Scot, not overly welcoming but she can cook, her cake is better than Mum's. Trefor asks John how I'm going.

"I'h his au right." John surely lied.

It's now milking time, John shows me how to put the milking machines together and the way things are done at Camsgill. 'I'd been in a shippon lots of times so this would be easy.' I thought to myself. Each cow had a name, 'Now they're having me on.' O.K. Tommy Fletcher had Winnie and Hilary but this is a proper farm.

My first contact with the cows was to draw milk from their teats into a small can to check for mastitis, I squeezed the cow's teat and nothing happened. Was there something wrong with the cow? Or was I useless? It turns out I was useless and John explains how to draw the milk from the cow.

"Tha puts thi hand on't tit and tightens tha fingers one at a time round it." John patiently explains, while giving a demonstration, milk pours from the cow.

'Why's it so easy for him and so hard for me?' I'm thinking as we move on to the next manoeuvre, placing the milking machine suction cups onto the cow's teats. 'How hard can this be?' I'm thinking as again, I make a fool of myself, air that hasn't yet been circulated is being drawn into the milking machine at an alarming rate because I simply don't know what I'm doing.

"No, tha's got ta kink pipe as tha puts it on't tit." John firmly explains in his ever-patient manner.

I'd come to Camsgill thinking things would be a breeze and on my first day, I discovered I was not suited to this life. I was hoping beyond hope I didn't bump into John when he was out with his mates and he'd told them how incompetent I was, I'd never live it down. Would I ever again mock a muck carter? Well, of course, I would but only when I became accomplished in the skills required to be a muck carter.

Trefor sees me before I leave and assures me I'll soon get used to things and asks me if I'd spoken to Mr Sanderson, "Not yet." I reply, still dreading the conversation I must eventually have with my boss. When I got home I couldn't wait to untie my dog and take her for a walk, to avoid that question that Dad was bound to ask, "How did tha go?" I'd only had to suffer this humiliation because he'd told me to go for the job, I should have known better.

27 A NEW CONCEPT

Two more Saturday afternoons at Camsgill and I seemed to have got a little more competent in the tractor reversing and cow milking department. I had not shown much in the courage department at Woodlands Nursery. It was my last Saturday morning, and I hadn't yet plucked up the courage to tell Mr Sanderson I had another job and wouldn't be there on Monday.

The payday ritual was upon me, and as Mr Sanderson dragged my five quid from his pocket, he quietly said, "We won't be needing thi on Monday." I'm sure I was about to tell him I wouldn't be there but I was too late. I'd been trying with all my heart to get out the news for weeks now and he already knew.

Not only did he know but he had someone ready to take on my job. How could this be? I'm sure he didn't know Trefor and if he did, I felt sure he wouldn't have socialised with him, as he didn't socialise, at least not to my knowledge. Rene had told me about the Freemasons and their secret ways, that's how he'd heard, Masonic tittle-tattle. Just as I'd kept my leaving secret (I hadn't had the guts to tell him.) he'd kept his knowledge of me leaving to himself. None of this made me feel good.

My motorbike had been getting harder to start, so on Sunday before I was to start at Camsgill, I thought I'd better do something about it. I turned to mechanical mode, after all, I'd fitted it with new piston rings under Mr Sanderson's guidance. Fitting a new magneto would be child's play. Didn't turn out that way, I forced something and cracked the crankcase. As a result of this, I never rode my motorbike again. This made me reliant on my friend Richard to get me around, which was pretty much how it was anyway. If we went anywhere together it was now always on his bike, this worked well for me as Richard, since his brush with death had become a very competent rider. I, on the other hand, was useless and had had a couple of spills that hurt. I never liked pain much.

I soon got into a rhythm at Camsgill and enjoyed the work and Trefor's company, he was an intelligent man who, unlike many of his peers could read and write. Another way Trefor was different to the other farmers in South Westmorland was his size. Trevor was about five foot six with his boots on and lightly built, most important was that he was dapper and always looked smart, he wore his flat cap with aplomb.

Trefor spoke without an accent, a little strange as he was of Welsh heritage and had spent most of his life in Westmorland, no sign of either in his speech, it was as I've said before, a little posh. I mentioned Trefor's size in his boots, I'm sure this would have been less without his boots, he wore an enormous pair of 'hobnailed' boots, it seemed, everywhere. His rhythmic stomp accompanied him where ever he strode and I can assure you, he strode, and at a pace, I was proud to match.

This was it seemed, where I belonged. My father had been right to steer me in this direction, not that I was going to tell him so. I was confident I'd found my place in the workforce and this work was going to be my life. How wrong I'd been to think I could be a gardener when this was what I was born for. I now fitted in the spot that was made for me, I was a round peg in a round hole.

Richard and I soon found a pub or two where I could get served, not an easy task as I still looked fourteen. Richard however, looked to be in his twenties, he was a little follicly challenged, not bald, but follicly challenged which helped his case. This was another thing I knew I was made for, swilling beer in a pub. My body, however, had other ideas and I could spew at the drop of a hat and I suffered the worst hangovers. When I turned up for work with one of my monstrous hangovers, Trefor was none too pleased, but to my surprise, understanding. This probably happened too often but I worked my heart out for the next week to make up for my sins.

I was to discover a new - to me at least - concept in the workplace working for the Jones's paid holidays. When I worked at Woodlands, I'd got my five quid a week come hail or shine but there'd never been any mention of 'holidays'. I'd never worked on Bank Holidays but no one did. So when Trefor asked when I wanted to take my holiday, I had to give it some thought.

I consulted Richard who, it seemed was familiar with this concept. A date was selected, this was pretty easy as Richard was a farmworker too and holiday time was the same on most farms, after haytime. Richard, I'm sure, decided on a motorcycle trip around Scotland, he had relatives there. Sounded exciting to me as I'd never been outside England before and Richard painted a nice picture of Scotland in my mind.

Two seventeen-year-old lads took off on a 90cc Honda motorbike for what, for one of them a least, was an adventure of his short lifetime. It was sometime earlier in our friendship that Richard had told me he was adopted and knew nothing of his mother and somewhat less of his father, and he had relatives in Scotland. His adoptive father was Scottish so they were his relatives. Glasgow, where these relatives lived was to be our first stop.

My first time, being almost alone in a real city, I may have been overwhelmed, I certainly wasn't impressed, by the city at least. I was however impressed by the way Richard managed to find his Gran's place, every place in this long street looked the same to me. A long grey wall, four storeys high with windows in it and doorways all along atop, steps from the street.

A culture shock was about to happen. In our little corner of the world, everybody lived in houses, with upstairs and downstairs and gardens back and front, even the little place Richard hailed from in Troutbeck had an upstairs. Richard's Gran's place was something else, it was two storeys up and seemed to me to be just one room. It was, obviously more as apart from Richard's Gran, there was an uncle and various others who lived there and we were to be slept there too for at least one night, maybe two.

This wasn't a place where people could be expected to live surely? It was merely a drawer in a giant chest of drawers, one room with doors in the wall leading into what were, no more than cupboards. However, this place was full of love and incredibly, happiness. Yes, Richard may have been adopted but he was embraced so strongly by his adoptive relatives, that it made me envious, I had no relatives who loved me this much.

While in Glasgow we attended a soccer game, Rangers playing someone, my first time in a real stadium, it was huge and we were miles from the action, but we were there. The rest of Scotland was something of an anti-climax, the weather was Scottish, which on a motorbike is not good. I got to see my first beach, one with sand and blue water, I loved that. Back in England, all I'd seen was the seaside. Now, the seaside is not like a beach, it is what it says it is, besides the sea and it has endless mudflats when the tides out and brown wavey water when it's in, people paddle in it.

We stayed in pubs as we toured and always got served so there was a bit of drinking amongst the sightseeing. We crossed the Firth of Forth Bridge on a 90cc motorbike, we weren't wimps. I'm sure we stopped, got off the bike and just took air when we were back on terra-firma, it had been scary. We were well on our way home now, my first journey into a foreign country was behind me. It had been an adventure, I'd seen another culture, heard another language and seen a proper soccer match live, but for me, that beach was the highlight.

I was so glad to get home to the security of well, that house in Goose Green with upstairs and downstairs and Mum and Dad and my sisters and normality. Back into my round hole where I fitted, my job at Camsgill with Trefor and Mrs Jones. I didn't want my life to take me too far from home.

28 THE GOOD LIFE TURNS BAD

My life and work at Camsgill were making me sloth-like. I loved the work and enjoyed Trefor's company when we worked together, which was most days. Mrs Jones cooked the best food and I was introduced to things I'd never eaten before, I think roasted parsnip was my all-time favourite. The food wasn't complex but just a notch up from the scrag-end that Mum was forced to cook, simply because we couldn't afford better. Lunchtimes were my favourite time, Mrs Jones's cooking and they had the radio on. For some reason, the BBC chose lunchtimes at Camsgill to replay some of their best programmes. We had a full sixty-minute lunch hour regardless of the season and after lunch, we three, Mrs Jones, Trefor and myself just sat a listened to the radio, a longtime friend of mine. Even with the generation gap, we all liked the same things on the radio, The Forsyte Saga and My Word were two of the programmes which had me riveted. I, it seemed was almost one of the family as Trefor and Mrs Jones were childless.

My hard work and less frequent hangovers kept me in the good books most of the time. We'd got through silage making, haytime and sheep clipping it seemed, seamlessly. The sheep clipping had little to do with me as for the first time, Trefor hired contractors to clip the sheep. He was getting older and I would have to be taught that new skill.

His logic was that if he hired professionals it could be all done and dusted in a day and he wouldn't have the work and pressure of teaching me. The contractors were two brothers I knew from the Young Farmers, George and Robert Bell from Commonmire, a local, rather rundown farm. As I said, I knew these men, I'd worked with Robert at Woodlands when he'd come to help with extra work, he was rough but an honest worker.

When I was told that the Bell brothers were coming to clip the sheep, I expected two scruffy blokes to turn up and for them to be pretty disorganised. How shocked I was when two rather smart young men turned up and soon told Trefor how they wanted things set up and went about their business. What would once have been a major chore on the farm was over and done within a few hours. My judgement of the Bell brothers certainly went up a notch that day.

I seemed suited to farm work, it was dirty, hard and as I'd expected didn't require too much brain work. Some jobs however required skill, drystone walling was one such job, I'd messed with this at home as we had drystone walls around our small acreage. When Trefor took me out to teach me how it was done I was shocked.

As I carefully placed the stones to build the wall, Trefor just dumped them, in what seemed to me to be a pile, I must confess it worked but it looked terrible. How such a dapper fellow could make such a mess of a wall was beyond me. He seemed to take so much pride in his appearance yet none in how his work looked.

As the first year wore on I learnt so much (Drystone walling aside.) dipping sheep was a pretty major job. This was done to protect the sheep from 'fly strike' when the sheep get infested with maggots and die. At Camsgill, Trefor had a 'state of the art,' sheep yards and sheep dipping facility. This took me back to the time I'd accompanied Dad with the sheep from Cox Bank to be dipped at Camsgill.

This was a little different now, I wasn't a little kid watching his hero, I was the farm lad hurling the sheep into the deep bath to be bathed in a kind of disinfectant, they didn't like this process so made it as hard as possible for the hurler. No sooner had Trefor's sheep been dipped than the new neighbour from Cox Bank came over with his sheep. It seemed the tradition had been passed on.

By now I knew the new owner of Cox Bank as he always gave us a lift when we were walking home, that is Mum, Barbara or myself. Jack Beck was his name and he was a brash young farmer and from the look of his sheep a very good one too. One could compare Jack's sheep with Shetland ponies, they were huge, no hurling with these sheep and dragging was more the order of the day. Now, this was hard work. That day I got to know Jack Beck a lot better than I had, and I think after dragging his sheep to the dipping bath I gained his respect too.

One of the most boring and least satisfying jobs on the farm was mowing thistles. This was done by driving the tractor around the fields with a mower on the back cutting the thistles, a prickly weed that the cows and sheep wouldn't eat. The strange thing about this is that once they'd been cut the cows would eat them, they were just as prickly and to me looked less appetising. The cows would make something they'd grazed around for weeks, suddenly look tasty and would make a point of showing you how tasty they were, tossing them around as they ate them. Easy as this job was it did seem heartless as the thistles grew back the next year.

I guess a heartless job brings on a mind which doesn't care or isn't there. This day must have been one when my head was empty. Trefor's tractor was, as I'd learnt on my first day, not easy to start, it needed to be heated to start, even on the warmest of days. As a result of this, I found it easier to leave it idling than stop it and have to go through the restart procedure.

I was cutting the thistles in a hilly field just across from the house and farm building this day. For some reason or other, I needed something from the buildings or had I been called in for afternoon tea, for the life of me I can't remember. As I said my head was empty. I left the tractor idling on the hillside and went to the farm buildings.

Now, this tractor didn't have a handbrake as such, there was a half-moon-shaped piece of steel that when activated would hold the brake pedal down, quite a clever device.

As I made my way back to the tractor, it was probably two hundred hilly yards away. It started to move, slowly at first, as it wasn't on a steep part of the hilly field. My heart sank as it did reach a hilly place and picked up speed, neck break speed, it flew through the hedge at the bottom of the hill and into the air and landed upside down having ploughed through two hedges. The engine was now screaming as the muffler had broken off. I was terrified as I was sure it would explode, I didn't know what to do.

Trefor took off at a trot in his hobnail boots and turned the engine off, he returned, grim-faced and for the first time in my tenure there raised his voice to me and said, "What the hell were you thinking." I was speechless. The tractor was a write-off. Things between Trefor and I remained speechless or pretty much speechless for the next couple of days. I was sure I'd lose my job, Mrs Jones was dourer than before and lunchtimes lasted forever.

The remaining thistles had to be cut with a scythe, I guess as a punishment, but I rather enjoyed it. The old TVO Nuffield tractor had to be used for everything now and it was a monster with dodgy steering, now, that was a punishment. My work rate lifted to repay my maintained employment and things slowly returned to normal.

29 THE WEDDING

Becoming eighteen seemed to be a big thing for my generation, the legal drinking age would have been the biggest thing, I'm sure the ability to vote had absolutely nothing to do with it. For me, a veteran of underage drinking, this leap into legality meant nothing. I rarely if ever took advantage of the fact I could now drink legally in a pub. I became an almost abstainer and only on the odd occasion had a drink with my friend Richard. I can only assume that my desire to snub authority was the driving force in my drinking habits, now it was legal if I drank, I would be conforming to authority. I can only philosophise, but I did become a pretty boring person when I turned eighteen.

Richard's life was moving on and he acquired another set of wheels in the form of an Austin A35 van, about as uncool a motor vehicle as one could own. It was dry and comfortable but certainly didn't have the appeal a motorbike did a couple of years earlier. He'd moved back to live with his parents and put his muck carting days behind him, he was driving a truck in a quarry near Troutbeck.

Perhaps I should have done something like that but I was so comfortable at work and home, I had no desire to leave my cocoon. All around me my peers were getting into these four-wheeled things, my old schoolmates Stephen Hunter and Dennis Atkinson now had cars and were souping them up. They hadn't spent their sixteenth and seventeenth years in pubs and dance halls.

I was at eighteen, lining my cocoon, cultivating my reputation as a good and now reliable worker, keeping out of the house as much as I could at home so that I was more likeable on that front and dressing, a little spiff-like. I rather hoped the local girls would notice me, the new me, they didn't or if they did they kept it to themselves. I was in a good place, I had a good job (I thought.) a safe and secure home and no reason to travel far from where I'd been born. I dreamt yes, but those dreams never took me beyond the horizons of the parishes of Preston Patrick and Preston Richard. Oh yes, I was a bore of the highest order but I couldn't see it.

I don't know why I was keeping out of the house, as the Watsons now had television, I think we were the very last people in Britain to get a television. From my first sense of that black-and-white flicker in the corner of my eye, I had been addicted to television. Now, I was eighteen and it was actually in our house, I didn't give it a second glance. Perhaps it was how we acquired the television that caused the disinterest.

My older sister Marion had got herself a boyfriend, and he was a television salesman. It's fair to say I didn't like him much, it's accurate to say I didn't like him at all. His name was Fred and he had a rather snappy minivan(Envy is a sin.) and of course, the thing I disliked the most, a Lancashire accent. We, the Watsons had never been able to afford a television so when this flashy television salesman lands on our doorstep via my sister and we suddenly have a television. My dislike of the television and the man who brought it to our door can only intensify. Fred and I had nothing in common but he was, at that time, one of a growing number of people.

It wasn't long after Fred brought us the dreaded television that he took my older sister. There was a time when I would have accepted the swop, but that was in my days as a television addict. Well, he, actually did the right thing and married her but I was surprisingly close to my older sister and didn't like to see her go. I say we were surprisingly close but we never seemed that way, quite the opposite, we seemed almost distant but she was my big sister and a part of the comfort wall I had been building.

The wedding was to be held at Preston Patrick Church on 4th

November 1967, my parent's twenty-fifth wedding anniversary, they too had been married at Preston Patrick Church. There was to be a reception at Preston Patrick Memorial Hall. I was half excited, nothing this big had ever happened in the Watson household in my lifetime. Add to the prestige of the wedding and its reception in the Memorial Hall, I had never been to a wedding so this would be, really something. As an afterthought, or at least it seemed that way to me, Richard and I were asked to be ushers at the wedding. This sounded important but I had no idea what an usher does at a wedding. I went to Mum for advice and she told me, "It's easy you just tell people where to sit in Church." Sounded easy enough to me.

Before the big day, my now-accountant sister and her intended, bought a house, a new house. This sort of thing was unheard of in the day, young married couples rented a house and saved for years before they bought a house. This brand new house was miles away in Burton and needed quite a bit of cleaning up done around it before the young couple could move in. It seems the bride-to-be's brother was ideal for this job.

As a result of this newfound handiness, I think I became a little closer to my big sister and her intended husband. I was ferried back and forth in the back of the minivan whenever I was needed to do the allotted manual work around the place, I didn't mind this work and felt rather useful. Being friends with my big sister was a whole new experience for me.

The big day arrived and I was quite excited, this was to be the first wedding I'd attended and I was to be an usher, wow! This was not what I expected, the ushers looked quite dapper in their suits, pity they didn't perform the job that well. Nobody seemed to notice the ushers and took their seats without our assistance. If I was boring, I was in the right place, because I was rapidly discovering that weddings are boring.

I didn't like this Church service one bit, but I sat through it in the hope that the reception would be the thing, it wasn't. The idea of me getting blotto at my parents' expense had rather appealed to me but from what I saw this was unlikely to happen. Mum hadn't done the catering so the food was uninspiring. All the people were old and nobody wanted to know or acknowledge me. It may have been my sister's day but it certainly wasn't mine.

I'm pretty sure it was long before it would have been deemed acceptable, I turned to Richard and said, "Let's get out of here." We did, into his van and off to our old haunt the Plough at Lupton. We were welcome there, recognised and I for one got duly blotto, at my expense when it should have been Dad and Mum's shout.

30 BEEN GIVEN MY NOTICE

Boring and bunkered down in my comfort zone, life was great. I was working hard and eating well, Mrs Jones was feeding me good and interesting food at work and Mum was feeding me all my favourites at home. Two women were looking after my stomach but none seemed to care for the rest of my body. To be fair I wasn't doing much to attract the local girls in my now, rather reclusive mode.

It was probably one afternoon in November when I was working away, filling up a hay rack for some bullocks and Trefor was wandering through the 'hull' to feed his calves, that he stopped. Trevor put his buckets down and said, "I'd like a word with you, Thomas."

Knowing I'd done nothing wrong, I felt this a little strange. "Yes?" I replied questioningly.

"Mrs Jones and I have decided to give up the farm." Trevor started, "We're not getting any younger and it's getting a bit much for us both."

'But you've got me' I would have countered if I hadn't been so dumbfounded.

"Don't worry, it won't be straight away. We will have to organise a sale to get rid of the stock and machinery and I will need to get a job and a house for us to live in. You, of course, will have a job here until we sell up, which I would say will be towards the backend next year. If you find yourself a job in the meantime, we will understand and you will be free to go, I will give you a reference, of course."

This seemed a strange place to break this news, and in front of these bullocks who would be long gone by then. Trefor seemed a little emotional and I can imagine now, may have rehearsed these words many times, after all, we had sat listening to the radio at lunchtime and nothing had been said. It was perhaps the best place and best time to break the news to me, we were busy with our work and I had my mind on the job at hand and there was the milking to be done.

That overcast wintery afternoon, the comfort zone I had for too long been creating, fell in a heap around me. Its walls, which I had drawn around me like a cocoon were suddenly smashed apart as I grew. Only one person knew about this sudden spurt of growth, this new horizon that lay ahead which was way beyond the horizons I'd viewed from my cocoon in Preston Patrick. That person was me.

I went home and told Mum and Dad the news of my impending unemployment.

"Tha'll be right, lad." Said Dad and not much was added.

I now took to reading the Westmorland Gazette and especially the situations vacant column, in those days it was on the front page of the paper and as far as job opportunities for me, it was almost a waste of time. Yes, there was the odd advertisement for a farmhand but none for me, as I had grown out of my cocoon, I was looking for a job that required a better class of muck carter. I was wasting my time because the harder I looked the more the same sort of advertisement appeared 'Dumb muck carter required, Thomas Watson need not apply.'

It was about the time when I was ready to give up on this fruitless search, that the advertisement I'd been looking for appeared. Well, it wasn't quite the advertisement I'd been looking for but it was a job I thought was worth applying for, for the life of me I don't know why. The advertisement stated: "Farm manager required for a farm in Western Australia." This wasn't the job, I was looking for, it was the only job that offered up a challenge to me, "Apply in writing to:" It continued. For the life of me, I can't remember who I had to apply in writing to but I do know it was someone who lived in the south of England somewhere.

I did as I'd been summonsed to do and applied in writing, at last, that business letter we'd been taught to write in primary school came to the fore. One of my first-ever letters was posted in the letterbox under the chestnut tree in Goose Green. This whole process was carried out as if by a robot, not the least bit of thought or research had gone into this act of stupidity. I had no intention of ever going to Western Australia and I was neither qualified to do the job nor if successful, able.

Two weeks after posting my job application, I got a reply I wasn't even expecting. I hadn't got the job, 'but would I please call the man who had placed the advertisement as he would like to talk to me', why? I thought to myself. My dog walk that night took me to the closest telephone box, which was in Gatebeck, did this man know the trouble I was going to? He probably thought everyone was on the phone like, now we had television everyone had.

I hadn't used the phone much or ever in those days so mastering the button 'A' and button 'B' was something of a mystery but I managed and got through to the man. The man seemed very nice and said I wasn't, really suitable for the job but he might have a job for me. I told him of my circumstances and out of the blue, he suggested that I apply for an assisted passage to Australia. He said to see how things went and his job offer, not the one in Australia, still applied if I wanted it.

In the less, than the mile walk home, I decided I was going to do exactly what this total stranger had suggested I do, apply for an assisted passage to Australia. On arriving home I searched through the old newspapers to find an old 'News of the World' as they always had an advertisement for assisted passages to Australia. For poor people, we always seemed to have lots of old newspapers, so I soon found that 'News of the World' I needed. This was the simple bit, fill in your name and address on the little slip, cut it out and post it off to Australia House in London.

"What's tha up to?" came Dad's booming voice as he walked in the door.

"Just sending this thing off to get an assisted passage to Australia."

"Well, tha knows what tha's doing." Was his rather strange reply.

Two weeks later I arrived home from work and Mum put my tea on the table and pointed to a package at the edge of the table, near the window where we had sat as children, "The's post for you." Mum had examined this package extensively long before I got home and knew it was from Australia House, she was not happy. I'm guessing she was expecting me to leave for Australia next week sometime. I guzzled my tea down while ripping open my package. It was full of glossy brochures and a huge form to fill out, not a bit like the slip in the 'News of the World'.

This was the start of my perilous journey down the road with Australian officialdom. I'd got this far, not very far at all really, but in my mind, there was no turning back. So far, the only people who knew I was taking this crazy path were my immediate family, Mum, Dad and Barbara. Marion was no longer at home but she would find out soon enough. I wanted to keep it that way because if it didn't work out, I could rapidly go down as a loser.

As I worked through the form, I came to a section that required me to have three independent referees. So much for keeping this quiet. Over the next week, I had to talk to my chosen referees and tell them why I wanted to use them as referees. I chose Tommy Fletcher, our neighbour and my childhood hero, Trefor Jones my current employer and Tom Sanderson my first employer. They were all very supportive and didn't mind keeping quiet about my plans.

I'm not sure when I had to part with the 'postal order' for ten quid, but as fighting my way through this form and the thought of no turning back was going through my mind, I'm pretty sure it was with this form. Posting this form wasn't like slipping the slip from the 'News of the World' into the Goose Green letterbox, this was serious stuff, and there was ten quid on the line.

My life was changing, from the moment Trefor told me of his planned retirement from the farm, I'd gained a new attitude. I no longer sought the security I'd clung to for eighteen years, I wanted adventure and I'd thrown myself onto the mercy of the government of another country to get that adventure. I'd read the rules, there was no turning back as I didn't have the return fare.

31 LAST OF THE SUMMER WINE

The summer of 1968 was one of those endless English summers, which lie in the memories of children and nineteen-year-olds who are to soon leave the country and community of their birth. It was in probability, cold and wet, but in the memory of this nineteen-year-old the sun shone endlessly and every day was perfect. Work-life at Camsgill was a breeze, no silage making, no haymaking and days were spent painting machinery so that it looked good for the clearing sale in September.

My leisure time was spent wandering the lanes of Preston Patrick, dreaming of meeting a beautiful woman, just around the next corner perhaps. Of course, it never happened but dreams rarely come true. I was somewhat aloof and almost had a permanent smirk on my face, I for once, knew something the rest of Preston Patrick didn't know, I was going to Australia. My idea to keep my departure to myself and a select few was the best idea I'd ever had. It gave me that smirk which probably annoyed a few people. It wasn't set in concrete yet, as on one of those balmy days I got the letter that put it in doubt.

The letter from Australia House advised me that I was required to attend an interview at a hotel in Preston, a major town in Lancashire. These people had everything organised, I was to catch a train to Preston and go to a hotel close to the railway station to attend the interview. That may have sounded simple enough but for this farm lad who could get lost in his closest town of Kendal, it was a little daunting.

And how would I go with this interview? My endless summer was starting to look rainy. No trouble getting time off work, seems my first train journey was easy enough and I even found the hotel. At the hotel, I showed my letter and was told to take a seat in the foyer. The most glamourous woman I'd ever seen in my life approached me and asked if I was Thomas Watson, (Dreams do come true.) "Yes." I struggled out, flushed with excitement.

This gorgeous creature introduced herself, well that was a waste of time, as I was in no condition to remember her name or even hear it. We sat at a low coffee table and she fired questions at me as she lit up a Rothman's, 'God she smokes Rothman's, how sophisticated is that?' I thought. Carol Rainsford who lived up the road drove, and I thought that was sophisticated.

The interview was nothing like I'd expected, for a start, I was being interviewed by the most beautiful woman in the world and she smoked Rothman's. The questions that she asked were mostly answered with a nervous "No." and when she suggested I go to Melbourne or Sydney rather than my chosen Perth, I stuck with Perth. It seemed that everything I was doing was wrong and I wasn't going to come through this interview well. I could have taken my dog to the interview and she would have gotten through because I did, she, however, would have had to do six weeks of quarantine. As it was I had some wait before I was to leave.

The English summer to end all English summers continued. Sister Marion and her new husband Fred were booking their holiday in Ireland, would I like to join them? Well, I had no plans to do anything so I went along with theirs. I, of course, had not looked into this excursion over the sea to Ireland, I was just tagging along with my sister and brother-in-law with whom I had nothing in common.

Everything was set and off we went one dark night, (Most summer nights are light but this one wasn't.) we boarded a boat to sail to Ireland. Marion and Fred disappeared and I had to find my shared cabin. I soon discovered that there appeared to be no toilets on this boat, it stunk like a urinal. This is my first trip on a boat and it turned out to be a floating urinal, my shared cabin was none to flash either. Why I had chosen to go with the newlyweds was beyond me, as I rarely sighted them.

There were no young people on this tour, I think I can call it that as there were bus trips involved. We were staying in a hotel in Northern Ireland by the sea in a pleasant little town, I rather liked Northern Ireland. Of course, even then, people raved about the beauty of southern Ireland, Eire. One trip took us over the border and to Dublin, I disliked what I saw of Eire.

Not the best holiday of my life but I did buy the best pair of shoes I've ever owned in the little town we were staying in. Buckskin moccasins with a flat sole, and whether they had it ingrained in them or because I'd walked along the beach in them, they always smelt of saltwater.

As the summer of my life continued, the results of my interview came to light, not that I was given any results but the date of my departure, the day I would be leaving for Australia, Tuesday 22nd October 1968. It was still quite a way off and didn't, really fit in with my plans as the clearing sale at Camsgill was in September. I would need to find a job for a month, and the thought of taking a month to do nothing never occurred to me, I'd already had what had been termed a holiday so another would have been gluttony, plus I would have had to explain why I wasn't working to the world, well the people of Preston Patrick.

I spent a good amount of my time that summer at Cox Bank, the farm I knew as a child. It was different now, it was owned by Jack Beck who I'd become friendly with after helping to dip his sheep at Camsgill for the last two years. The best difference was that guinea fowls had been eradicated from the place, no more ducking for cover as they flew across the yard. The yard was no longer cobblestones but concrete, and the house had a newer feel, with no hams and bacon hanging in the kitchen. The Beck children were playing in the yard, just as the Watson kids had over ten years earlier. As there was no hay made at Camsgill that summer, I helped at Cox Bank, this helped me get that last month in Preston Patrick taken care of, I could work for Jack.

My best mate Richard was rarely sighted as the summer wore on, not only was he living with his parents in Troutbeck, he had acquired a girlfriend. Pretty serious too by all the accounts he gave me, she kept him busy as she lived in some town in Lancashire, St Helens, I think it was. Lots of travelling was involved as weekends were all the time they could have together.

"You've got to meet her." He would say.

Well, one Sunday afternoon I did, we went out somewhere and had a fun time. He'd landed on his feet I thought. He didn't have time to hang around, she had to be back in St Helens that night. Richard promised to take me to the airport when I left for Australia and we said our farewells till then, I kissed his girlfriend's hand in a gentlemanly manner, which surprised even me, and she pashed me, which shocked me even more. That's why he put up with her God-awful Lancashire accent.

The clearing sale at Camsgill came and went, it was the strangest two days of my life. On the day of the sale, everything was in place. The machinery was laid out in the field down from the yard, the cattle were in their stalls and hulls and the sheep were in the sheep yards. It had been quite a morning setting all this up. On the afternoon of the sale, I became redundant, I had nothing to do, and people, it seemed had come from everywhere to help and I felt useless. No milking that evening as the cows now belonged to someone else.

The next morning there was the cleaning up to do. The place was ghostly, with no animals, not even a dog. Once cleaned up I went to see Trefor, I got my last pay packet and an envelope with my reference in it. We shook hands, there were tears in eyes and Trefor asked me to write and tell him how I was going when I got to Australia, it was still a month away.

32 UP, UP AND AWAY

My last month in England saw my parish torn asunder or it seemed that way to me. This activity had been years in the planning, strange men with tripods had been striding over fields for the last year and in my last month work started. The extension of the M6 motorway from Carnforth to Penrith was becoming a reality. I had never seen anything like what was happening, hills I'd grown up with were being dug up and moved into the valleys I'd grown up with. Farms were being cut in half and some were to become unviable. We all knew this was going to happen but none of us had seen such things in our lifetimes.

Of course, this activity meant very little to me as I wasn't going to be around when all this motorway construction came to fruition. But I do remember standing agog, as the giant machines moved my hills into valleys and people who knew nothing of Preston Patrick were tearing the parish apart, invading land that had been in the same hands for generations. Perhaps it was just as well I was leaving because the land I had loved all my life, would never be the same again. Regardless of all my maudling talk, this was an exciting time and these new people were making their way into the local pubs and the Gatebeck Working Men's Institute in Endmoor. I, of course, was oblivious to the good things this could do for the local economy and would have been with the doomsayers, who knew this was the end of the world as we'd known it.

As all the activity was going on around me I was, basically somewhere else, floating on a cloud that was to carry me to Australia. I was working for Jack Beck at Cox Bank where my Grandfather had farmed in my childhood. This was just a fill-in job till the day came when I was off, I didn't need to impress anyone or work toward anything. I felt free and as a result, worked harder than I had ever in my life.

That last month at Cox Bank was great, I was part of the family. Jack's wife Ann was eight months pregnant and under that strain, so it was part of my job to dress the youngest girl or, at least correct the dressing she had done herself and make sure the middle child Linda was smart enough for school. The eldest boy was now around eleven and had no interest in coming down to the shippon like the girls. This was not part of my job description but the girls made it my job and I enjoyed it.

The day eventually came when I was to say goodbye, Tuesday 22nd October. True to his word, as always my best friend Richard, arrive to take me to, well it turned out London. I'd said my goodbyes to the Becks the night before, it had been rather emotional as Linda had come running down the lane as I was leaving, in tears, she had just realised that I wouldn't be there for milking in the morning. I must have said the right words to her as she trotted off back to her waving parents. Sister Marion and her husband Fred had called in that night too, and goodbyes were uttered.

My case, a cumbersome thing made of cardboard with extendable fasteners had been packed, I think, by Mum so everything was there. I was ready, this morning was the big one. Sister Barbara was off to school, I think we hugged and she took off on her bike. We Watsons aren't very touchy-feely, did Dad put his hand on my shoulder? I think that would have been it, I know he said those meaningful words, "Tha's doin' right thing lad." Mum with tears in her eyes but holding up well said, "You'll write won't you?" And gave me the biggest hug and we were off in Richard's trusty Austin A35 van to Oxenholme station.

It was when we got to the station and Richard bought his ticket to London and took my itinerary from me, I knew I wasn't going to get out of this. The train ride to London was direct so Richard could have let me hang on to the itinerary a little longer. This was the longest train ride of my life and it seemed to go forever, through green countryside and dirty grey towns and cities.

To my amazement most of the countryside was flat, I'd grown up with hills. And there was Crewe, a nondescript town in Cheshire where all the train lines in England met, this may not have been fact, but it seemed all trains went through Crewe and everybody had heard of Crewe. It turned out to be just a huge acreage of railway lines and a huge disappointment to a country lad. We arrived in London in the afternoon and had another train to catch to the airport.

It was now when we had something simple, like catching another train to do that Richard kicked in, his possession of the itinerary was a Godsend. As this would have been where I got confused, lost and missed the plane and went home with my tail between my legs. This seemed to involve some walking through London and I instantly thought, 'What a God-awful place. This can't be where Wordsworth wrote his poem.' (Upon Westminster Bridge.) We got the train and arrived at the airport in good time.

I had the stuff to go through with the Australian people. Present the Document of Identity I'd been issued with, with the passport photo my sister Barbara had taken up against the wall at Ivy Garth, would I ever see that wall again? There was a wait for the plane, Richard had come prepared, he had his camera with him and got someone to take a photo of us both before I left. It was now time to board the plane, Richard and I shook hands and hugged, would we ever see each other again?

It must have been a walk across the tarmac in those days and then the steps to climb. I had no idea what to expect as I stepped through the doorway of the plane. To me, it was just like the Stainton's coach we used to go on for school and Young Farmers' excursions. This was to be a much bigger excursion and I didn't know a living soul on this aeroplane. It seemed like forever before the plane took off and I could have waited much longer.

The take-off scared the living daylights out of me, I don't know if anybody else was as scared as me or if anyone noticed my fear, but nobody said anything. There again, nobody said much now we were in the air and we had tea coming and I was a bit hungry. Our first meal was steak and salad, I'd never seen food like this, we'd never had steak at home and the salad was full of foreign objects as far as I could see, I was familiar with lettuce but that was about it. There was a large slice of a red thing and some bits of green and red stuff, I was very careful eating any of this food, it looked nice but I wasn't sure, I pretty much stayed hungry.

There were two young blokes sitting next to me on the plane who seemed to know each other and didn't, really want to know me, the odd word may have been spoken but begrudgingly. We did, however, have someone who didn't mind everyone knowing his business, this chap was emigrating to Australia to find a better life for his boys. It wasn't long before I took a dislike to this loudmouth and we had a long way to go.

We flew and flew and slept and no sooner had I fallen asleep than we are told that we will be landing in Bahrain. 'Where the hell's that.' I thought. We were told we had to leave the plane and get back on later, this was a refuelling stop, we were then told we could get a drink in the airport and stretch our legs.

They, however, didn't tell us how hot this place is, even in the middle of the night. As I stepped out of the plane I was struck by a wave of the hottest air I'd ever experienced and I'd worked in glasshouses. Well, we sure needed a drink by the time we reached the terminal. I had hung on to my two fellow travellers of the silent type and bought them a drink with my English money, my change was a selection of washers. I still didn't get much out of them, and certainly not a second drink.

Back on the plane, and the next stop is Singapore, there was daylight coming through the window which was not close to me. I wasn't so scared of this take-off but it would still class it as scared, more of the same. I'd become a veteran flyer by the time we got in the air in Singapore and then for some reason they told us what to do in case of an emergency. Why now? Damn it we were almost there and then they tell us we may crash into the sea and never be seen again, what would they tell Mum?

33 AUSTRALIA

Well, it turned out we didn't need the life jackets after all. We landed safely in Perth at twenty past twelve on the morning of the twenty-fourth of October. Was I glad that was over? No more take-offs and landings and being cooked up in this plane I was beginning to dislike. It was pretty cruisey through customs and emigration for most of the passengers, but not me. I had to confess to having worked on a farm and had to have my boots cleaned, I think they had to be sterilised as it took a while. I had two electric razors stuffed in them, as I'd heard that electrical goods were expensive in Australia and thought I could make a quid selling them. The customs officers came back with my boots and the razors, (Why must these officials always work in twos?) 'I'm done for now,' I thought. The boots and razors were returned and the customs officers grinned broadly at my obvious embarrassment.

In a state of flusterment, I found my way to the front of the airport where my two travelling companions were standing with another young man. A flashy-looking car was there too, seems the addition to the crew was our chauffeur/sponsor. The new young man was a member of Apex, a young men's organisation that did charitable work in the community.

Apex, it seems was our sponsor and we were its charity for that day at least. We pile into the young man's car and travel off into the darkness, we end our journey outside an old-looking hotel, the Crystal. We, the three musketeers, are told by the young man that someone will pick us up around seven tonight and show us the city. We are booked into our room and told breakfast will be served in the dining room. I don't think my companions like the idea of me being their companion but there we are, all in one room.

We rise in the morning none too early, breakfast, I meet Weeties and rather like them. I stick with my newfound 'friends' as they seem to know what they are doing. I, on the other hand, have no idea what I should be doing. Off we go to the bank to change our money.

I like this place the sun is shining and it's so new looking and the streets are so wide. We land at the ANZ Bank, flash as, and new looking. My companions, obviously knew to come here because they are treated like royalty, they must have sent their money here from England and accounts are opened and passbooks handed out. Then the farm lad with his few quid steps up to the counter and asks if they will change it for him, they do begrudgingly and ask if I'd like to open an account, "Nah, not now." This is a rather rude reply.

The next place to visit is the Commonwealth Employment Agency, it's a bit of a walk and I don't think we've taken a short way. It's getting hot and we're passing a pub, "Would you like a drink?" I offer, "Oh yeah." comes the reply. Here I am at the bar again, wasn't I there in Bahrain? "Three beers," I say. "Sorry son, you're not old enough." Is the reply from the middle-aged barmaid, "Bullshit, I'm nineteen." Is my retort, as I reach for my Document of Identity. "You've got to be twenty-one to buy a drink in this country son." Comes the rather relaxed reply from my newly adopted mother. Not sure how old my offsiders were but they sure as hell didn't offer to buy a drink.

Onward to the Commonwealth Employment Agency, this is a bit like the bank, two of us are treated like royalty and the other, that's me, is told to come back tomorrow afternoon, "We may have something for you then." 'And pigs might fly.' I think to myself, these people haven't impressed me.

I seem to be on my own in this big city, my offsiders were drawn into the welcoming arms of the public service job finders. As I meander back towards the Crystal Hotel, I notice small plaques outside the doorways of what appear to be staircases. These plaques, in some cases, are advertising employment agencies. I decide to try one of these staircases, and sure enough, there, on the first floor is a door with the name of the agency on it, I knock and I'm invited in by a woman of about forty, who I discover, knows exactly how to cross her legs for the best effect. She is so nice and so understanding but can't find a job that I would be suitable for, she is telling me I'm unemployable in the nicest way she can. This woman or her sister is at the top of every set of stairs I climb and by the time I get back to the Crystal, I am aware, that I am unemployable in Australia.

It's evening time and the three young lads from England are outside the Crystal Hotel waiting with bated breath for the young man from Apex to pick them up for their city tour. And true to their word the man from Apex is there with his flashy car (The cars here are something.) to give them the tour, I think it's the same bloke who picked us up from the airport. Off we go, King's Park, a view of the city, up and down the main streets, points out Pinnochio's nightclub, the place to be if you're twenty-one. We're not a lot wiser, at least I'm not, it's dark and streets are hard to follow in the dark, it was a nice drive and we shunted another car and nobody seemed to bother, a lot more relaxed than England.

The next day and I'm on my own, with more employment agencies, more knockbacks and then a glimmer of hope. I wander into Pastoralists and Graziers employment agency near the ANZ Bank, no stairs to climb there, it was almost a basement, down a few steps.

"We haven't got much at the moment but there's a bloke at New Norcia looking for somebody." And this is a man speaking now, and he doesn't cross his legs for effect.

"He's only offering twenty dollars a week and he won't be down until tomorrow afternoon." This man doesn't sound too positive and twenty dollars a week doesn't sound too good either.

"Drop-in in the morning and I'll have spoken to him by then, and we can see how it goes."

I can see it's not going well.

I leave Pastoralists and Graziers and wander across the road, through some nice shady gardens, it's warm again, across another road and find myself by what, our guide last night, described as the river. This is the best, palm trees, lawn and the sun beating down, my employment status seems to drift from my mind as I soak up the pleasantness of my surroundings. I could live here, I could certainly daydream here because that's what was happening. Back in the world of the living, I had an appointment with the Commonwealth Employment people.

Back to that God-awful building with its sad people and drab decor. The news here is good, they have found me a job. I'm sent off to a place called 'Oat Street' seemed a strange name for a place. They gave me instructions on catching the train etc: and off I go. It's Friday afternoon, I get off the train at Oat Street station and try to find this place of employment, but I find nothing, to me, this whole area was deserted. Dejected, I return to the city and the Crystal Hotel and what is now to be my room. My 'friends' are putting the last of their possessions into their cases.

"You leaving?" I ask.

"We've got jobs, we're not staying here." Was their reply.

Not sure what these blokes did but it sure as hell wasn't farm work like this unemployable.

To say I wasn't too happy with myself would have been an understatement. As the evening wore on and darkness fell, I was now really in the dumps. It was then I remembered my best friend in England, my tranny, my transistor radio. Would it work here? Did they have radio here? Only one way to find out, give it a try.

I turned on the switch and low-and-behold there's bloody horse racing on, 'What sort of carrots do they feed their horses here? it's pitch black out there.' Is the thought going through my head. I turn the dial and hear pop music, I turn again and more pop music and again and again. This certainly was somewhere I could live, the gardens, the river and half a dozen pop radio stations. Perhaps I'll find that job tomorrow and then I'll know I've landed in heaven.

34 THE BLOKE

Saturday morning comes around, at long last, I can't get my breakfast down fast enough. Of course, Pastoralists and Graziers won't be open until nine but my life is hanging on this job, they may have for me. I wander down to Pastoralists and Graziers and my best friend in the whole world recognises me.

"No worries mate, that bloke from New Norcia will meet you at the Crystal at two this afternoon." My friend advises me.

'It's alright for you no worries, but I've got hours to kill in this strange city.' Is the thought going through my head.

This street I'm in seems to be closed, St George's Terrace, it's full of banks and insurance companies so I guess they don't open Saturday morning, I'm thankful that Pastoralists and Graziers did. I remembered what I'd done the day before, wandered through those nice gardens and down to the river. This seems a good idea for today too, the gardens are cool and the sun shines forever in this country.

I walked and dreamt and soaked up the sun for a few of the longest hours of my life. I was back at the Crystal Hotel by one and still had an hour to wait, two o'clock came and no bloke. I've never done late, something my parents drummed into me, this bloke is late and I want a job. Twenty past two and a young bloke with jet black hair strides into the foyer of the Crystal Hotel, I'm losing faith and this bloke's too young to give me a job.

"Tom Watson?" he asks.

"Yes." I meekly answer.

"Dennis Halligan" he announces,

"So you want to come and work on the farm do yah?" he asks rather rhetorically.

"Yes, I've got a reference," I mutter and dig out Trefor's reference. Dennis flits through the reference and hands it back.

"Your hands look as if they've done a bit of work." He states and follows up with, "Would you like to come and see Viv?"

I must have said yes, as that's what we're doing a few minutes later. We walk up to Dennis' pick-up, which I later learn is a 'ute.' "Hop in," says Dennis, and off we go.

Dennis explains he's down in Perth to straighten up his in-law's house as they have been to England for a holiday and are due back next week.

"Viv's brother was supposed to look after the place but it's a fucking mess, so we've got to clean it up."

We take the scenic route to South Perth, down the freeway, beside the river, 'Wow this place is fantastic.' I think to myself as Dennis talks and asks and drives in the most layback manner. We pull up at a back gate to the smell of newly mown grass and enter the house from the back too, I think it's a farm thing, straight into the kitchen.

"This is Viv," announces Dennis.

"This is Tom Watson Viv, he's coming to work for us." Until now, I'd always been Thomas Watson. We have a cup of tea and cake and I get to meet the Halligan's young son Gavin, a terror if ever one was born, and Viv's brother Gwyn, who shows no shame in his neglect of the garden.

Gwyn is my age, I'm not sure what he does but it wasn't gardening or house cleaning, he's into guns and brings one out to show me (I'm not into guns.).

"This is the sort of gun you'll be using on the farm," he tells me, both Vivienne and Dennis say nothing but look rather downcast. A bit of small talk with Dennis and Vivienne and Dennis drives me back into Perth, over the Causeway for the return journey and I'm still liking what I see.

"I'll pick you up about two tomorrow afternoon," Dennis tells me as I close the ute door. I'm on cloud nine as I enter the hotel, I go to my room and flick on the radio and life's good. That evening I decided to explore the nightlife of my new city, yes, it was mine now. You can have a shower whenever you want here, and it's Saturday night too so there's no excuse, I've never been this clean.

I venture out onto rather deserted streets, 'I'm not doing those shady gardens at night,' I think to myself 'only well-lit streets for this boy.' I find, what appears to be a dance hall, it's got Anzac House over the entrance, 'this looks like me' I think. I enter but do not linger, everyone looks paired off and something in me says I should have an early night as tomorrow I go to the farm, where ever that is. I return to my room and find solace in the radio, it just goes and goes, what great company.

Sunday has arrived and I have to kill time until two this afternoon, more long hours, how many times can I sort out my case? I'm more than ready at one and descend to the foyer, I discover I have a bill to pay, was I stretching it to think it was in the ten quid? Two o'clock comes and goes and my mood is glum. And then I see the ute with the lawnmower on the back drive past, 'that is the one I was in yesterday, isn't it?' It seemed such a long time later that Dennis strides into the Crystal and grabs my case and says, "Let's go Tom." Dennis throws my case into the back of the ute and off we go to New Norsha as Dennis calls it.

The ute was quite luxurious to me, much flasher than English cars and Dennis seemed to drive it with ease. As we drove out of Perth the houses became further apart and on smallholdings and most were new or newish. I saw my first house with a bright blue roof, there were in fact, lots of them and they all seemed to have a small vineyard alongside. Soon the houses became miles apart and older and I wondered how much farther we had to travel.

Dennis kept a kind of conversation going, asking questions of me and explaining the landscape as we continued the journey. We pull into a garage, I would have called it, turns out it's called a roadhouse here, get filled up with fuel and Dennis goes to pay and returns with icecreams and drinks, drumsticks and choc milk. These were new to me but very pleasant on what is becoming a hot day. We were at Bullsbrook, a new-ish-looking town (No more than a village really.) that houses an Air Force base Dennis informs me.

The place names fly off Dennis' tongue, and we pass through them just as fast, the gaps between are huge. I'd never travelled this far in a car before, or at such speed, I glance at the floor of the ute and notice that Dennis is now barefoot and had his feet crossed over the accelerator pedal, and I'd been feeling safe.

We reach New Norcia and I get a quick rundown on the place as we drive through, I get the feeling that it doesn't impress Dennis. Finally, we pull into a house just like the ones I saw with the bright blue rooves, dogs barking and a bit of a farm feel but no real farm building. We enter the house and an engine somewhere starts up, (It was the electricity generator.) we have a cold drink, Dennis throws some frozen meat to the dogs and my case is still on the ute, isn't this the farm?

We get back in the ute and head off down a gravel road, Dennis asks me to look behind us, and I see my first cloud of dust. Through a couple of gates and along a dusty track and I see an old shack, as we approach Dennis slows down and breaks the news that the job I've got with him isn't that good; "Yah know Tom, farmworkers in this country are pretty much rubbish and not thought much of." My new employer reports, "Yah'll be right." He adds with a smile. I move into my new home, a corrugated iron lean-to with a semi-dirt floor covered with a rug, a shearer's bed with a kapok mattress and a wardrobe of sorts.

Sheep are being brought in by Mary, Keith and Leone. I gradually meet each one, Mary is a large woman and full-on, Dennis' mother and to be my carer. Keith is Dennis' cousin, a farmworker elsewhere but helping Dennis out this weekend. Leone is Keith's wife and a little hotty in my eyes, and then she opens her mouth and knocks the edge off my attraction.

Once the sheep have been drafted and put in the shed ('That's a loose description of the building.) we all sat around the table and had tea. The new Pommie had to hear all the snake and earthquake (An earthquake had flattened Meckering two weeks earlier.) stories and hear how this was the worst time of the year for snakes. I'll sleep well tonight knowing a snake may slither under my bed and the building may collapse around me as I sleep.

35 TO WORK

I awake to a sunny Monday morning and my first day's work in Australia. I dress just as I had the previous Monday morning: jeans, shirt, belt, knife, socks and boots and head into the kitchen for breakfast. "Chops or cereal?" asks Mary in her cheerful manner. 'Chops for breakfast?' I think to myself, "Cereal thanks." I reply. There's a gravel dragging sound outside – Dennis' ute drawing to a halt - and seconds later Dennis charges into the kitchen.

"No snakes in your room Tom?" he asks with a laugh.

Dennis warms some milk on the stove and then pours it on his weeties, my stomach rolls at the smell of warmed milk.

"Well best get up to the shed." Says Dennis after wolfing down the weeties.

"You have worked in a shearing shed before haven't you Tom?" Dennis casually asks as we stride up to the shed.

"Well, sort of." Is the best I can come up with.

"Never mind you'll soon get the hang of it." Dennis shoots back at me.

Seems we'd been the last to leave the breakfast table, we enter the shed and there are three other blokes already there; two messing with their sheep shears and another joking about something.

"G'day guys, this is Tom Watson, he's just arrived from Pommieland." Announces Dennis, "This is Slim O'Callahan our rousy and these two are Lionel Parkes and Peter Black our shearers."

The shearers all but ignore me and Slim laughs. (On reflection I think my mode of dress may have been the cause of Slim's hilarity.) 'Friendly bunch.' I think to myself.

"Best get started," Dennis says as he walks over to an old-looking engine which until now had been hidden by the shearers. Dennis takes a crank handle and spins it twice and the engine leaps to life, the shed shakes and the shearers grab a sheep each and start shearing them. The shed doesn't stop shaking and the engine isn't quiet, and the rattle of the shears adds to the cacophony of sounds.

I'd seen sheep shorn, but this was so different from my experience in England. In what seemed like no time the first shearer had finished his sheep and Slim picked up the fleece and threw it onto, what I was to learn was the wool table. My turn next, as the second shearer finishes his sheep I go to grab the fleece as I'd seen Slim do seconds before. I pick up two handfuls of wool and the fleece remains on the floor.

"We'd better teach you how to do that Tom." Says Dennis with a grin.

The day isn't getting any shorter as I slowly learn to pick up a fleece and skirt it, I have patient tutors in Dennis and Slim.

"Can you duck down the house and get 'smoko'?" Dennis asks, but it's, actually an order. On my return, the shearers have knocked off and that monstrous engine has been stopped and the shed has stopped shaking and all is strangely silent until a sheep loses its balance on the grating and causes the others to run around and create a moment of havoc. I sit on the floor of the shed and have my first smoko and wonder how I'll make it through the day. I did, and my fleece throwing and skirting were showing signs of improvement.

Knock-off time arrived and the shearers and Slim disappeared, the shearers to have a bath and Slim went home.

"We'll just press up a couple of bales of wool." Dennis casually informs me, "Here, hop in the press and tramp the wool will yah."

I clamber into a hessian bag inside a rickety steel frame and duly tramp the wool as Dennis hauls huge armfuls into the press. Dennis then shows me how this process works and I see my first finished bale of wool, so square, so neat, it seemed a miracle that something like this could be produced in a broken-down shed, out of a rickety steel frame. And then, it was to be carefully weighed and branded, I wasn't allowed to brand that first bale or lots after it as this had to be done with precision. Once we'd pressed enough wool we headed down to the house for tea.

There was a conversation over tea which I didn't understand, not that the Australian accent worried me, I rather liked that. It was that they were talking, to my ears at least, in riddles, they were, in fact talking about things I didn't know anything about so it was a blur. I was politely drawn into the conversation and asked questions about England, England had completely slipped from my mind and I'd only been working here for one day.

The shearers left the table and retired to their room, I was left with Dennis and Mary. As if out of nowhere Mary asks, "Are you going to kill a sheep?"

"Aw, shit yeah," answers Dennis, "I'll do it now, d'ya wanna come Tom?" I look around in a kind of haze and innocently ask, "What do you want to kill a sheep for?"

"You wanna eat don't you?" was Dennis' sharp reply.

We didn't just go out and kill a sheep when we wanted to eat in England, we had butchers and abattoirs and saleyards and civilisation. I thought it best not to mention this to Dennis and followed him up to the shed.

"I haven't been doing this long, dad used to do the killing," Dennis tells me and then explains that his father died in April and he'd got the farm and its debts.

A sheep was duly selected, the way it fought I have a feeling it knew what was afoot. The sheep wasn't the only animal with a premonition of what was about to happen, the dogs were staying close and foolishly, looking sheepish. I witnessed my first sheep killing and it wasn't pretty, hygiene was last on the list of priorities.

The sheep was killed on the dirt floor of the shed where we had earlier pressed wool, Dennis wasn't a nimble knifeman but got the job done. The dogs waited patiently and were rewarded with the heart, liver and kidneys. The sheep was left hanging on the gambrel and covered with a sheet and we again retired to the house. We went into the kitchen and Dennis told Mary he'd cut up the sheep tomorrow morning.

"Do you want a bath?" Dennis casually asks me, 'No, I'll be right," I answered. The Englishman was coming out in me and I realised I didn't know where I was living, "What's my address?" I asked, "I'll have to write home."

"Belarbrook, New Norcia." Dennis swiftly replies, "and the postcode is 6509."

"Is that all?" I ask, a little puzzled as it was only two lines and addresses in England usually went to almost a page.

Now I was going to sit down and write home as I had promised Mum I would, not sure what I'd tell her in this first letter, there wasn't much to tell really.

36 LEARNING TO DRIVE

Friday comes around and the shearing week comes to an end at half-past five, Lionel doesn't hang around, he's got a wife in Perth and he's going home for the weekend. Slim too takes off, after a few words with Dennis, I think they are, "We won't need you Monday."

In my first week, I've managed to become a reasonably accomplished rouseabout and with only a couple of days of shearing to go, Slim won't be needed. I have wool to press and I can now weigh and brand the bales only partially supervised. What a week it has been, I've learnt new words like sheepo, smoko, woolaway, sheila and of course, bullshit. Bullshit was, obviously an abbreviation of the term we'd used in England, 'bull arse and bracken'.

That first week I met many of Dennis' friends and relatives, it seems shearing time is a good time to visit farmers as you always know where they are, in the shearing shed. Much as Dennis had told me that my position was, in the eyes of most people that of a 'low-life' he introduced me to everyone as an equal.

One of the people who intrigued me was Dennis' half-cousin Len Halligan, Len was a bachelor in his fifties and seemed to be a family 'elder statesman' with an eternal smile. When we first shook hands he said, "You've got a good grip on this country my boy." I didn't realise it at the time but he was referring to the size of my feet, size ten, the largest part of my slender body.

The shearing week may have ended but my working week was to continue through Saturday and there were jobs to be done around the place. The second shearer, Peter Black was staying at the place over the weekend as he had no real home, he was a New Zealander, a Kiwi, I was to learn. He had his washing to do, five pairs of greasy jeans and five singlets, I would have called them vests but it seems in this country they're singlets. It had me quite bemused that men worked in their underwear, I always found vests to be one of the most uncomfortable of garments. Men doing their own washing seemed foreign to me, but I had lots to learn.

Dennis got on quite well with Peter, Lionel, on the other hand, disliked Dennis and treated Peter with a little disdain. Lionel was a shearer who was trained to dislike farmers (Cockies I would later learn they were called.) and shearers who were just doing it as a fill-in job as Peter was. Peter had his name down for a Conditional Purchase block in a place called Esperance and was working any job he could find, the last couple of weeks it had been as a shearer, he wasn't that good.

As Saturday afternoon wore down Dennis asked Peter if he was going to pick up his mail on Sunday, knowing that Peter had his mail delivered to a farm he'd worked on some miles away. Peter answered that he was.

"Can you take young Tom with you, and give him a look at some of that country?" Asks Dennis.

"That'll be fine by me." Replied Peter, seems it had to be fine by me too but I don't remember being consulted.

Sunday comes around and I seem to have the day off to go to someplace I'd never heard of, Dalwallinu. I was soon to learn that I had to learn place names by hearing them as most I'd never be able to pronounce after just seeing them in the written form. Off we go in Peter's ute for miles, little is said, Peter isn't a conversationalist and I'm simply mesmerised by the miles and miles of what seems like nothingness.

We pass through Bindi Bindi, Miling, Dalwallinu and Perenjori, place names in England don't end in 'I' or even 'u' and they are pronounceable. We eventually stop at what must be a big farm, there are huge sheds filled with huge tractors and combine harvesters and what must be disc ploughs.

"Have a look at this lot," says Peter, "I'll be back soon."

And Peter disappears for a small eternity and I'm left in the middle of nowhere surrounded by the most monstrous machines I've ever seen.

Peter eventually returns with an armful of miscellaneous letters and packages.

"Can you drive?" he asks.

"No," I answer, as I'd never learnt to drive a car and anyway, I didn't have a licence.

"Course you can, I saw you drive yesterday." (I'd moved Dennis' ute about a hundred yards the day before.)

"The gears are just the same as a Falcon." Peter continues.

I try to protest and explain I don't have a licence but Peter wanted to read his mail. He gets out of the driver's seat and marches around to my side and says.

"Move over and get behind the wheel, in and down for first, up for second and straight down for third. Now get on with it, it's a piece of piss."

What could I say? I take off smooth as you like, I progress through the gears and in no time I'm doing sixty miles an hour along a single strip bitumen road and my driving teacher is reading his mail. What would have happened if there had been a car coming the other way? I dislike imagining as both cars would have had to move over and have the two lefthand wheels on the very unstable gravel verge. How far I drove that day, I have no idea, I do know that was the only driving lesson I ever had and calling it a driving lesson is drawing a longbow.

There were more firsts to come in those first two weeks working for Dennis. I had my first haircut, done with the sheep shears, not as scary as it sounds. I sat on an oil drum, Dennis wound the engine of the shearing plant with the crank handle and Lionel cut my hair with his handpiece. Nice way to end shearing, Dennis' wife Vivienne didn't think so but we'd had a laugh.

With the shearing out of the way, there was one very important job that had been neglected, the ploughing of firebreaks. Dennis started me off, "Just plough around each paddock and then move on to the next, you know how to open a cockie gate don't you? I'll pick you up for lunch." I soon find that a cockie gate is a tangled length of ringlock fencing wire, hanging between two strainer posts and the fences on this property aren't in very good condition. There are two and a half thousand acres of paddocks to plough firebreaks around so the job isn't done in a day.

If I thought the weather was hot when I arrived in Australia, it was nothing to what it had become while I'd been sheltered in the shearing shed away from the sun. I was now out in the sun, the legs cut off my jeans and my shirt on the tractor seat, it felt great. This was a great job just sitting on the tractor dragging a fourteen-disc plough around endless paddocks dreaming my life away and getting sunburnt beyond belief.

And then I saw my first snake, now this wasn't your ordinary everyday snake, it was a proper snake. It was way bigger than the tall stories I'd been told around the table on my first night on the farm and that's saying something. This snake took up the whole width of the firebreak I was to plough and it was between the fence and a huge salmon gum tree, I was terrified. For some reason, the tractor came to a halt - perhaps it was scared too - the snake lifted its head as if to strike. I turned the tractor into the crop and gave the snake a very wide berth, flattening the crop as I went and terrified it may give chase.

When Dennis came to pick me up I told him about the snake and its size feeling sure he wouldn't believe me. Dennis just burst out laughing, "That's just that old carpet snake on Marlborough hill, he won't hurt you." I was neither amused nor convinced that that snake was harmless.

37 EXPOSING MY SPORTING PROWESS AND MEETING PHYLLIS

The sunburn I received in those first few weeks in Australia was legendary, at least the Halligans got great joy from telling everyone about it and if I was handy I had to expose it. I was almost a medical exhibit, an example of what happens if you leave a Pom out on a tractor for a week with no shirt and cut-off jeans.

It didn't worry me, but I had no social life outside that I shared with the Halligans as I couldn't go anywhere. I couldn't drive on the highway as I didn't have a driver's licence, it's obvious that hadn't mattered a few weeks earlier when I was driving down the highway for Peter Black. But there's the law and now if I drove it would be in one of the Halligan's vehicles.

Mary, Dennis' mother and my landlady took it upon herself to get me that little bit of social life. There was a badminton night at the Waddington Hall on Tuesday nights and it was just starting up again or was it just finishing? Either way, Mary determined to take me with her to badminton knowing nothing of my sporting prowess or my desire to play sport.

The sum of my prowess and desire amounted to zero but the knowledge that Keith and Leone (Whom I'd met that first night on the farm.) would be there gave me the incentive to go along. The chance to see Leone, the only female of note for thousands of miles over-powered my passionate dislike of sporting participation.

There I was again, showing off my sunburn and exposing my

lack of sporting prowess, the night was what one could call a disaster. There were a couple of handy sheilas there, which reminded me of the Commandment regarding coveting someone else's wife, Keith could keep his wife, these girls had enough to keep my interest in badminton going. It was, however, plain to see that conversation with these girls was nigh on impossible as I was a lowly farmhand with no knowledge of what interested country girls in Australia. I'm not sure which happened first, my lack of desire to play badminton or Mary giving it up or perhaps it was the end of the season, vale the shuttlecock.

I was captive to Belarbrook, it was where I had to spend all my free time, not that I minded, the weather was great and I didn't have much free time as I could always find jobs that needed doing. I worked, slept and wrote home every week, the writing home was the easiest task, as someone who worked and slept I had an awful lot of news for Mum. I remember how at school I'd get halfway down a page and seize, no matter how I tried I couldn't think of anything else to write. Now, when I wrote home to Mum the words just flowed and finding enough room on an aerogramme was a chore, an extra sheet of paper was often slipped in. I became a part of the Halligans' extended family, I was included in most things they did.

I was to meet Vivienne's parents, those people Dennis had had to clean up for before they returned to Australia from their holiday in England. They were introduced to me as Lawson and Francis, not as Mr and Mrs Lewis as they would have been in England. They were rather English and found the farm to be quite a novelty. They took a shine to me and wanted me to be a fellow Englishman, this I found hard as they were from the south of England and I was from the north of England. They were nice and Lawson had recently retired or was on long service leave from the public service where he had been a photographer. It was obvious, that Lawson hadn't retired from taking photographs as you couldn't move before you appeared in a photograph, it could get annoying but it had an upside, I always had photos to send home.

It's said there is a 'black sheep' in every family, in the Halligan family it was Dennis' sister Phyllis. Dennis was at pains to warn me about

Phyllis, she had married a bloke who Dennis didn't approve of, I understood this as my sister married a bloke I didn't approve of but I still tolerated him. The main gripe Dennis had with his sister was blain of all family relationships, money.

Dennis had been left the farm and its debts in their father's will and the care of his mother, and Phyllis had been left a lump-sum payment which the estate didn't have. Phyllis and her husband (I think the emphasis here was the husband.) wanted to get their hands on the lump sum. Mary continued her happy relationship with her daughter, oblivious, it appeared to me, of the siblings' dispute. Phyllis was to visit her mother and was bringing the kids much to Mary's delight.

I was left wondering what sort of a dragon Dennis' sister was, as I found it hard to believe anyone could dislike Dennis and pre-visit Mary had regaled stories of Dennis and Phyllis as kids and what playmates they had been. In the few weeks I'd been here I had realised that Mary wore rose-tinted glasses so took her stories with a pinch of salt.

A mini minor car came cruising over the hill one Saturday afternoon, drawing to a dusty halt just where Dennis normally parked. The doors flew open, and out came the largest child screaming "Nana Mary, Nana Mary." And ran into Mary's welcoming arms, that done the next two kids released themselves from the back seat and followed suit with the same cry. Next, a rather laconic figure emerged from the other car door and hugged her mother. This, of course, was the infamous Phyllis, a not unattractive woman, about thirty I guessed.

For the life of me, I can't remember why I was witnessing this scene, but I was. Phyllis turn to me and said, "You must be Tom, I've heard about you." There was a glint in her eye as she uttered the words as if to say, 'I'll get to you later.' The, I'll get to you later look, made me feel a little embarrassed and also a little fearful of this, what appeared to me to be a harmless mother of three of the cutest kids I'd ever seen.

I took off to whatever it was I should have been doing when Phyllis arrived and she, I presume had a healthy reunion with her mother. Bathed, I reported to the kitchen for tea, the kids had tired of Nana Mary and I was to be their next plaything. They climbed on my knee, they showered me with questions and Mary introduced me to them, Lesley, the eldest, Donelle, the middle and cutest and Michelle, the least enthused by me.

Phyllis talked, but mostly to her mother, occasionally chastising the kids, which they ignored. I took my leave and retired to my room, turned on the radio and got the scratchy sounds of 6KY, the radio station with the best reception. Disrobed and climbed into bed thinking, 'Phyllis isn't as bad as Dennis claims, she's sure as shit got cute kids.'

I'd left the door ajar as I usually did, I disliked feeling locked in. It must have been half an hour later when a head came around the door.

"Hope you're decent." It was Phyllis.

"This used to be my room." she said, "I suppose my brother has told you all those bad things about me." She continues, bearly taking a breath and plonks herself on the end of my bed, which I'm guessing she's slept in before.

Most nineteen-year-old boys only dream of a twenty-nine-year-old woman sitting on their bed and chatting them up. And here I was having it happen to me. Did Phyllis realise she was sitting within inches of a nineteen-year-old hormone balloon, who was naked under this sheet and blanket? If she was aware of the situation it didn't phase her, she just talked and talked and I just listened and discovered I could talk to her too. She told me how she had young girls boarding with her and tells me about each one. I should meet these girls and when I go down to Perth I must stay with her and I probably will meet them.

How she worked on the farm before her brother was old enough, how she loved driving the truck and hauling bags of super. I don't know how long we talked but I'm sure Mary had long ago stopped the lighting plant and called goodnight to Phyllis. The hormone balloon had been deflated only moments into our somewhat one-sided conversation and replaced with admiration and friendship.

"I'd better get to bed, mum will be wondering what we're up to, good night love." Phyllis finally ends our conversation and leaves my room. I'd made my first real friend in my new land.

38 EVERY DAY WAS PARADISE

Life at Belarbrook went on without much input from me. Yes, I worked hard and was conscientious but I cared not for a social life as there wasn't one to be had. I was living miles from anywhere and knew only the people I was living with and their friends and relatives, most of all I was happy. Mary had been sent out to buy me shorts and singlets, the farmworker uniform of the time. I disliked wearing singlets as I never felt comfortable in them. This was part of not thinking for myself, I didn't need to. I was taken to Moora and told where to open a bank account, advised who to avoid and who could be a good friend - that had been shot to pieces when I met Phyllis - my existence was almost child-like.

My work life was very much man-like, in England, I had dipped two hundred and fifty sheep, here in Australia I dipped two and a half thousand in much harsher conditions. One paddock was the size of the farm I worked on in England, everything was bigger here. Perhaps my mind was so busy coming to terms with the enormity of everything around me. I was only too happy that others could do my everyday thinking for me.

Harvest time arrived and I was to meet what I thought was a combine harvester, it was, I was told, a header. How long was it going to take me to learn this new language, which after all was only English? I was to operate the header, a new secondhand one drawn by the tractor. I'd only ever seen the likes of this machine in a self-propelled form in England.

I discovered it was called a header because it was designed to only take the grain-bearing heads of the crop. This meant the operator had to raise and lower the 'comb' (Another new word.) in line with the height of the crop. I managed this job with ease, I had to as there were hundreds of acres to harvest.

I'd now been driving the farm utes for a month without a licence or a care in the world. I, of course, had no idea how to get a driver's licence here. In England, I'd had a licence for a motorbike and a tractor but not a car as my chance of owning a car was remote. It seemed here in Australia a driver's licence was essential if you wanted to go anywhere. I hadn't given getting a licence any thought, enter my thinker, Dennis.

"We're going to have to get you a licence, aren't we?" Dennis tells me one day out of the blue.

Mary now pushes herself in, "I'll get him a book, next time I'm down the Mission."

This is another new word I was picking up, 'the Mission' is New Norcia, so-called because it was established as a Benedictine Mission before my time, and Dennis' and Mary's for that matter.

The 'book' Mary had referred to is what we would have called the highway code in England. Mary duly delivers a copy of the book and I study it and as I thought, it's pretty much the same as the highway code. I'm then told the basics of getting my licence, "You've got to reverse into the police station gateway and know the one-way streets in Perth." Mary tells me.

An appointment is made for me and Mary stays in charge, she'll drive me into the Mission as she knows the local policeman and that will go in my favour. I learn the one-way streets in Perth, Hay Street, Murray Street, Barrack Street and William Street. 'What have the one-way streets in Perth got to do with my driving ability?' I think as the day draws closer.

The afternoon of 11th of December 1968 arrives and Mary chauffeurs me to the New Norcia Police Station, in real terms, the policeman's house. I have to produce my English driver's licence covering a motorbike and tractor and my Document of Identity. If Mary 'knowing' this bloke will make things easier, I don't know how things would have gone without introduction. I do my theory test and yes, the last question is; 'Name the one-way streets in Perth.'

The practical driving test comes next we hop in Mary's ute and off we go. "Turn left here, and turn right here," Constable Wake directs, "now stop here." We're on a slight incline heading up to the Hotel.

"I want you to do a hill start here."

'Nobody mentioned a hill start, this thing hasn't got a handbrake.' I'm thinking. I've never had a driving lesson but I do know you are supposed to use a handbrake to do a hill start. I've had to do lots of hill starts without a handbrake around the farm so no panic, but what if he picks up on the car having no handbrake? 'Just do as you're told', I think, and all goes well.

"Now back to the station." I'm instructed.

"Pull up just beyond the gate, will you? Now reverse into the gateway." Instructs Constable Wake. I can't believe how well I managed to reverse that ute into that gateway. "O.K.," says the policeman with a sigh and gets out of the ute. I follow suit and ask, "Well did I pass?"

"Well yeah," drawls the cop, "Yah a bit heavy-footed, yah'd better watch that."

'I met your daughter at badminton a few weeks ago, and she's hot, yah'd better watch that too.' I think as I follow him into the station come house and complete the paperwork and get the spiel about P plates, "You'll need to have them for the next twelve months." He advises me.

Christmas is drawing closer and Mary wants to go Christmas shopping in Perth, I get the job of chaperon. Dennis is very unsure about his mother driving to Perth alone, as it is she won't drive into Perth but leave the car at Guildford and catch the train into Perth. This turns out to be a day off work which is much harder work than, actually working.

As we glide through Bindoon, I seem to recollect the name of this place. 'That's where Lesley Evans is coming to.' I think. I remember this from a letter from my sister Marion who works with Lesley's father. I too, knew Lesley's father as he caught our school bus to work every day, but Lesley less so, as I only remember her fleetingly from the Preston Patrick Young Farmers.

I relate to Mary that I know a girl who has come out from my part of England to work for some Scottish people in a place called Bindoon.

"Oh I know where they live, we can drop in on the way back." Mary swiftly advises me. Mary isn't someone you can negotiate with when she's on a mission.

I'm towed around Perth by Mary, the streets I remember from two months earlier. The shops, now that's another matter, I'd never been in any of them and keeping tabs on Mary wasn't easy, she wasn't a methodical shopper. It didn't take long for me to find I had a better understanding of the streets than Mary as she traipsed me the long way around to every shop in Perth. We had lunch at Coles, a must for everyone from the country I was told, I found it hard to warm to the cafeteria.

Oh, was I glad to get on the train back to Guildford? Shopping with Mary wasn't my forte. Off we go, 'I'm sure we're going the wrong way', I think but have faith that Mary knows where she's going. No sooner had we got in the ute than we pull into a non-descript house just off the road. I immediately dread Mary reversing back onto the road when we leave. We are visiting Mary's brother completely unannounced, thankfully it's a brief visit. Mary drives back towards New Norcia and I'm in a haze, she seems to have grown another leg and is at her energetic best when we reach Bindoon.

"Let's go and see that girl you know." Mary blurts out as we drive through Bindoon with its Hall and tractor yard. It's obvious that I have no say in this matter and we pull into a house, which to me seemed, unlike a farmhouse. I knew Lesley was going to work on a farm so thought we were at the wrong place.

Now Mary, in her stays and high heels and now fading make-up, appeared a formidable woman, especially now with her newfound spurt of energy. Mary marches up to the back door and announces herself to total strangers and drags me along. The Youngs, I discover these people are, are delighted to meet me, Lesley seems less enthusiastic, I find out she has just arrived in Bindoon and has just had two strangers land on the doorstep. I had felt a little embarrassed throughout this ordeal, Mary didn't bat an eyelid.

39 KILLING A PIG

Christmas is fast approaching, my first Christmas in Australia, I don't know what to expect, 'Will it be just like England with goose and roast potatoes and Christmas pudding?' I'm thinking in one of those moments of thought I rarely had. It seemed the goose was to be replaced with pork.

There had been a sow and her four or five piglets wandering about at 'Dump' (An abbreviation of Dumpingerry the homestead I lived in.) since I arrived. I was told by Dennis that they had been left behind when all the other pigs were moved to the new pig yards, at the end of the farm where he lived. This sow had just given birth to her piglets and it was thought unwise to move her. It turns out she was pretty resourceful, as I had never seen these pigs fed or watered and they were in good shape.

Gwyn, Dennis' brother-in-law, had come up to the farm from Perth with his girlfriend and I think a gun. I don't know if this was planned, but Gwyn's visit coincided with the harvesting of what was to be our Christmas dinner. The copper had been boiling all afternoon, the copper being our only hot water at Dumpingerry.

Dennis and Gwyn arrive in Dennis' ute with the usual cloud of dust, I'm lying in wait so Dennis just calls "Hop in," and off we go. Being last in it leaves Gwyn in the middle of the bench seat of the ute, just as well really. As we tear off down the track to where Dennis knows the pigs are, Gwyn casually asks, "Ever killed a pig, Tom?"

"No," I reply.

It seemed to me that Gwyn was something of a veteran of pig killing. No time for thinking, the pigs are in sight, Dennis screeches to a halt turns off the ute and leaps out calling "We want the little boar," I leap out the other side of the ute and give chase, there's a dog involved and Dennis captures his quarry, the little boar which isn't that little.

"Grab that rope out of the ute, will yah Tom." Dennis orders.

About now Gwyn gets out of the ute and comes to inspect this newly captured pig, "He's a beauty." Comments Gwyn. Dennis hog-ties the pig and we carry it back to the ute. I'm elected guard and sit in the back of the ute with the pig, as the ute takes off the pig urinates on me, if you think pig shit stinks, you haven't been pissed on by a young boar.

I'm rather dreading the next bit, the killing of the pig. From the stories I'd heard of pig killing in England, it was a noisy and messy affair, with the pig squealing its head off and blood everywhere. I was somewhat disappointed when Dennis took a claw hammer from the back of the ute, and then calmly struck the pig at the centre of its head just above the eyes. It appeared stone dead but was just stunned, Dennis then took his knife and stabbed the pig through the heart, and now, it was dead.

Now we needed the hot water from the copper, we carried this up to the shed in buckets and suddenly discovered that the washtub we were to scald the pig in was just a smidgen too small. As a result of this miss calculation, we had to dip first the back of the pig in the cooling water and scrape like hell and then the front of the pig and scrape like hell. It didn't work well, and the other thing that didn't work well was Gwyn, he was bloody useless. Kettles were boiled, razors were called for and eventually, the black Berkshire pig started to turn white though, slightly piebald, as darkness fell it was deemed we could do no better than we'd done. Christmas dinner had been harvested and the pig was duly gutted and the dogs rewarded.

The next day Dennis arrived early to cut up the pig, it looked a lot worse than it had the night before but, as Dennis put it, "The women are only going to see it in small pieces."

"We're going down the dam for a swim this afternoon, do yah want to come?" Dennis asks as he leaves with his share of the pig.

"I'll be in that," I reply, I think I'm getting into this new language.

Dam bathing was one of the new and wonderful things I'd discovered in my new land. It was so disappointing that I still couldn't swim but I could splash around and get cool in muddy water. It was one day I took a sip of dam water that I found out just how muddy it was but it had a cooling effect on a hot weary body, just don't drink it.

Dennis had taught me the art of dam bathing, it seems you run over the side of the dam, rip off your clothes once out of sight and run flat out into the water making as much noise as you can. This terrifies the sheep and wildlife for miles around and perhaps warns any women in the vicinity that there's a naked man in the dam.

This planned afternoon dam bathing was rather different from the male after-work cool-off, there would be women present, Vivienne and Gwyn's girlfriend, who I was yet to meet. I prepared myself for this bathing by wearing my work shorts, I didn't have any swimming gear, which I learn are called bathers in Australia.

I report to Dennis and Vivienne's house for this afternoon 'swim' in Mary's ute and we all pile into Dennis' car, a Ford Zephyr. The others have towels and bathers and generally, look the part, Gavin, Dennis and Vivienne's son, is stacked in the car on top of me. I'm seated in the back between Gwyn and his girlfriend with Gavin on my knee, I've never been this close to a woman with so few clothes on as this in my life. My cheeks are aglow.

To the idle observer, this looks for all the world like an outing to the beach, it is, in fact, a quick drive around the corner, perhaps a mile, half a mile if you were a crow. Rather than the usual run over the bank of the dam, we saunter over the bank and the three swimmers dive into the water, Vivienne and I are left with Gavin who is soon in the water. Vivienne is six months pregnant so is choosing not to swim, I wade into the dam I usually throw myself in and just cool off moving away from Vivienne and Gavin and trying to look, well, adult but looking very much like I can't swim.

As I stand in the water looking helpless, I'm suddenly aware that I've just been circled by 'Bubbles', Gwyn's girlfriend. Her name wasn't Bubbles but I think the name suited her, not that she had a bubbly personality, she didn't seem to have a personality. She did have a bubbly body and a very brief bikini, did that have bubbles on it? Perhaps that's why I'm calling her Bubbles.

"Can't you swim?" asks Bubbles.

"No," I reply, "I had stacks of lessons at school but still can't swim."

"Let me help you." Standing alongside me she puts her arm in front of my chest, "Lay on my arm and I'll hold you up."

She does exactly what she said she'd do and I'm now laying flat in the water

"Now take a stroke."

I do and she gently lets me go and for the first time in my life, I can swim, what a fantastic sensation. "It wasn't that hard was it?" She asks of me.

"No, it was easy, thanks for that."

I know, I should have hugged her and kissed her but no sooner had I swam my first stroke than Vivienne can be seen on the bank of the dam with one of her disapproving scowls on her face. She had seen Bubbles manhandling me in the water and knew, as a girlfriend of Gwyn's no good could come of that sort of thing. Seeing Vivienne's face Bubbles squeals.

"He can swim, he can swim."

Vivienne smiles reservedly and says, "Well done, that's a first, someone learning to swim in our dam."

The rest of the afternoon is a blur, I'd learnt to swim and my body had been touched by a nearly naked woman, this new land was giving me so much. Back on the tractor tomorrow and swim in the dam afterwards.

40 MY FIRST CHRISTMAS

Christmas 1968 was organised for me, as was much of my new life in Australia. I was to have Christmas with Vivienne's parents, Lawson and Francis Lewis at 104 Ryrie Avenue in South Perth. Dennis, Vivienne and son Gavin left for South Perth on Christmas eve with our lunch in the boot of the car, a leg of the pig we had killed just a few days earlier. I was to follow on Christmas day after feeding and watering the pigs, in Dennis' ute.

I managed to find the Lewis' house and the lunch was a very English affair, they being English, albeit twenty-odd years prior. The most memorable thing about the Christmas of 1968 was that it was the then hottest on record, forty-two degrees. At the time I think they were boasting the temperature in Fahrenheit, one hundred and five degrees. If the radio hadn't told us I would have been none the wiser. I was now getting used to hot days so one more made little difference to me. I set out for New Norcia late that afternoon after having a thoroughly lazy day in blistering heat.

After Christmas, it was back to harvesting and the everyday chores of the farm, although work in my new land never seemed a chore and the sun shone every day. Vivienne was by the end of February, very pregnant and Gavin came with Dennis for work. Being only three Gavin required care in the work area, a duty shared by Dennis and me. I will confess to enjoying doing my share of the child-sitting, although there wasn't much sitting involved.

Towards the end of March Vivienne gave birth to a bouncing baby girl, Kylie. As I remember it a holiday was called for this occasion, I was to visit Vivienne in hospital. I was equipped for this visit with a kangaroo Mum had knitted for the newborn child, when Mum wasn't sending letters she was sending parcels for her antipodean son. It was obvious Mum thought I'd found a home with the Halligans and a baby present was in order.

On this visit to Perth, I was to stay with Phyllis, Dennis' much-maligned sister. This was my first visit to 9 Adrian Street, Phyllis' home and my first true meeting with her husband Don. I'd met Don briefly one day when he'd visited the farm in the middle of harvest and thought he didn't seem as bad as Dennis had painted him.

I was welcomed into the Overington household with open arms, especially by Phyllis who was thrilled to see me again. Don welcomed me warmly but I could feel the warmth wasn't as genuine as Phyllis', his was a little too welcoming. Phyllis' house was chaos, children running wild, the promised young girls wandering to and from their rooms in various states of dress and the radio blaring from the (To me at least.) ultra-modern radiogram. The girls may have been an attraction but the radiogram stole their show, with me at least.

When Don had gone to the pub, Phyllis introduced me to the girls who were boarding with her, giving me a glowing reference to each. The reference that Phyllis was giving these girls wasn't what they wanted to hear. I'd driven up in a dirty farm ute and looked boring, I wasn't the man for them. It had filtered down to me that these girls were mostly 'Wards of the State' and Phyllis was being paid to care for them, a responsibility she didn't take as seriously as she should have. Although the girls weren't attracted to me, the idea of a wild young girl was attractive to me. I returned to the farm the next day with a degree of reluctance.

Since I first arrived at Belarbrook, Dennis had told me two things he felt were important for me to be aware of: firstly that farmworkers were the lowest of the low and secondly, it rained like hell here in winter. Well, here I was having the time of my life being a farmworker and I'd been here for six months and never seen anything that looked like rain. Dennis' viability was looking bad, and then, about Anzac Day (I didn't know anything about this day, its significance or that it was a holiday.). It rained, not the rain Dennis had promised, but that miserable English rain I'd left behind six months earlier. I was cold and wet and miserable and I reported for work as usual and was told, "It's Anzac day, we don't work today."

I had been ready to work, I returned to Dumpingerry rather dejected with nothing to do. I went to my room and picked up an old 'Elder's Weekly' and thought, 'I've read this before, what else is there to read?' My reading to this time had very much centred on old Elder's Weeklys the odd Countryman or an old copy of the West Australian newspaper. Elder's Weekly was an advertising vehicle for the major stock firm in Australia, the Countryman was the weekly farming news magazine and the West Australian was the daily paper, I mostly looked at the pictures.

There was a book in my room, I've no idea where it came from but it was super thick, not something I'd normally give a second thought. I presume it had been there for the six months I'd been there and it was only now on this day of miserable English rain that I ventured to pick it up. The weight of this book alone would once have kept me from reading it, the title didn't draw me in either, War and Peace, part one. 'What's this shit?' I'm thinking. Something inside me said, "It's a bloody challenge, I bet you can't read it from cover to cover." With a challenge thrown at you like that, what can you do? All I could do was take up the challenge, it wasn't much later that I discovered that this hadn't been a challenge at all, this book was what I'd been looking for all my life.

With the rain came seeding time, the time I'd been waiting for for months or it seemed like months. The duel wheels had been waiting beside the shed to be fitted to the tractors, tractors would get bogged regularly and I would see real rain, flooding rain and the dams would fill up from the runoff. It had me mesmerised all summer how these dams would ever fill as they were to me, merely holes in the ground. I was to do the ploughing and working the ground afterwards to effect a weed kill and Dennis would seed the crop, wheat and oats.

It was cold and to a degree wet but nothing like Dennis had promised, we got through the whole cropping program without having to fit the duel wheels to the tractors. We never got bogged once, and just as I thought, the dams didn't fill with water. This was a very unusual winter, Dennis was at pains to tell me almost every day, or the days we saw each other, we were working our individual, patches and most days we just worked and slept. One night I just worked through, lights were bobbing around paddocks every night and men wore stubble and all-in-one overalls. The seeding of 1969 was the most successful season in living memory.

Dennis' neighbour, Tony Mauritz was so excited by the way the season had gone he threw a party, a 'bucks party' I remember it being called. This party was held in a gravel pit, a hole in the ground where the shire road maintenance crew had taken gravel to repair the road. A sheep had been sacrificed for this party, a plough disc barbecue built and a couple of cartons of once cold beer laid on. Most importantly, a tree had been set on fire earlier in the day and we had a nice warm centrepiece for the party.

I got my first real taste of Australian beer and wasn't the least disappointed. I think the preparations for this party started around four o'clock that afternoon, I know we got our invitation in the early afternoon. It was a blast, and although it was attended by only farmers and farmworkers, not one tractor got a mention. Let's say, Tony knew how to throw a party. A good time was had by all and even the hangover I had the next day was acceptable.

41 MY NEW UTE

With seeding out of the way, life on the farm returned to normal or as normal as life could be working with Dennis. Lambs to be marked, tailed, castrated and earmarked, blood aplenty. This was a merino stud farm and Dennis bred rams to sell to other farmers so some of the lucky lambs snook past the castration. These lambs were selected for their wool quality and conformation, something Dennis involved me in. Dennis told me that there was a living to be made just classing wool, perhaps I should look into it. Since my arrival at New Norcia, Dennis took every opportunity to point me in the direction of improving myself. This wool classing thing seemed to strike a chord with me, but I had bigger fish to fry.

I had seen an advertisement for the latest Ford Falcon, it came in four body shapes: sedan, coupe, station wagon and ute. I had set my heart on the ute as all the young blokes drove a ute, and let's face it I wanted to be one of the young blokes. I was cashed up, as I'd spent very little since my arrival in Australia and just banked my paycheques as they came in.

Dennis didn't pay me weekly, it seemed to be whenever the chequebook and I were close, Dennis would write me a cheque. This didn't worry me and Dennis was a good bookkeeper, in that regard anyway, I was always paid my dues. I told Dennis of my plans to buy a new ute and he just said, "We'll have to check it out next time we're in Moora." I wanted a new ute as I'd had the experience of buying secondhand when I had bought my motorbike and it hadn't gone well.

To my amazement, we were in Moora the next day and I had my latest paycheque in my hand. Dennis took me to the Ford dealer in Moora and did my talking for me, they'd have a new Falcon ute there next week, the colour wasn't discussed, but it would be white. I then went over to the Commonwealth and opened my first cheque account, with my latest paycheque and most of the money from my savings account. I was issued with a chequebook and felt so rich, you could buy anything with a chequebook I thought.

The next week seemed to go on forever, I'd only seen a picture of my ute-to-be and couldn't wait to see it in the flesh. Dennis got the phone call, my ute had arrived in Moora, Dennis, it seemed, was more excited than me and we were off to Moora that day.

Well, we'd ordered the ute, (Dennis and I.) I hadn't paid a deposit or anything, it was a very loose agreement, I'd been taken on Dennis' word, which must have meant something. It was now time to sit down in the office and get down to the nitty-gritty, the ute would cost two thousand, four hundred dollars. I had one thousand, two hundred, which left a shortfall of one thousand, two hundred dollars.

"No problem." Says the salesman, "We can get finance for that, how old are you by the way?"

"Twenty." I proudly replied.

"Oh, we're going to need a guarantor, you've got to be twenty-one to get finance."

My heart sank, the dream of my new ute was in tatters. Before the tears could well in my eyes, Dennis standing at the back of the office proudly announced, "I'm his guarantor, where do I sign." It was now my turn to sign, the cheque for twelve hundred dollars, I carefully wrote out my first cheque, one thousand and two hundred and signed in the bottom right-hand corner. If my chest had puffed out anymore, it would have burst, I was now the proud owner of a brand new XW Ford Falcon ute.

I now had to drive to Calingiri to pick up the number plates. I'd seen the ute on the way into the office but that was about all, I'd handed over my money and now I opened the door of my first car. It was amazing, it had rich burgundy upholstery and trim and, a radio, in all my life I had never dreamt of owning something as elaborate as this. I turned her on and my hand went straight to the radio, and low and behold the faint sound of 6KY, my favourite radio station.

I followed Dennis to Calingiri as I'd never been there before and got the licencing details out of the way and drove back to Dumpingerry and parked outside my room. The ute stayed there for the rest of the week, the first flush of ownership was over, it had suddenly become just a car.

It was about a week later, that Dennis got a call from the Ford dealer in Moora, my cheque had bounced, or they had had a phone call from the manager of the Commonwealth Bank telling them that he couldn't clear my cheque. I was to go into the bank and see the manager and he would explain the problem to me.

I now didn't have to rely on Dennis to get into Moora, I had a ute of my own and could do my own thing. Dennis let me go saying, "I don't think it's much, you'll sort 'em out." I presented myself at the bank and was ushered into the manager's office.

"It's only a small thing, Thomas, you haven't written dollars after the one thousand, two hundred."

I just looked blankly back across the desk and thought, 'Well.'

"Can you just write the word dollars in and initial it?" said the bank manager as he slid the cheque across his desk.

"Yeah, is that it?" I asked rather abruptly. "Yes, that's it, Thomas." The bank manager politely replied.

I left the bank less than impressed. 'All that fucking way for a bloody word.' I think as I turn the ute around and head back to New Norcia.

The successful seeding was showing signs of fruition as the crops grew, but the pasture paddocks never showed much. Truckloads of sheep were travelling down Great Northern Highway every day, the news was, that most of these sheep were being sold for fifty cents ahead, not enough to cover the cost of transport. The word drought was being uttered and at Belarbrook it looked like a bumper harvest but there was hardly any water in the dams. I was soon to complete my full farming year in Australia, shearing time was to come around again.

Shearing this year would be a little different, Dennis wasn't going to pay a shearing contractor to supply shearers and shedhand. He had become aware that he'd have to get through this shearing on a shoe-string. Dennis knew an Aboriginal shearer who worked around New Norcia with his brother and was pretty reliable, he'd get him. Dennis caught up with Arnold Pickett and an agreement was struck. Arnold and his brother Manuel would shear Dennis' sheep at a better price than he had been charged when I arrived.

Much was said about Aborigines and none of it was favourable, Mary protested but Dennis assured her these blokes wouldn't steal or make trouble, the Aboriginals' main claims to fame it seemed. I'd hardly seen an Aboriginal, up close at any rate and never spoken to one so when these men turned up and spoke and acted much the same as white men, I was most surprised.

This year I was to be everything, rouseabout, presser, penner-upper and when Dennis wasn't there fill-in woolclasser. I soon got in the swing of things, the skills I'd learnt the previous year seemed, to come naturally to me even though it had been twelve months since I'd last used them. Throwing and skirting fleeces at speed, was a breeze, my classing had to be looked over but I could now press, weigh and brand a bale of wool unsupervised.

It was perhaps now that Dennis' idea of me becoming a woolclasser was starting to make sense. I enjoyed working in the shearing shed with the disciplined two-hour shifts, half-hour smokos and one-hour lunch break. Not that these times applied to me as I had work to do in smokos and lunchtime to keep up with things, but the theory was good. It wasn't too hard, as these shearers weren't very fast and even when they brought their nephew along to learn how to shear I could still keep up with the wool handling.

Once shearing was out of the way, the sheep had to be dipped as the year before and then harvest time returned and this year the crop was huge. Although, the now-declared drought had taken its toll on the livestock the crops around New Norcia were very good but seeing the stock short of water was heartbreaking and summer had just begun.

42 MOVING ON

1970 was to be a big year for me or otherwise depending on how you looked at things. I was registered for national service (It was compulsory.) and I'd also put my name down to do a woolclassing course by correspondence. I dreaded the thought of national service as I thought my life had been an adventure for the last fourteen months, and now it was time to get on with my life. Good fortune looked down on me and my birthday wasn't one of the ones balloted for national service.

I was finding out that they did some quaint stuff in Australia and the selection of army recruits was one of them. If your birthdate was picked out of a barrel you had to do two years of national service, if not you were pretty much home free. The two years of national service included being shot at in Vietnam, a country I'd barely heard of, this didn't appeal to me in the least. The woolclassing course looked challenging and the thought of doing it via correspondence was daunting. School and things scholastic had long since departed my thoughts, I'd had a passionate dislike for both.

My life in New Norcia was getting trying, things were tough on the farm due to the low water supplies. One of my daily jobs was dragging dead sheep out of drying dams, it was depressing. I was now pretty much my own boss and did what needed doing without any supervision. Dennis' main concern was excessing a reliable water supply. He did this by having a bore sunk at his end of the farm. In my opinion, it was taking more of his time than was necessary, I became frustrated but hung in.

It was one hot January day and I was driving back to Dump for my bath and tea, feeling just a little pissed off as there was a lot of harvesting yet to be done and Dennis was looking down a hole at the other end of the farm. Just before I got to the boundary of the Dumpingerry block, (Dumpingerry had once been a separate property.) I noticed that some sheep had somehow got into the best crop of wheat on the farm. I could have rounded them up and got them back to where they should have been, but I was knackered and fed up with things. I turned around and raced back to where I knew Dennis would still be gazing down his bore.

My ute screeched to a halt not far from Dennis, without getting out I yelled, "I'm finished here, the fucking sheep are in the crop. That's me, I'm finished!" Before I could drive off Dennis rushed over to me, "What crop? What sheep? We can sort this out, come on, we'll sort it out." Dennis hopped in the ute and off I drove back to the scene of the crime, how Dennis calmed me down so quickly is beyond me. We managed to round the sheep up and return them to their paddock and fix the fence which they'd pushed over, without too much crop damage being done.

"Not that bad after all Tom," Dennis says as we drive back to his place.

"I don't care, I'm finished Dennis, I can't take any more of this shit, I'm leaving now," I answer.

"I don't want you to go, you know that don't you?"

"Maybe, but I've got to go," I reply with tears in my eyes.

"Well take me home and I'll pay you up," Dennis mumbles.

We return to Dennis' house, he gets the chequebook and returns to the ute, writes my cheque and hands it to me.

"You know you've got a home here anytime don't you?"

Those words drove me over the edge and the tears poured from my eyes, I may have mumbled "Yes," I'm not sure, we parted with the same handshake he greeted me with fifteen months earlier.

I returned to Dumpingerry, packed up my stuff, broke the news to Mary and sped off to my only friend in the world (Or so it seemed at the time.) Dennis' sister Phyllis. By the time I reached Phyllis' place, it was dark, she was expecting me as Mary had rung her. I was welcomed with open arms.

"Well, you've finally had enough of my brother, have you?" She queried as I walked through the door.

I had no reply to give her, I'd just left her brother's employ but I'd also left behind my other best friend, mentor and supporter for the last fifteen months. I couldn't bad mouth the man who gave me a break in a land that seemed so unwelcoming on my arrival.

A bed had been prepared for me and I was welcome to stay as long as I liked, husband Don was ever so welcoming too, offering me a beer. I declined the beer but still had to hear about how he was now my new best friend, as he drank his beer, after all, I was a friend of Phyl's. Even as my new best friend, Don didn't impress me.

The phone rang, it was for me, "Lawson Lewis," Phyllis says with a smile as she hands me the phone. Vivienne's father had rung to try and persuade me to return to the farm. It was a futile exercise, not only wouldn't I return, I couldn't.

It was not long before I got homesick for New Norcia, perhaps two days. Perth was boring, yes there were the girls, but they worked during the day. I had a great excuse to return, I could take Phyl's kids up to see their Nanna Mary. No argument from Phyl, so off we went me and the three girls. Mary was thrilled to see the kids and not unhappy to see me. It was like going home, it was really, as it had been my home all my time in Australia. That was one day of boredom relieved.

On my return to Perth with the girls, I realised I hadn't said farewell to what were my first friends when I first arrived, Keith and Leone. I took the opportunity to go up on Saturday when Keith would be home, didn't seem right to visit Leone when she was home alone (Perhaps there had been a time when I would have been tempted.).

Keith and Leone were thrilled to see me, I think they were pretty lonely living in the old Waddington post office with only a roar of passing traffic. I'd now been living this carefree life for almost a week so when Keith asks me "What are you going to do now?"

"I guess I'll have to look for another job." I replied, "hadn't given it much thought."

"Well I was talking to my old boss the other week and he said he was looking for somebody."

"He's an arsehole." Squeals Leone. "He's alright," continues Keith, "I did some work for him the other weekend."

"I might give it a go, where's he at?" I ask.

Keith tells me the bloke's name is Basil Blee and he gives me directions. I bid my friends goodbye and decide to strike while the iron's hot.

I continue up the road to Moora and follow Keith's directions, I find the olive trees Keith told me about so I know I'm there. I tentatively turn into the driveway, it's a track to the house and I pull up outside a workshop that looks inhabited, it is. There's a bloke under the bonnet of an old Ford Zephyr ute. "G'ay," I say, "Basil Blee?"

"That's me, who's asking?" "Tom Watson, Keith Stevenson told me you were looking for somebody to work for you."

"Well, I may be, what have you done before?" Basil asks me.

The job interview goes on and I get the job.

"Can you start Monday?" Basil asks, "I'll show you your room."

I wasn't expecting this, there's a shower, a washing machine, toilet, this is sheer luxury compared with my room at Dumpingerry with its semi-dirt floor, thunderbox and copper. Perhaps I'd landed on my feet with this job, Leone's words seemed to have a little truth in them, "He's an arsehole." This bloke did seem to have a cold side but Keith thought he was alright and I think Keith's name had got me the job, that was enough for me.

Back to Perth, and a waltz around Canterbury Court tonight, Canterbury Court had become my dance hall of choice on my odd nights out in Perth since I got my ute. I didn't know anyone at Canterbury Court but was working on knowing somebody soon. Back to work on Monday and to a new life in my luxury accommodation.

43 THE NEW LIFE

Sunday evening I presented myself to my new workplace and my seemingly luxurious quarters. I had to make my bed with my bedding something foreign to me, as at home Mum had done it and I'd had my bedding supplied at New Norcia. Perhaps the luxury was only visual.

Basil rousted me out of bed at quarter to seven the next morning. Feeding the pigs was the first job, this was done by driving the old Dodge ute down to the pig yards loaded with the feed for the day. That may sound simple but the Dodge ute had to be started first. "You pull the choke out three-quarters of an inch," starts Basil, "and then you press the accelerator pedal twice, turn on the key and press the starter button. If it doesn't start you have to crank it." If the bloke hadn't been so sincere, I would have thought he was pulling my leg.

He knew what he was talking about as the ute started. It seemed that the sole purpose of the Dodge ute was to feed the pigs, my head was starting to spin but at least I had a job. I was to discover that most of the engine-powered machinery on this place had a crank handle.

The next thing I found out was that every day was organised, there was a starting time and a finishing time. This was very much unlike my experience with Dennis where everything was disorganised and easygoing. As the first week wore on I discovered my new boss had mood swings and picking them wasn't easy. One moment he was jovial and easy going and the next simply, impossible. It was obvious Leone had seen the latter in him and her judge of character was pretty close to spot on.

I got my new address and was soon writing home again and getting letters, much to Basil's displeasure, to me it seemed anyway. I had also started my woolclassing course on correspondence which created more mail. I have a feeling that at times I got up Basil's nose, especially with my woolclassing course as it was bad enough that I could write, trying to improve myself was way over the top.

Basil was living proof of what Dennis had told me about farm-workers being the lowest of the low, he treated me that way. So in my second week, after carefully picking my time, I asked Basil for a week off so that I could attend a woolclassing course that I had booked and paid for. The course was at the end of February. There was an eery silence and then the answer came, "Well yes, but I can't pay you for that week you understand?" Basil begrudgingly answered.

"Of course, that's fine," I said and left it at that.

I didn't find the work hard at Olivedene, I think that's what the place was called, but I did find the boss hard to get on with. Remembering how hard it seemed to be to get a job when I first arrived in Australia, I hung in and learned to roll with the punches, or was it selective deafness?

It was in my first few weeks at Olivedene that I got two important items in the mail. The first was the confirmation that I didn't have to do national service and the accompanying papers, it seemed piles of them. If things changed, I could still be called up at any time and basically, I hadn't gotten off free, didn't like what I read but that was the worst scenario.

The second item of mail that felt important was a letter from my good friend Richard Berrie asking me to be the best man at his wedding. Naturally, if I was to attend I would have been the best man there, but I couldn't possibly do it as I hadn't yet done my two years in Australia. If I returned to England I would have had to have paid, not only that fare but my original subsidised fare, way beyond my means. It was with much regret that I had to write to Richard and say I couldn't be the best man at his wedding.

I think it may have been that day that I realised that there would now, be no going back for me. My next letter was to my sister Marion, asking her to send my saving from England, by no means a fortune but probably enough to pay off my ute.

My week off for the woolclassing course was now coming up and so was my twenty-first birthday, I was a little excited about both. I decided to have a party for my twenty-first, not a lot of organisation was needed as I didn't have any friends to invite. It would be a small do, at Phyllis' place, I determined before I asked her.

For this party, I'd need a sheep, I knew a bit about catering, that's what we'd had at Tony Mouritz's party and that went well. The hard part about this was, that I had to ask Basil if he would kill one for me, to my surprise he said yes and the deal was done, I'd pick it up on the Saturday of the party.

I really shouldn't have gotten excited about the woolclassing course, it wasn't for the likes of me, it was for farmers and that's mostly who attended it. There were perhaps a few sessions that focused on wool-classing, but the main thrust of the course was to encourage farmers to buy wool futures, to offset any fall in wool prices when they sold their wool. The thing about wool futures was pushed so hard, that even I knew what wool futures were by the time we had finished, not that it was of any benefit to me.

The week staying a Phyllis' place was more exciting than the rather boring woolclassing course. I got to know some of the girls who boarded there, all young and to my eyes attractive. I too was attractive to them, not because of my extremely good looks but because I had wheels, these girls found my ute very attractive. "Hey, Tom can yah take me to…?" was the question most asked of me, and how could I refuse those fluttering eyelashes?

This must have been how I got to know Rhonda a bit better than some of the others. I remember taking her to visit her parents or grand-parents, but I'm not sure which. They lived in what looked to me like a one-room shack in Jandakot, no wonder she was a ward of the State. I couldn't see she had other problems and that week I helped her move to a place in Scarborough where she was to work as a live-in childminder.

The Saturday of my twenty-first birthday arrived and I was out of the blocks early. I had a sheep to pick up in Dandaragan and I thought I'd invite Lesley Evans and her boyfriend to the party. The only people I knew who I thought were invitable. I had made Bindoon and Lesley one of my stops on my trips up and down the Great Northern Highway and got to know John, her boyfriend at a dance in Bindoon and my stops there.

My stop at Bindoon, with my invitation, meant a detour on the return trip from Dandaragan, yes they'd try and make it. Now I'd stop off at Rackich's and pick up a couple of flagons of wine and a carton of king browns, liquor sorted.

I returned to Phyl's place with a rather warm sheep and the liquor, thankfully Phyl's husband, Don was brought up on a farm and so knew how to cut up the sheep. That job was soon out of the way and the chops could cool in the fridge.

The evening of the party arrived and I had to pick up my other invitee, Rhonda. This was rather exciting for me as I'd never taken a girl out before, may have met and pashed, but not taken one out in the true sense. Don and Phyl had invited a few friends and the party got going, John and Lesley arrived and I was falling into a flagon of wine. Things didn't go well, I was able to take Rhonda home and promised to see her the next day.

The next day I went to see Rhonda as promised. I was met by her new boss and told that I wasn't welcome and to leave Rhonda alone. For the life of me, I didn't know what I'd done but I just let it go and drove back to Dandaragan for work on Monday.

44 ANOTHER MOVE

Back at Dandaragan, life continued on its dull course. I had found one new challenge, my younger sister Barbara had sent me a copy of Dostoevsky's Crime and Punishment. I had written and told her how much I enjoyed reading Tolstoy and was looking for books of the same ilk, Dostoevsky may have been Russian like Tolstoy but his Crime and Punishment certainly wasn't in the same ilk as the Tolstoy I'd read. I found it almost impossible to read but being bored most nights gave it a shot.

It may sound strange, but I was finding that Basil and I had something in common, a dislike for each other. I being a Pom, got up Basil's nose simply for being a Pom, it had long been the custom for Australians to dislike Poms and Basil wasn't going to break with tradition. I disliked Basil because he was a moody know-all who only smiled when I met with some sort of misfortune.

This lighter side of Basil came to the fore at crutching time (When the sheep get their bum wool trimmed to prevent blowfly strikes.) two shearers came for this operation and I acted as general dog's body penning up and the like. The second morning Basil handed me two shiny-looking plums, well I thought they were plums.

"Try these," smiled Basil.

I should have smelt a rat but just thought Basil was showing the shearers how nice he was. I think the shearers had been tipped off, I popped one plum in my mouth and almost immediately spat it out.

"Aw fuck!" I exclaimed.

Basil burst out laughing and the shearers followed suit.

"What's that shit?" I asked.

"They're olives, haven't you seen them growing on the trees?" replied Basil still smiling, this trick was going to keep a smile on his face for at least an hour and had records been kept, broken all records, smiling wasn't Basil's forte`.

I got on quite well with the shearers who could see I worked pretty hard and got no thanks from Basil. The other men who came to do work at Olivedene were the tank builders, they came to build a concrete tank next to one of the property's many bores. These tank builders worked weekends and asked if I'd give them a hand, I must have done alright as they offered me a job. They may have noticed that I wasn't getting my due reward with Basil, and for some unknown reason, I knocked the job offer back. Perhaps it was because I'd got into the woolclassing course I was doing by correspondence and perhaps I felt, for some strange reason, secure working for Basil.

I was starting to go 'gangbusters' with the woolclassing, it wasn't hard as I had the textbook and most of the assignments were covered in the textbook. I was getting really good marks and my tutor was paying me compliments, and then the next assignment's marks came with a little advice.

I should get a job in a shearing team and perhaps I could start on that path by going to see a shearing contractor he knew, Synott and Dunbar, they had an office in Outram Street, West Perth. I needed no further encouragement, on Monday morning, I plucked up the courage to front Basil, amazingly he was in one of his rare good moods.

"Urr, Basil," I snook out, "I'm afraid I'll have to leave this weekend as I've got a job in the shearing teams."

This of course was a lie, as I didn't have a job in the shearing teams to go to but I did have an address. It was obvious that Basil wasn't thrilled by this news but took it like a man and said, "You get used to it." I took this to mean there had been a few before me who had quit.

After saying my farewells to Basil, Mrs Blee and their numerous children, (I know Mrs Blee and the kids haven't had a mention but Mrs Blee was virtually invisible and the kids, were encouraged to avoid me.) I was on my way to Phyllis' to spend some time in the city and find this job.

This stay with Phyllis saw me make friends with another of her boarders Robyn. Robyn wasn't a ward of the State and had a few good records I enjoyed listening to, she was also good company and never short of a boyfriend and we became mates.

Of course, I had the serious business of finding this job in the shearing teams, and about Wednesday I got to it. I had to find Outram Street in West Perth and Synott and Dunbar's office, I did, it was hardly an office, it was a room in a dingy little house, at least that's how I saw it. Someone was manning this room and I stated my case and mentioned Mr O'Rielly, my tutor, but that didn't seem to make any difference.

"We could have a job starting soon but the truck has left and you'd need your own transport." I'm told.

I was a little puzzled as I thought everyone who worked in the shearing teams had their own transport. I explained I had transport and the deal was clinched, I'm sure I was never asked about my experience or what you'd think would be asked.

I was then told that the job was at Bullara Station, "Just south of Exmouth." And shown the place on the map on the wall, didn't look that far away. It turns out it was nine hundred miles away, I'd never driven that far or anywhere near that far but I was living an adventure.

I determined to leave late Friday afternoon to start work on Monday morning, in the meantime I needed supplies. I think it was Don who advised me I'd need coconut oil soap "as the water isn't too flash up there," and a few other things.

It was dark by the time I reached New Norcia and as I crossed the Mission boundary I saw the lonely light bobbing across the Belarbrook highway paddock. I pulled over and wandered across the paddock and waited for the tractor to arrive on its next lap. I had long ago made my peace with the Halligans and Dennis was aware of my plans to head off to the shearing teams. The roar of the tractor subsided to an idle and a voice in the darkness called out.

"The bloody things you could run over and nobody would know about, what the bloody hell are you doing here Tom?"

"I'm heading up to Bullara Station, I've got a job with a shearing team there. I was wondering if I can get my mail sent here while I'm away and perhaps Viv could redirect it for me."

"Well you don't do things by halves, do you, Bullara, how far's that then? Yeh, Viv'll sort your mail, I guess we'll see you when you get back." Dennis smiled in the darkness, we shook hands, I headed back to the road and the tractor roared some more.

I drove off into the darkness, passing through towns I'd only heard of and soon looking for a place to pull over for a bit of sleep. Sleep wasn't easy to come by, there was a mixture of roaring trucks and excitement drawing me out of any sort of deep sleep. As the first daylight of my journey came over the horizon it was time for a fuel stop, for both ute and body, I was at the Shell roadhouse just outside Geraldton, I'd gone nowhere.

The journey continued with my eyes scanning every aspect of the landscape, the agricultural land was now waning and the station country looming large. Miles of scrub and the straight open road that seemed to go forever. There were two roadhouses between Ajana (The last settlement heading north.) and Carnarvon, the Billabong and the Overlander and nothing else.

I took another turbulent night's slumber south of Carnarvon and then I entered into the last leg of my journey. Heading towards Carnarvon (Which I thought was a town in Wales.) in the early morning was quite depressing, the short brown scrub and the flat boring land did not inspire me.

Driving out of Carnarvon was, however most impressive, banana plantations, and deep green grass and I saw my first emu. Left at Minilya roadhouse and on to gravel road, I was used to gravel roads but wasn't prepared for a hundred and fifty miles of it. It did keep you alert and if you tended to fade there were always the cattle grids to brighten your day.

It was mid-afternoon as I turned off to Bullara Station, suddenly I was driving up steep red sandhills and sinking over the other side. After three or four of these sandhills, the land flattened and I found myself in an oasis of green and red and white. The green grass, the red dirt and the whitest of white tree trunks on the beautiful little gum trees dotting the landscape. This beauty was scarred by corrugated iron rooves on ramshackled sheds, the shearing shed and the shearer's quarters.

I drew to a halt in front of a smart young man. "I'm looking for Tony Waldron," I announced.

"That's me." He replied.

"You must be Tom Watson, our new rousabout, that's a pretty flash vehicle for a rousabout," continued the smart young man.

"Well, I'm actually, a woolclassing student." I tendered.

"Oh, have you worked in a shearing shed?" Tony queried.

"Oh yeh," I replied.

"And what have you done?" came Tony.

There was an easterly zephyr bringing the whiff of sheep shit to my nostrils, which lifts the ability of all men, "I've worked a shed for three shearers on my own." I put forward.

"That's pretty impressive, we'll see how you go tomorrow." Tony may have been young but he'd been around shearing sheds long enough to pick up on a story. "Park up your ute and I'll find you a hut," said Tony.

We wander around the back of the main block of huts and there are two newish huts, I get the only hut left which is unoccupied and it's one of the newer ones. A hut to myself, pretty good I thought. Well, it was almost to myself I had to share it with the bed, the standard chain-link gate on folding legs with a kapok mattress, not sure when the floor had been swept last.

"There you are a hut to yourself, tea's at six-thirty I'm sure you know the drill," Tony tells me. And there we are, the bed and I.

I open the lid of my suitcase, make my bed and take a shower, shit I needed that. I go for tea and it's the usual roast of mutton, no one much says anything, perhaps there was a, "You're new aren't you?" Did I need to get used to the rhetorical question? I'm not sure but there would be more to come. I return to my hut and decided to write home to Mum and report on my progress in my new pursuit and give her my new address, which was my old address six months earlier.

As I settle down to write, there's this sort of thump at my open door.

"Dooyah want a ticket mate?"

"Nah, I'll be right," I replied.

'I've only just got here and this bloke wants to sell me a bloody raffle ticket.' I thought.

"You've got a ticket have yah?" the now rather gruff voice comes from the dark doorway.

"No, but I don't want a ticket." I impatiently replied.

"Mate, you've got to have a ticket to work here, it won't cost you anything the classer will charge it to your account. Now let's have your name and you'll be sweet."

I became a member of the Australian Workers Union. I thought I may be working amongst intellectual genie tomorrow, as I knew the ticket wasn't going to cost me anything because the classer would charge it to my account.

And the morning came around, breakfast out of the way and I head up to the shed. Tony organises us rousabouts, well me, as the others are used to this system.

"You can manage this side of the table can't you Tom? That's Barry over the other side, he knows what to do. I'll leave you to it." Tony quickly tells me as he takes off to start the engine for the shearing plant. I was used to this time when the engine starts and the shearers try their handpieces and the sounding of the bell, but not on this scale.

There were six shearers in this shed and when the first fleece landed on the table, it had done just that, landed on the table, a twisted, tangled pile of wool and I was supposed to skirt it. I quickly straightened it out a little and was skirting when I felt the pain in my right hand, "What the fuck!" I shouted.

"That's the neck, it goes in the bin over there," Barry tells me with a smile.

These sheep have been marching through spinifex and all the thorns gather under their throat and are discovered by innocent rousabouts having their first day in the station country.

I soon got the hang of things and got through that first day with a couple of new friends, Barry my fellow table hand and Rocky the piece picker. It wasn't easy as the board boys still had to learn how to throw a fleece. I discovered that Rocky was a farmer's son and doing woolclassing too and Barry was from Victoria.

When we knocked off Barry announced that he had to kill a sheep, would anyone like to give him a hand? 'Why not,' I thought, I'd seen Dennis kill a sheep loads of times. As we walk to the killing yard (A slab of concrete with a gantry to hang the sheep on.) Barry says in his finest English, "Dunno how I got landed with this fucking job, I'm not very good at it, but you do get a dollar a sheep."

"I've never done the job so I don't know what help I'll be," I confess.

The unfortunate sheep passed away, an autopsy would probably have said, "Of a severe neck wound." Barry and I set to skinning the sheep, I'd seen it done, we took a back leg each and cut off a slither of skin and in with our knives. We were pros, we hauled the sheep on the gantry and continued to push the skin off with our hands, all seemed to be going well until we looked back on our work. The sheep was beginning to look like a naked mud wrestler after a particularly bad bout. It seems you should hold the skin in one hand and push it off with the other, Barry and I had changed hands. "Fuck it's a mess," I exclaimed.

"Not as bad as the first one I did," returned Barry.

On day two, something was going on, the shearers shore one sheep each and everything came to a standstill.

"What's going on?" I asked no one in particular.

"There was a shower of rain last night and they think the sheep are wet," answered Rocky.

I believe that shearing wet sheep is a health hazard and so a vote was taken, the sheep were declared wet. The shearers returned to their huts, the rousabouts would still get paid regardless so work was found for us.

It seemed as if out of nowhere some butts (A butt is a loosely packed woolpack.) of flyblown wool appeared. The flyblown wool was to be carried onto the roof of the shed and spread out to dry. If shearing wet sheep is a health hazard, spreading flyblown wool on the roof of a shearing shed should be a reason to call the flying doctor.

The spreading of flyblown wool on a shearing shed roof is, to say the least, character-building and team bonding, it's also a bloody dirty rotten job. I now start to hear about the ride up to Bullara on the back of the truck. I'd seen the truck parked outside the classer's hut but thought nothing of it, the shearers and my fellow rousabouts had been transported to Bullara on the back of this truck (It's late June.) it has two rows of wooden seats back to back on the tray of the truck and a frame which can be covered with a tarpaulin in case of rain. I was led to believe that the tarpaulin doesn't keep you dry.

I could understand the rousabouts being conned into this prehistoric mode of transport but surely not the shearers. It's now I remember I'm not paying for my union ticket, yes, they're not the brightest bunch. More comes out, last week the shearers went on strike because there wasn't a fridge on the camp and they're rationed to two bottles of beer a night. They got their fridge but it was to keep the meat in, I don't think they got to put their beer in it.

I think the shearers started work after lunch that second day but not before another vote on the condition of the sheep. I was somewhat confused as to why these men were here, they didn't want to work and the conditions were far from good and to a man, they liked a beer, just as well they didn't like three. Rousabouts were allowed one bottle of beer a night if they were twenty-one, I was in that category but didn't partake. On day three I was sprung, the nice gentleman who sold me my union ticket had my details and worked out I wasn't claiming my beer. I was approached to claim my beer and sell it to the shearers, how they were going to split this bottle of beer I have no idea. I declined the offer to buy my beer and was not that popular, for a day at least and then they got over it.

45 THE GOOD LIFE

I was enjoying my time at Bullara, it was the first time I'd worked and lived with a team of men, although the term team was perhaps stretching things a little. There was a gap between roustabouts and shearers, roustabouts were thought of as inferior beings and treated that way most of the time. This didn't worry me as I was beginning to see that this team of shearers weren't too superior to me.

As I grew in confidence I bounced out of bed each morning dressed and took off to the kitchen for breakfast, "Morning Cookie," I crowed. Our cook was a pleasant lady in her early forties and she scrubbed up well. My confidence was shattered a split second after my words had been uttered.

"Mrs Robson to you my boy, and don't you ever forget it."

That pleasant face had turned to a scowl and I had had my first lesson in respecting the cook.

The weekend flew around and Tony was under pressure from the shearers with the two bottles-a-night rule. Whether he chose to take the shearers into Exmouth, some seventy miles away or they requested he take them I'm not sure, but take them he did.

I don't remember being invited along but some of the other roustabouts went, so I presume I was. I had seen country towns at night and I'd seen the bright city lights, I preferred the latter and stayed in camp. I can only relate to what went on in town as it was told to me, I'm sure reliably.

As you now know our team of shearers were strict unionists and shore to the union rules, few teams in the early seventies shore to the rules and they used what were called 'pulled combs'. This was the standard shearing comb, with the teeth on the outside of the comb heated and stretched out, giving the shearer around half an inch per blow advantage over the standard comb which our shearers used. Unionists felt this was wrong and a crime against fairness, punishable by a damn good beating.

Well, off to town the truckload of shearers and roustabouts went, driven by our trusty classer. When they arrived in town they descended on the only nightlife in Exmouth, the pub. It just so happens, that there was a team of shearers working at the neighbouring station, Yardie Creek, they were already at the pub. Not only did these shearers from Yardie Creek have their own cars, but they also used pulled combs. They probably found it amusing that the shearers from Bullara had ridden seventy miles on the back of a truck, to get to the pub.

Shearers are known to suffer from a disease called ovinus excreta branius, known commonly as 'sheep shit on the brain'. This causes the shearer to start talking about shearing the moment he tastes lager. And so it was that night, two teams of shearers at a bar talking shearing and before long, the subject of pulled combs came up, it was on for young and old. An all-in, all-outside donnybrook. Whether Tony had witnessed one of these events before, I'm not sure, but he rounded up the roustabouts and headed back to camp leaving the shearers to their own devices.

Who won the blue, will probably, still be in dispute but our shearers were told to leave town (I presume by the local police.), and as they had no transport, were bundled into a taxi and ferried the seventy miles back to Bullara. Of course, the shearers had no money of consequence and Tony had to be dragged out of bed to pay the taxi driver.

Well, no one seemed that much worse for wear the next morning and life continued until the next weekend. What was Tony thinking when he decided to take the shearers to Coral Bay for a day? (Perhaps he was once again trying to ease the beer rule.) Coral Bay was a new development on the coast that promised lots and was all of a hundred miles from Bullara. Again I was probably invited but declined, just as well I think.

As I said, Coral Bay promised lots, but in reality, was just a pile of sand with a bar and a beautiful beach. From all accounts, the shearers had a great time, but when it was time to return to camp, they chose to purchase some beer for the trip back. Reality struck, the bar didn't sell packaged beer. They did, however, sell flagons of wine, each shearer equipped himself with two flagons of wine to enjoy on the journey back to camp and perhaps top-up his two-bottle beer ration.

Thankfully the next day was Sunday and the shearers would have time to recuperate, they didn't. The remains of the first flagon had to be had for breakfast and the second drank in the afternoon. These men were hardened drinkers but the McWilliams sherry took them down. I imagine that Tony booked out about a carton of Bex powders on Monday morning.

When we finished at Bullara, the squatter put on a barbecue and it was chops all round and the two bottles a night rule was forgotten.

I now got to see Exmouth before we started at our next shed. Exmouth was nothing like the other country towns I'd seen in Australia. Perhaps this was because it was basically, an American town in Australia. Most of Exmouth was built to house U.S. personnel who worked at the nearby Northwest Cape American base. A lot of the cars were lefthand drive and were plainly American and the place looked so new. I was rather impressed with this new-looking town but there wasn't much there.

Our next shed was Ningaloo Station, almost due west of Bullara and I was informed it was on the coast. I drove into Ningaloo in the late afternoon, accompanied by two shearers, what a drive, the sun was blinding and finding the road after you left a creek bed was touch and go. As we headed down to the shearing shed, the sight was in stark contrast to my arrival at Bullara. The terrain was flat and covered with short scrub which looked black, there were giant sandhills behind the flat black scrub. It looked so desolate and dry.

The huts and the shed looked kinder than those at Bullara and they were more comfortable but the landscape still looked foreboding, as we looked inland from under the sandhills. I knew we'd landed in hell when I took a shower, my carefully purchased coconut oil soap wouldn't get close to a lather, and the water, in my opinion, was saltier than the ocean. Here, I was sharing a hut, I think with either Rocky or Barry, at least the company wasn't bad. We settled in had tea and went to bed, the usual lights out at nine.

Our first morning, breakfast, "Morning Mrs Robson," I knew my place.

"You can call me Mary now." came the now, very pleasant voice of the cook.

Obviously, I'd earn my stripes. I wander up to the shed, happy, I can call Mrs Robson Mary, but not happy in my surrounding, this place looks like the end of the earth. I enter the shed through a side door and like Bullara, the end beyond the press is open. And how open, the next stop is in South Africa. There before me is the finest beach I'd ever seen, and by now I'd seen a few West Australian beaches. The bluest ocean with the gentlest waves lapping the white sand, I'd landed in heaven.

There was the usual scuffle of the sheep's feet on the grating, the start of the engine and the rattle of handpieces and we were off. The first fleece lands on the table and half of it disappears through the mesh of the table. No necks here, but the fleeces are full of sand, it was a full-time job cleaning up the sand. Even in heaven, there are drawbacks.

46 FINDING A NEW FRIEND

Our weeks at Ningaloo were so different to our time at Bullara, we all seemed much friendlier with each other. I was fascinated by the wool press, the press I'd used at New Norcia was just a metal crate with cables. The wool presses at both Bullara and Ningaloo were structures, they were Ferrier wool presses. They had two steel pillars on either side of two wooden boxes into which the wool was loaded. One box was hauled onto the top of the other box by a pulley system where the presser rode down on a rope aided by a bag of sand. Then he proceeded to drive the plunger down via another pulley system with a crank handle, when the pressure was too much for the crank handle he went to the leaver, a six-foot-long solid steel handle that brought the plunger to its final destination. Quite a simple operation once you got the hang of it and a good way to keep fit.

The presser was a log of a man who spoke rarely, coming up to smoko he would have the press filled and ready for the crank handle and leaver part of the operation. This was just waiting for me, innocently fascinated by the machine, so on our second day at Ningaloo, I asked if I could 'take it down for him,' "Go for your life" he mumbled.

And so my smokos were full, grab a sandwich and a pannikin of tea, go for a swim in the ocean fifty yards away, take down the press and barrow a sheep. Barrowing is starting to shear a sheep for a shearer before the bell rings to start the run. It was probably about then that I realised I would never make a shearer. I'd seen Tony shear a sheep quite well and thought if I wanted to be a classer I'd have to be able to turn my hand to any job in the shed and I was mostly in love with the Ferrier wool press.

Barry and I only killed one sheep at Ningaloo, the rest of our protein was drawn from the ocean. From somewhere the shearers produced a net and set it up out from the beach. I honestly didn't think these men were capable of such things, I was wrong. The shearers seemed happy at Ningaloo (Who wouldn't be?) I have a feeling they'd supplemented their beer rations with a supply from Exmouth between sheds. I saw a couple of them laying on the beach on the weekend, beer in hand and one on a string in the ocean cooling, life was grand at Ningaloo.

Tony informed Rocky and me that he wasn't going on to the next shed as he had a big job organised down south. "I'd like you two to work with me there instead of wasting your lives with this mob, what do you reckon?" Both Rocky and I leapt at the offer, even though we were currently in paradise the draw of civilisation was too much to refuse.

We rousabouts, Rocky and I at least, had become friendly with Mary the cook and even helped her wash up in the evening. Mary was a motherly ear to vent our complaints on.

"The water here is so salt I'd be better off washing in the ocean," I complained one night.

"You should try that and see how you fare," replied Mary.

I think she may have tried washing in the ocean as it was bloody worse.

"Shit it's hot at night here." I again complained another evening.

"You should come and sleep in the sandhills with me, it's beautiful up there," came Mary's reply.

I innocently continued drying the dishes, not realising that I'd been given the invitation of my life.

Our time in paradise came to an end all too quickly and a parting of the ways was in order. Barry was put in charge of the truck and the remainder of the team. Fancy that, a rousabout being given authority over the shearers, just shows how much Tony thought of them. Mary, the presser and a shearer who I believe had taken up Mary's offer headed south in the presser's ute. Tony, Rocky and I were last to leave in my ute. It must have been mid-Friday afternoon when we finally left, with me at the wheel.

It was starting to get dark as we drove past Carnarvon and I was starting to get nervous about the kangaroo population, there seemed to be a lot of them. Rocky was starting to get a bit toey, I wasn't driving fast enough.

"For fucks sake Tom, let me drive, we'll never get home at this rate." Rocky finally burst out.

It was fair enough really, I wasn't used to this sort of driving and Rocky had been brought up with it, probably been driving since he was twelve. I pulled over and we changed places, off we went at a now steady pace, must confess home seemed closer now. Just as we were getting comfortable a mob of roos crossed the road.

"Shit that was close," I remember saying.

And then bang, "What the fuck was that?" I queried.

"Must have been a roo," said Rocky, "I didn't see it."

Rocky pulled over and steam was coming from under the bonnet, all else look fine. On closer inspection, we could see the bumper was caved in and the radiator was buggered, no way could we go any further. We discovered the roo we hit was little more than a joey, yet it had done enough damage to strand us.

Tony now drew himself up to his full height and stated, "I can't stay here, I've got to get back to Perth."

In what seemed like no time a truck pulled over heading south and Tony was in it with a, "See you Sunday night at the Ozone Hotel, you know where that is?"

That left Rocky and me with the ute in the middle of nowhere, and I at least had no idea what to do. It was just coming daylight when a truck travelling north pulled up.

"You blokes want a tow into Carnarvon?" came a voice from the truck.

"Yeah, that sounds fine," I replied.

"How much?"

"Breakfast," came the swift reply.

As we are hitching up the ute, we discover there are two in the truck, so that would be two breakfasts.

"We'll tow you to our yard in Carnarvon and pick the ute up on the way back and drop it off in Kewdale for forty bucks." Two breakfasts and forty bucks down I now had to trust these blokes.

Breakfast done, Rocky and I now had to get to Perth, well me to Perth, Rocky to Darkan a bit further. We hauled our ports out of Carnarvon to the junction where the road south is. We spent most of Saturday at that junction trying to hitch a ride with no success. It was early evening when a truck finally pulled up and offered us a lift. This bloke took us as far as Dongara where he was turning off to go elsewhere. It was well and truly dark by this time and truly cold. There we were frozen in the dark and liftless, we lit a fire, I don't know how as neither of us smoked.

We eventually got a lift and this bloke was going all the way to Perth. As daylight came I was starting to see familiar territory, Moora, Walebing, Waddington and as we drew close to Belarbrook, I just had to call the driver to a halt, "Can I get out here mate," I asked.

"Yeah no worries," was the reply.

I thanked the driver and left Rocky with a, "See ya Monday." I dragged myself up the driveway to the house and round to the back door. I was greeted by Dennis in his pyjamas.

"Tom, what the hell are you up to? Where's the ute? You want some breakfast?"

I then poured out my sorry tale, Dennis the ever-optimist, came out with the reassuring, "You'll be right mate, we're going to sort the cattle out today, do you want to hang around."

The idea of working with Dennis again was too much for me to resist.

"Too right," was my instant reply.

I worked all day with Dennis and showered, had tea and found myself on the road outside Belarbrook again hitching. I seemed to wait forever, I finally got a lift. Of course, I had to tell my tale of woe to the driver, this time I'm in the comfort of a car. Whether this bloke felt sorry for me or was simply generous, he dropped me at Phyllis' place. It must have been around ten when I tapped on the door of 9 Adrian Street, regardless there was the hug and the, "Come in love your bed's ready." And was I ready for bed?

47 IT'S COLD IN WILLIAMS IN AUGUST

It would have been just after six when I left Phyl's place, with my port and the prospect of hitching a ride to Williams. I had no chance of making it for the seven-thirty start but I knew Tony would understand.

There was no time to stand and hitch, I had to progress, so I was walking with my port and hitching with my thumb. I must have got a ride to Albany Highway and then on to Kelmscott, where I was again picked up. This lift was a winner, as the bloke who picked me up, knew where I was going, but I didn't. All I knew was the shed was a big one just out of Williams, I would have known where to go, had I met up with the rest of the team at the Ozone Hotel at six on Sunday night. This bloke who picked me up was a wool buyer and took me straight to the shed, I think my tale of woe helped.

I walked up to the shed with my port and wearing my street clothes and entered all smiles, "Where the fuck have you been?" were the first words to leave Tony's mouth when he saw me.

"I've had to hitch all the way down here," I pleaded.

"So did Rocky and he managed to get here on time, so where the fuck were you?" Tony wasn't happy and I didn't get to plead further as Tony quickly told me to, "Get a hut, get changed and get your arse back here quick smart."

That was the first time Tony had really bombed me and it put my tail between my legs as I thought, I'd done pretty well to be there and Tony would understand. Obviously, he didn't. Was this a sign that I wasn't going to like this shed?

Come lunchtime, I understood why Tony had left us in such a hurry after we hit the roo, his wife was the cook here, she was gorgeous, and amazingly, could cook too. My first night in Williams was awful, it was bitterly cold and I didn't have enough blankets, I awoke, opened the hut door and was welcomed to a ground covered in frost. I thought I'd left that in England. A few days earlier I'd complained about the heat and been swimming in the Indian Ocean, I didn't like this place.

I soon acquitted my late arrival with my work rate and by week's end was back in the good books with Tony. Rocky had been home while I'd been working at New Norcia and was now equipped with his car, he drove me back to Perth for the weekend. My ute had been transported to Kewdale, Phyl's husband Don, had picked it up and repaired it, (He and his brother had a smash repair business.) I was free again.

This shed at Williams seemed to go on forever, it was an eight-stand shed so we must have been putting a lot of sheep through, but they just kept coming. At one point we split into two teams and worked at other farms the cocky owned. I enjoyed that part, as I was with the team which included Tony and his wife. I now found out that Tony's wife was not only a cook but also a hairdresser too, I got my hair done.

I stayed down at the shed that weekend and went to a dance in Darkan as suggested by Rocky. This would be the last country dance I'd attend, these things weren't meant for the likes of me, a mere rousabout. Rocky was surrounded by sheilas, but, of course, he would be, he was a cocky's son. Country girls have all been warned about shearers, rousabouts and the like, 'all wasters'.

Tony had news for me, the shed was coming to an end and I and a couple of other rousabouts wouldn't be needed beyond cut-out. I wasn't unhappy about this, although I'd enjoyed working with Tony, this contractor he'd been working for was someone I couldn't warm to. I think the feeling was mutual. Before we parted, Tony advised me to, "Get the paper first thing Saturday morning and if you see a job ring up straight away, I'm talking six o'clock," he said.

"There's not much work around and lots of people looking for it," he continued.

We parted company with a smile and a handshake.

I took Tony's advice and had the paper by six, found a job and rang the bloke, he didn't sound too happy after being dragged from his bed.

"Can you come round to my place this morning and we can have a chat?" this rather gruff voice asks.

"Now?" I ask.

"Hell no, about nine will do." The gruff voice answers.

"We're at 796 Canning Highway, can you manage that?"

"No worries," I confidently reply. I had no right to be confident as there had only been one job in the paper for a rousabout. At a quarter to nine, I headed off to 796 Canning Highway, a largish brick house on a corner block. I knocked on the door and was welcomed in by a nice middle-aged lady who seemed to know what I was there for. The house was pretty bland inside and I was ushered into a room where a rather oriental-looking man was sitting behind a desk. 'This couldn't be the gruff old bastard I was talking to on phone,' I thought.

He opened his mouth and I knew it was, "Take a seat, mate." I could see this bloke wasn't a great conversationalist, he asked where I'd worked, and whether I had transport.

"The job's at Annean Station just south of Meekatharra, can you manage that?" he tells me and asks me in the same sentence, "the man to see is Snowy Herbert, can you get up there for Sunday night?"

"No worries," I reply.

'This bloke only ever asks questions,' I thought as I left with a new job in my port.

A night out at Canterbury Court and an early start for Annean Station tomorrow. The trip wasn't without incident, I broke my first windscreen just south of New Norcia, got what was described as a temporary windscreen at the New Norcia roadhouse (It was a sheet of plastic.) and then dropped in to see Dennis and Vivienne, had a cup of coffee and drove on.

This drive north was different to my first, it was the inland route and the country was different, through the northern Wheatbelt and over a cattle grid and suddenly I was in station country, red dirt and scrub for miles.

I arrived at Annean in time for tea and met Snowy Herbert. Snowy was a man in his fifties or more, solid, not tall, white-haired as expected and he walked with a pronounced limp, I was to discover he had a permanently whitened face due to his white stubble. Snowy found me a hut, the last it seemed and asked a few questions and ignored my answers with a sort of, "I've heard it all son" look on his face. I liked this bloke.

I seemed to share my hut with someone who didn't exist, at lights-out, my hut mate materialised, grunted something and climbed into his bed, not an outgoing person it seemed. I was later to discover this shy retiring bloke was Snowy's son-in-law and spent his time with Snowy and Mrs Herbert(Mum, Snowy always called her.) our cook. At tea that night, I'd found the atmosphere pleasant, more homely than the other teams I'd worked in. I was now able to be aware, that tomorrow is another day and most of these blokes are here to make a quid and it would be fatal to stand in their way. Perhaps the atmosphere could change.

48 MY FRIEND THE FERRIER

I'd made a good judgement on my first night, this team were a friendly bunch and I seemed to slot in straight away. I took my now standard position as table hand and all went smoothly. At smoko, I met the presser and asked if I could, 'take the press down' as I'd done at Ningaloo.

"No worries mate, you like pressing do yah?" he replied.

"Yeah, it's alright," I answered quite casually.

This bloke wasn't like the other pressers I'd met, those had been the big, strong, silent types, a sort of standard stereotype in the day. Les, I discover his name to be, was perhaps not as tall as me but carried a load more muscle and was quite loquacious, we hit it off straight away. Perhaps it was because he had a ready-made helper at smokos.

This was the first shed where I had a fellow Pom working with me. He must have caught my accent and latched on to me like a leach.

"I saw you talking to the presser," he said, "you want to watch him." I got the idea that he didn't think much of Les and had something against him. I later found out that he had shared a hut or had been in the hut next to Les when the shed started, and Les picked him up in a flash. He regaled stories of bestiality in New Zealand and how the pigs had squealed and then finished with.

"I think you'd be alright, I haven't seen you in the showers have I?"

David, Dave we called him, took fright and locked himself in his camper on the back of his ute and was never seen in the showers before Les had left.

On my second or third night, I was laid back on my bed with no one to talk to, as my roommate was never there. I heard the conversation in the next hut, not unusual as the huts were divided by corrugated iron which only went up to the eves, leaving a gap to the gable.

It was between two shearers, one of them was a learner and getting all the lowdown from the older guy. They got to the topic of pulled combs, a no-no at my first two sheds.

"Well all the shearers except me, went into Exmouth this night and they met up with a team of union shearers," the story started, "and well" laughed the storyteller, "a fight broke out and these other blokes had gone into town on the truck and their classer took off and left them behind and they had to get a taxi back to the station."

"I was in the other team," I called out and walked around to the next-door hut.

"Dennis Cherry," said the storyteller as I entered the hut.

"Tom Watson," I replied, with a firm handshake.

"Small world," said Dennis.

This was followed by more stories and laughs and perhaps when I heard about Les and Dave.

I had to take my ute to Meekathara the first weekend to get my windscreen fixed, Snowy had told me where to go, so I was fine there. The problem was the return journey, as the ute wouldn't be ready until the following weekend. My, newfound friend Dave, was going into town so he would give me a lift back.

The main road into Meekathara was a single strip bitumen road, the sort of road I'd first driven on. Dave had taken others into town so I was relegated to the camper on the back of the ute for the trip back to Annean. First, I could say Dave was none too houseproud, secondly, he didn't seem too savvy on how to drive these roads. For the endless miles, we travelled back to the Annean turn-off, Dave drove with two wheels on the bitumen and two wheels on the gravel shoulder at well below the speed limit.

For the passengers in the front, this was probably a little frustrating, for the two of us in the camper it was downright scary. We were glad to get onto the gravel road to the station, where we were carefully manoeuvered over each corrugation. I'm not sure how long Dave remained in Australia, but he still had a lot of adapting to do.

I remained with Snowy's team until my woolclassing exams came up, and then I got leave for my exams with the promise of work straight after. I'd got on well with Snowy, he had favourites and I'd made my way to be one of them. Sometimes Snow would impart some of his knowledge to you in those quiet moments, "All shearers lie," he'd say, "never seen one who could shear as many sheep as he said he could." And the one that got home to me was the, "If you're twenty-one and still a rousabout, you're a no-hoper." I was twenty-one and still a rousabout, I had to do something about that.

Les had given me as many tips on pressing as he could, he'd shown me how to pin a cap on the giant twin box presses, how he fastened the flaps with one fastener and then four to get a neater bale (The standard was two and three.). Most importantly, to place the classer's stencil neatly on the lefthand side of the bale, "They get the shuts if it's not just so." He was a Kiwi.

I returned to Phyllis' place as was now the norm when I was in Perth. On this stay, Phyl had a new boarder, Karen. Karen was obviously part aboriginal, I had been warned that white men should not cavort with aboriginal girls, if you did you got the moniker 'Gin Jockey', I didn't want that.

Karen was pretty, sweet and bubbly, it was too much for both of us, I didn't care if people called me a Gin Jockey, I was in something beginning with 'L'. I waltzed through my woolclassing exams and had now to head to Thunderlara Station for my next job. Departing this time meant farewelling Karen, I left, saying I'd be back for Christmas and I'd write.

I was heading off to join 'Youngie's' team, the boss, the number one team, I had no fear, I'd climbed to piece picker with Snowy's team, top rousabout rating. I was cocky and confident even though I'd been warned I'd be up against the best, Pud and Henry. Pud was forty-something and still a rousabout so Snowy had him covered. Henry was seventeen, full of life and had taken his name from a jam tin, literally, Henry Jones IXL a famous jam company at the time. His real name was Norman Jones but he never liked it.

I walked up to the shed the first day, not knowing what to expect, I guessed I'd be at least a table hand. I was approached by Youngie, Bill Young the boss.

"Mate, can you pick a few bellies and pen-up?" said Youngie in his usual questioning manner, which meant that that is what you're going to be doing.

'Pen-up and pick bellies,' I thought, 'who the fuck do you think I am?'

"Yeah, no worries," I answered.

Penning up and picking bellies was the lowest job a rousabout could do and, yes, I thought it was below me but I had to prove myself in the number one team. Needless to say, I had two clear lines of bellies (The belly wool of the sheep.) and the word sheepo was barely uttered.

The presser at this shed was in fact, a shearer, a giant of a man called Snowy Owens. A raconteur of the highest order, I could have listened to him for hours, he was probably a pretty good shearer, the one thing he wasn't much good at was wool pressing. He got snowed under (No pun intended.) and I was so busy trying to impress with my belly-picking I didn't show off my skill on the press.

A proper presser was called in, it was Les. Les had been driven up (He didn't have a car.) and I was quite surprised to see him.

"G'ay mate." I welcomed him with, there wasn't the usual smile on Les' face, but a scowl.

"What the fuck am I doing here, you useless bastard, you could have done this job standing on your head, what's wrong with yah." Les let out, never breaking into his usual smile.

I sort of blurted out some weak excuse about being new to Youngie's team and added that I didn't think I'd be able to manage. I think Les forgave me as we continued to get on and he had now secured the job of presser in the number one team, I had secured my position as belly picker and penner upper in the number one team.

49 THE CHRISTMAS BREAK

Thunderlara was the last shed of the year, it would now be the Christmas break.

"I'll give you a call in January, alright mate?" Youngie said as I picked up my cheque.

"Yeah, that'll be fine," I answered and hopped in my ute and headed back to Perth.

The Christmas break meant two or three weeks with no income, not that that worried me as I was pretty well cashed up. When I started in the shearing teams, I didn't realise that I'd become an itinerate worker, your job security lasted as long as the sheep at the shed, no longer. I was pretty right, as I had Youngie's word he'd give me a call in January.

Returning to Phyl's place was great, Karen was waiting for me and my friend Robyn was on holiday. I was surrounded by women, a great feeling after having only the company of men for weeks on end. Oh, there had been 'Glad Bags', our wonderful cook but she didn't count. Karen was working during the day, but Robyn was free.

"Can you take me down the beach, Tom?" asks Robyn on my first morning back, "I need to get a tan and there's no one to take me," Robyn pleas.

"No worries," I reply, rather keen to hit the beach myself.

Robyn and I started at Port Beach and worked our way up to Scarborough. It was my job to drive and apply coconut oil to Robyn's body, a lesser man would have given his right arm for this job. It meant nothing to me, I was doing a friend a favour. Coconut oil isn't the best suntan lotion around and Robyn returned to Phyllis' place looking like a lobster. I was almost unaffected by the exposure to the sun, the new skin I got, after losing my first skin in my first few weeks in Australia, seemed almost impervious to ultra-violet rays.

Karen was her usual smiley self when she returned from work, she was sympathetic to Robyn's plight and said, "I don't go out in the sun too much or I just turn black." I got the feeling something wasn't quite right, Karen lacked her usual warmth. I wasn't very good at reading women's feelings.

The next day I caught up with Les in the city. He was staying at the Grand Hotel which was far from grand. It was cheap, I think they were called residential hotels, and a lot of Kiwis stayed at places like that. The time with Les gave me an insight into how Kiwi shearers lived in Perth, they had their haunts, like the Railway Hotel on Barrack Street. You could always get your cheque cashed at the Railway.

The GPO, the General Post Office, and most Kiwis got their mail delivered there and could call home on the bank of telephones they had there. They could call, it seemed to me, anywhere in the world as there was a veritable library of phone books there. I realised how lucky I was to have a base like Phyllis', even though I still had my mail sent to New Norcia. I bade Les farewell, knowing we'd catch up in the new year, as he would be the presser in Youngie's number one team and I'd continue as a rousabout.

It was straight after Christmas when I got the phone call from Youngie. This was unusual as I knew his teams wouldn't be starting work for a couple of weeks.

"Mate, do you think you could do a bit of gardening for me?" Yes, the ever-present question from Youngie.

'Could I do a bit of gardening for you?' I thought, in a state of excitement.

"Where at?" I asked.

'You're not the only one who can ask questions,' I thought, re-straining my delight.

"My place, can you make it tomorrow?" asks Youngie.

"Yeah, I can do that," I replied.

The deal was done, and I was thrilled, I loved gardening and hadn't had a chance to get into anyone's garden in my time in Australia.

I was at 796 Canning Highway bright and early the next morning, Youngie showed me the tools and the garden.

"I've got a fridge full of cool drink, help yourself when you get thirsty," said Youngie as he departed for his place on the coast.

It was as hot as Hades and there was a fair amount of work to do. The cool drink got a fair hammering the first day, the second day the fridge got emptied and I suffered for it, but the work had been done. I could barely move without the need to urinate, my stomach was bloated and I may have gotten a touch of sun. I wasn't as happy as when I took on this job, I didn't remember any offer of payment, although I'd cut out a reasonable slice in the cool drink, and no word from Youngie either.

By the end of the first week in January, I'd still not heard from Youngie and was needing to get back to work. I got the paper and went to the 'situations vacant' section. I found only one job in a shearing team. 'Woolpresser wanted for four stand team.' It was advertised by an employment agency in Perth, 'I reckon I should give that a try,' I thought and headed off to Rural Enterprises in Perth.

I was armed with my liar's hat and my fingers crossed because I knew that the starting weight for a woolpresser was around twelve stone, I could merely muster ten stone in a wet army coat with the pockets full of rocks. Obviously, the bloke at Rural Enterprises didn't know or care and fell for my bullshit, I got the job.

It was like going home, the job was at Summer Hill, just up the road from Belarbrook at New Norcia. I knew the cocky from my time up there and didn't like him, but I wasn't working for him, I was working for the shearing contractor, Tom Waters.

I had to go out and buy a bale hook, any presser worth his salt owned a bale hook. I got myself up to the shed on Sunday night for a Monday morning start. Tom Waters looked at me strangely, he knew the starting weight of a presser and could judge I was a little short of weight. Luckily, I carried a fair amount of bullshit in my pockets and could talk the talk, I just had to do the walking. I got by with ease, I thought.

We were a few days into the shed before I sighted the cocky, or more correctly he sighted me.

"You're not a woolpresser." He exclaimed when he recognised me, from my days at Belarbrook working for Dennis.

'Fuck off you arrogant bastard,' I thought but said nothing, I think I just pointed to the stack of bales I'd pressed and left it at that. As I said I didn't like this bloke, obviously the feeling was mutual and he had wanted to put me down in front of my new boss. I never saw him again, don't think he liked being proved wrong.

When the shed came to an end, I got my cheque from the contractor and was asked.

"You be right for the next shed?"

I didn't even have to think about my answer.

"No mate, I've got a six-stand shed starting with Bill Young next week."

That was a barefaced lie, as I hadn't heard from Youngie and I certainly wasn't going to be working for him as a presser. I was looking to my future as a woolclasser when I gave that answer, knowing that a presser with a four-stand shed was on a wage not that much better than a rousabout. I knew I'd get a call from Youngie and much preferred working for him than Tom Waters with his 'cocky run'.

Back in Perth, the call from Youngie came.

"You can press can't yah, mate?"

"Yeah," I answered.

"I've got this shed at Wongan Hills, starts Monday, think you can do it?" continues Youngie.

"I'll give it a go," I replied, not believing this conversation was taking place.

"Can you drop round and I'll fix you up for that gardening you did, thanks for that mate?" Youngie still managed to make a question out of a statement.

50 THE NEW PRESSER

Shearing sheds in January, tend to be hot, this one Youngie had sent me to, didn't buck the trend. From memory, it was a five-stand shed and I was again working with Snowy Herbert. I got through the shed, I think I was being tested, as when I got back to Perth after cut-out I got a call from Youngie

"I've got this shed at Carbla Station, you know where that is?"

"I'll find it," I replied.

"You live in Palmyra, don't you mate?" Youngie continues.

"Yeah," I reply.

"Do yah think you can pick Glad up? She lives down there, Zenobia Street, yah know that?"

"Yeah, no worries mate."

Youngie finetunes Glad's address and the arrangement is made.

Gladys Shaw is the cook for Youngie's number one team, a mature-aged lady with grown-up kids, a veteran of the shearing teams and a bloody good cook. I now realise I'm the presser with Youngie's number one team and transporter of the cook. I pick up Glad and find her to be good company, I have worked one shed with her before so we knew each other. By the time we reached Carbla, I knew more about Glad than Glad did. By the time I reached my hut, I'd forgotten most of what I'd learnt about Glad.

Carbla Station was the only place I worked in the north where I never saw the 'donkey' lit. The donkey, by the way, is the hot water system. One, or sometimes two, forty-four-gallon drums plumbed into the water supply and heated by an open fire, lit each lunchtime by the rousabout who's doing the fatigues or chopping the wood. The reason the donkey wasn't lit was that we didn't need hot water, it was quite hot enough without it. Luckily they had a hydraulic wool press which took the pressure off me.

One weekend we headed down to the beach, some took fishing gear, others bathers. It was a waste of time taking anything but a shovel and bags. We had landed on 'Shell Beach', I believe they call this stretch of coast Useless Loop and for good reason. There were no fish, the water was foul and stagnant looking, and there are stromatolites were sticking out of the water.

The beach wasn't sand but shells, starting with tiny ones at the water's edge to thumbnail size shells where the sandhills should have been. I'm sure if we'd bagged these shells we could have sold them in Perth. I'd never seen anything like this before. It was then that the stories came out, about how the homestead here was built with blocks of shells cut from the shell hills back from the beach. One amazing thing about shearing teams is that someone always knows something about something, usually that something is exposed fairly late in the piece. If those in the know had explained, that there were no fish at shell beach and the water wasn't suitable for bathing, I for one would never have seen that phenomenon.

I was still scratching my head as to how I had managed to get this job, less than two months earlier I'd been picking bellies and penning up. Now I was in line to earn some serious money, at times having the opportunity to ring the shed, that is, to be the highest-paid member of the team. I knew my friend Les had this job in his back pocket when I'd last seen him, where was he?

One evening I was talking to my newfound friend Henry, he of the jam tin fame. In reality, Henry was talking to me, he could be rather loquacious at times.

"Fucking Youngie," he started, "Rang me up just after Christmas and wanted me to clean up his fucking garden, I told him to fuck off."

Henry continued, obviously feeling a little superior, having had the nerve to tell Youngie to 'fuck off.'

"He rang me too," I put in, "and I did it, got two days' pay too," I laughed.

"Well, there was no way I was going to clean up his fucking garden." Ended Henry.

I had an awful thought, that perhaps I'd got this job because I'd cleaned up Youngie's garden. I quickly threw that thought aside and I knew I'd got it through Les, he must have been the one who told Youngie I could press.

After Carbla we all returned to Perth for a cool down. I'm sure I was walking with a pronounced swagger, now I'd become the presser in Youngie's number one team. I really needed someone to tell this news to and Karen wasn't very interested, let's face it she didn't really know what I did. She did know, that I took off for weeks on end and perhaps wrote her the odd letter. Let's face it girlfriends are for pashing, groping and seriously messing about with, not serious talk. Yes, I could listen to her prate and it was like beautiful music but I couldn't remember the lyrics.

My friend Robyn, would understand, her dad was a shearer and she had some idea of what a woolpresser was. By now, Robyn had moved out of Phyllis' place and was living in a share house in Subiaco. I rang her at work, she was delighted for me.

"I've got tickets to see Russell Morris and the Bee Gees tomorrow night, do you want to come," Robyn tells me.

"Sounds good to me, who's Russell Morris?" I answer and question in the same breath, "it's my birthday too," I continue.

I had Robyn's address as she at least wrote to me, Karen didn't, so it was just a matter of when I should pick Robyn up.

In 1971 the Bee Gees were a band on the wane, their best was behind them and 'First of Me' was now a distant memory. Hence they were touring Australia and performing at the Beatty Park Aquatic Centre, a swimming pool built for the 1962 Commonwealth games. I must now confess, that I didn't know that I was going to a swimming pool to see the Bee Gees, had I, I may not have gone. Not only were my experiences at swimming pools less than inspiring, but the acoustics were always terrible and that echo still terrifies me.

Robyn's tickets for Russell Morris, for that's who she was going to see, must have been bought for a boyfriend she'd dumped and I was the lucky recipient. As we walked up to the entrance of Beatty Park.

"It's a fucking swimming pool, Robyn," I exclaimed.

"No, it's not," Robyn assured me.

Robyn thoroughly enjoyed, what I thought was a pretty ordinary show from Russell Morris. And then the Bee Gees came on, Massachusetts, To Love Somebody, New York Mining Disaster, I Started a Joke' I was blown away. These guys really rocked, what a birthday present I was getting. When I thought they were all done there was the encore, bang, bang, bang, feet stomping and this poor ten-pound Pom was hearing for the first time, 'Spicks and Specks'. My night had been made, I dropped Robyn off and returned home to Phyl's place to find Karen had gone to bed and didn't want to be woken. I'd wake her in the morning with a cup of coffee, she loved my early morning coffees, and I could tell her about the concert then.

To my amazement, Karen wasn't the least bit interested in my night out or the Bee Gees concert, she enjoyed the coffee, I'd be off to the next shed tomorrow, and I wondered if she'd miss me.

51 YATHROO

I was now living the life of Riley, the work was hard and the money was good. After most sheds, there was a break of a couple of days in Perth. I still classed Karen as my girlfriend but it seriously wasn't serious. On one occasion I returned to Perth and asked Phyllis where Karen was, "Oh she's left, she's gone to work for some people at Green Head," Phyllis told me.

I was somewhat heartbroken but not defeated, I had a couple of days up my sleeve, and I could check this Green Head out.

"Where's Green Head?" I asked Phyllis.

"It's up the coast somewhere near Geraldton, I think," replies Phyllis, with a lack of enthusiasm. 'Thanks for your depth of knowledge,' I thought and announced I was off to see her.

I set out for Geraldton, I could work something out from there. As I drove I spotted a couple of hitch-hikers, I could hardly drive past them after my hitch-hiking experience months earlier. Well, these guys were pretty harmless and they lived in Geraldton. I told them I was looking for my girlfriend and she was working for people at Green Head.

"The only problem is I don't know where Green Head is," I explained.

"I know where it is," pipes up one of them, "You can stay at our place tonight and I'll take you out there tomorrow," he continues.

These guys live in a less-than-salubrious place and I'm given a mattress on the floor and my wallet slept with me.

True to his word my newfound friend is up bright and early and directs me to Green Head, a fishing settlement or perhaps one could call it a shanty town, perhaps both words were stretching things a little. It wasn't a town and the dwellings were no more than shacks. Somehow or other we found Karen, she was walking along the beach looking gorgeous.

"Wow, you've found something here," my comrade exclaimed as we approach Karen.

Karen was her usual bubbly self and asked me to come and meet her employers. This is about where our relationship was to end, her new employers didn't like me and made it obvious. Mr Fisherman quietly took me outside and told me to leave and stay away from Karen, I took his advice, rather reluctantly and drove my comrade back to Geraldton and then I returned to Perth.

I think I beat myself up a bit, not so much about losing Karen but why these people had taken such an instant dislike to me. The beating I gave myself didn't injure me much, as I'd got back to Perth to attend my favourite hangout Canterbury Court Ballroom.

The sheds rolled by and there was a mix of hydraulic and manual presses, the sheds with hydraulic presses were easy. The sheds with the manual presses found my weight and size wanting but I got through. The one shed I was dreading was Yathroo, I'd been there earlier in the year for crutching, (When the shearers trim the wool around the crutch and pizzle of the sheep, to help prevent blowfly strike.) as presser it was my job to pen-up and at the end of the day press a couple of bales of wool shorn from the sheep. For these tasks I got the basic pressers rate, around eighty dollars, I hadn't worked for that little since my first shed as a presser.

It was fun, and I got to work with my friend Henry but already I didn't like this shed. This property only had wethers, which they kept for wool production and after their five years of useful wool production came to an end they were shipped to Singapore for meat.

At crutching time I'd seen the size of these wethers and was well aware of how much wool they would produce. Everything at Yathroo had been done the same way for years and they hadn't changed the press, it was a manual Ferrier press, in its day the finest. The Ferrier was the press that drew me to want to press wool all those months ago, it had a sort of romantic feel to it. The Ferrier was designed for the archetype presser of the day, the early nineteen hundreds, a man of around six foot and weighing around twelve stone plus. I was five-nine and ten stone, but I'd been getting by using a Ferrier.

My first day at Yathroo as the presser was much like the first day at any other shed; put the first woolpack in the press, check the press, set up my branding station, open the wool book and then wander down the board. The wander down the board would sometimes entail me grabbing a fleece and throwing it spectacularly onto the wool table, just to show the board boys, that I too had been there. Today there was no such show, I just chatted quietly to the shearers, knowing I was now on equal footing with them, I was going to ring this shed.

"You ready for this?" one asks.

"Fucking hope so," I reply and realise it's time to get to the press, one bin was already full of wool.

By the second run, I was snowed under with wool, I needed to lift my pace. The clock came into play, I'd used it before when I was under pressure. Unlike the shearers, I had nobody to time myself against, the clock was my only competitor and he was fierce. The first day ended late for me as I had to catch up to the wool. Glad had kept tea warm for me, bless her, she was a rock and friend. We had gotten closer as I took her to most stations and I enjoyed her company, she'd light smokes for me as I drove, the only problem was she slobbered all over them.

Breakfast, day two and I have my usual weeties and pannikin of coffee.

"That all you're having?" questions Glad, "You're doing a real man's job now, you should be having chops and eggs," Glad advises.

"Never done much breakfast," I casually reply and head off to the shed. I'm into it from the moment I enter the shed, there's still wool from yesterday. And so on it went, there was no relief.

I stayed up at camp on the weekends, it would have been easy to duck down to Perth as Yathroo was only about a hundred miles or less from Perth. I stayed, as there was wool to clean up and I was just too knackered to go dancing. I was tempted to go to Perth on the second weekend as one of the shearers also stayed on camp, a Kiwi who I found boring and I disliked his company. Sadly, I had the leftovers to press up and it meant I pretty much had to stay behind and be bored by this rather overbearing Kiwi. Being knackered didn't relieve the constant drivel from this man, feigning sleep seemed to work best and let's face it I needed rest.

I think we spent three weeks at Yathroo, I'd got a little quicker, I thought. At most sheds, the presser is thought of as a cut-out looms. On the last day or so the lambs or light shearing ewes come out and the presser can get cleaned up and out of the place not much behind the shearers. At Yathroo, there were no lambs or light-shearing ewes, just bloody woolly wethers. The shearers finished in the early afternoon and they were glad to get away, it hadn't been an easy shed for them.

The presser had a load of wool to clean up and was dying to leave this place too. Enter my little mate, Davy Rutherford, he volunteered to help me clean up, not sure if he knew what he was in for. We cut out at quarter to one the next morning, I'd held Davy to ransom as he didn't have a car, I was his lift home. I drove as far as Gingin and just pulled quietly over to the side of the road and said, "You'll have to drive Dave I just can't go any further." A still cheerful Davy drove on. Yes, I rang the shed, my tax bill rang the rousabouts wages, I'd achieved the unachievable, I'd pressed at Yathroo and was still alive to tell the tale.

52 YOUNGIE AND THE SILENT TREATMENT

After Yathroo, my body was weary and my head in another place, perhaps both were ready for a holiday, not just a couple of days break. Our next shed was Brickhouse, everyone on the team seemed to be looking forward to this shed. It was only twelve miles out of Carnarvon and it seemed my fellow teammates thought Carnarvon was a party town, I certainly didn't. For some reason, I preferred to be well out of country towns and well away from the city when I was working. Strange, as I loved the city, country towns did little for me. I'm sure the comradery of the team was much better when we were stuck in the middle of nowhere.

When I arrived at Brickhouse with Glad in tow, I got my first bomb from Youngie, "I don't want any fucking overweight bales here, you got that?"

"No worries Bill," I answered, remembering what brought that on, I'd pressed a real thumper at a station owned by the same people who owned Brickhouse earlier in the year.

"I don't want no worries, I want no fucking overweight bales, alright?" ended Youngie's blast.

'Aw fuck off you silly old bastard,' was what I was thinking but certainly not saying.

As I settled into my hut at Brickhouse I noticed a familiar ute had pulled up outside the huts. It was my old friend, (Well I'd met him twelve months earlier.) Dennis Cherry, our ways had parted when I joined Youngie's team. Dennis was his same affable self, relaxed and easy going. It was our first day that I realised Dennis had changed, he was shearing a lot more sheep. Dennis had been introduced to the team to shear against our resident gun, Steve MacKenna. A common tactic amongst shearing contractors, to get more sheep shorn, as the two top shearers would race each other, regardless of who or what they were, shearers just did that. Youngie was a master at bringing the right people together, to get the best results.

Dennis, Steve and I were the team guns, I'd rung the shed at Yathroo which put me up there. We were all twenty-two and had one thing in common, we liked work, I guess we had a touch of 'sheep shit on the brain' and got on quite well. Steve tells Dennis and me that he has a friend who skippers a prawn trawler out of Carnarvon and he'd been invited to join him for a trip out to Dorres Island one weekend, would we like to come along? Dennis jumped at this offer, he had a boat and loved fishing and the ocean. I went along with this idea because if I didn't, I'd be left in camp with only Glad for company. I liked Glad, but not that much. I disliked fishing, I rather liked the ocean, provided I can see land and this would be an adventure, I certainly wasn't as enthusiastic as Steve and Dennis.

Saturday came around and the three sailors were ready for the sea, two noticeably more ready than the third. I put my hand up to drive into town, the least I could do, as I wasn't going to catch any fish or show any of my nautical ability. I think the boat fare was a carton of beer. What a beautiful balmy day we had chosen, once onboard, we were given fishing lines. I took to this with much distaste, I slipped the fishing line over the edge of the boat and planted my arse on the deck, that was me for the afternoon. Dennis and Steve were fishing like mad but not catching anything. The Skipper was drinking the fare along with his crew, I think they may have been fishing too. For some unknown reason, a fish accidentally took the bait on my line and got attached to the hook. I now had to haul this slimy creature to the surface, fortunately, there were volunteers to remove it from the line. I'd caught a parrotfish I was told, it wasn't very big but it was the only fish caught that afternoon.

As the afternoon wore on we sighted Dorres Island, a sandhill in the middle of the ocean. It just happened that this sandhill is surrounded by reefs, our Skipper is now well into the boat fare. It would have been fair to say he was pissed, the boat ran aground on one of Dorres Island's reefs. Never before have I seen a man, go from drunk to sober, in such a short time. He got to the wheel of that boat and roared the engine back and forth until we were freed from that reef, it took a while but he succeeded.

After we had dropped anchor, Dennis and Steve took off to shore and started ripping some black things from the reef, they may have been mussels. I lay on the sandhill and almost fell asleep. The grounding of the boat had been the most exciting part of my day. We now had to sleep on this boat, the last time I'd slept on a boat was when I went to Ireland with Marion and Fred and I didn't like that. This trip hadn't been a good idea, for me at least, I was bored, my teammates were as happy as pigs in shit.

I can't remember how I killed or wasted Sunday but I do remember we didn't go back to Carnarvon as we should have done. I do remember catching up with another prawn trawler and a party being held, I was no part of this party. We did another night on this tub and I was woken at some ungodly hour to do something in the dark, I think it may have involved holding a rope or something. God, I'd had a terrific weekend.

On landing in Carnarvon we realised, we were going to be late for, not only breakfast but starting time. We piled in my ute and headed out to Brickhouse, around halfway, we saw Youngie heading into town, he was looking for his two gun shearers and his woolpresser. We must have been Youngie's most reliable workers and here we were, no better than the team's worst pisscat, who he expected may not turn up on Monday morning after a weekend in Carnarvon.

Youngie huffed and puffed but said not much, I think I copped the brunt of it as I'd been seen driving the others when he drove into town. I was put on, what we called 'the silent treatment'. It's quite a strong psychological tool, I always thought it wouldn't worry me, but it wears you down. Apart from the silent treatment, Brickhouse was a breeze for me as I was using a hydraulic press.

We moved on to Doorawarrah Station, I'd been there the year before and left to do my woolclassing exams. They had a hydraulic press here but it wasn't working so I had to use the reliable old Ferrier, it held no fear but was frustrating when there was a hydraulic press, standing against the wall of the shed. I was still on the silent treatment from Youngie, and it may have been starting to get under my skin. I'd met some shelia at Canterbury Court, just before we left for Carnarvon and written to her, I got the reply at Doorawarrah. It was a 'Dear John' letter as we called them, 'You're very nice but not nice enough, I don't want to see you again.' It didn't faze me as she was just some shelia. My head wasn't where it should have been, it wanted to be back in Perth.

I was complacent in my work, something out of character for me, as I lived for and enjoyed my work. One morning as I was swinging from the crank handle of the Ferrier to the leaver, something I'd done a thousand times before, I hit the leaver down onto the top of my foot. The Ferrier leaver weighs around thirty pounds and when swung down by the presser, another ten stone. This hurt like hell, I couldn't keep going, that hurt almost as much as my foot. I was advised by my teammates to go into town and see a doctor after getting the compo forms from Youngie.

I got the forms from a very unhappy and reluctant Youngie and headed into town. I saw a doctor and was more or less told I was a malingerer and he won't fill out the forms. I returned to camp and rested up my foot, it was now the weekend and there was wool everywhere in the shed. Our gun shearer, Steve MacKenna put his hand up to press the wool while I was crook, he did a great job as I found out on my return to the shed on Monday morning. I attempted to press that Monday morning but failed, my foot still hurt too much, I saw all the bales of wool that Steve had pressed on the weekend and felt defeated. My brain blew up, 'I can't do this anymore, I've got to go,' was what my brain was telling me. I marched or rather limped off to find Youngie, "You can stick your job up your arse, my leaving," were my words to Youngie as I stormed off to the huts to pack. I went to the kitchen and said farewell to Glad and was gone in minutes.

As I drove down the highway out of Carnarvon I could feel my foot getting better. This reminded me of when I'd left Belarbrook almost two years earlier, I was something of a hothead, I stopped off at Belarbrook to see Dennis and Vivienne before returning to Perth. They'd forgiven me, I wondered if Youngie ever would.

53 ONWARD AND DOWNWARD

My return to Perth was less than triumphant, I'd just thrown away the best job I'd ever had, or so it seemed. In reality, it had been the highest paying job I'd ever had, a stepping stone to a future, as I had a healthy bank balance. It had become all I knew, my trade as it were, there wasn't much else I could do. I took the rest of the week off and rested my foot, a week off was all it needed, the doctor in Carnarvon was right, I was a malingerer.

By the weekend I was ready to find another job as a woolpresser. I saw a couple advertised, one was just a phone number and the other Pastoralists and Graziers. I opted for the phone number first and rang the number. It was Spargo (Not sure of his first name.) and he asked me to meet him at his house in Shelley. I made my way out there, it was a bloody mansion, 'Has this bloke built this on shearing?' I thought as I entered the drive. I could tell this job wasn't mine as I introduced myself to Spargo, Spargo knew wool pressers weighed over twelve stone and were at least six foot and didn't have Pommie accents.

I'd failed on only three counts but it was enough, he told me about his teams and his run in the Goldfields in his gruff way and said he'd give me a call. 'Bollocks.' I thought as I pulled out of his driveway and headed into Perth and good old Pastoralists and Graziers who had given me my first job in Australia. This was a push-over, I had this job, pressing and penning up for a four stand team on the basic pay. How the mighty had fallen, never the less I had a job and could climb back up.

This new job was in Dandaragan, just off Rowe's Road, territory familiar to me. The dreaded Olivedene was on Rowe's Road and I'd disliked working there. The job was a breeze, probably too much of a breeze, the shearers were pretty much all learners and shearing around a hundred a day. I wasn't liking this setup, it wasn't what I'd become accustomed to, I was indolent in the extreme and getting snowed under with wool.

One day the classer approached me and said, "The wool truck's coming this afternoon do you think you could press five bales this next run, I'll get one of the rousabouts to pen up."

'Five bales a run, you're taking the piss,' I thought.

"Do my best," I answered.

I don't know if this bloke was just giving me a prod or thought five bales a run was beyond me, but it worked. I pressed ten bales for the run, my best effort on a manual press. I quit after that shed and decided that I'd get a job in Perth.

Back to the paper and the situations vacant column, 'Storeman wanted, apply…' it was someplace in Osborne Park I think. When I got there, there was a queue around the building, 'Fuck that, I'm not queueing for a bloody storeman's job.' I thought, I still had some pride.

Back to the paper, I must have dug further this time. This time my eyes fell on this strange advertisement, or strange to me, at least. 'Milkrounds available for lease. $800.00 deposit phone (You don't expect me to remember the number do you?) Sunnywest Dairies Pty Ltd.' I now knew what I wanted to do, I wanted to be a milkman.

I rang the number and got through to the man in charge, Jim Onderwater. "If you get down to our depot tonight about midnight, you'll meet a bloke called Phil Tucker, he'll show you the round," says Jim.

'This sounds very relaxed for someone who's putting eight hundred on the line.' I thought but turned up at the Sunnywest milk depot at midnight (I'd had directions as I had no idea where it was.) it was the only place so brightly lit at that time of night.

"You can't park there mate." These are the first words I hear as I park there.

"Where then?" I shout back.

"Anywhere over there, 'll do," came the reply.

After parking, I walked over to the voice and explained I was looking for Phil Tucker.

"He'll be here any minute mate," the voice tells me.

Any minute comes around, and a little off-white flat tray Toyota races into the yard of the milk depot screeches to a halt and reverses up to the loading ramp. There is a Sunnywest logo on the doors of this little truck and all the others that had come and gone, had been unidentified, I got the feeling that this could be Phil Tucker.

"This is Phil," the voice tells me.

I approach this rather disinterested-looking bloke and go to introduce myself.

"You're coming to look at the round, Tom is it? Phil, I'll just get loaded up and we'll be off," this bloke says as I almost force him into a handshake.

'At least he can shake a hand.' I thought as I'm released from Phil's firm grip. As Phil loads the milk crates onto the truck with some dexterity, I note that this thirty-something bloke, with super deep pockets (The pockets in his shorts protrude below the bottom of his shorts.), is noticeably light on his feet. "Hop in," says Phil after loading the truck.

Off we go in silence, we come to a halt just up the street.

"One in there," says Phil out of the darkness.

My mind is now in overdrive, 'I came to look at this milkround, not do, this milkround,' is my immediate thought, I'm sitting in the milk truck wondering what I'm supposed to do.

"One in there on the veranda," Phil repeats.

"Do I get it from anywhere?" I ask.

"Yeh, anywhere," Phil returns, his head falls to one side and I can tell he thinks I'm dumb.

Off we go again, take a sharp right into a driveway and stop again, "Two in there behind the concrete swan," says Phil.

And on it goes, the driving is somewhat erratic and at times I'm sure we're on the wrong side of the road. And then the street lights go out, "You might need this," Phil tells me, as he hands me a bicycle light on a belt.

Knowing I'm dumb, Phil explains how this apparatus works, "You just put the belt on and turn on the light." God, he really, does think I'm dumb.

Well before the street lights went out I was lost, if this bloke dropped me off now I'd never find my way back to my ute. I'd come out to look at this milkround, and now found myself doing this milkround, I wasn't dressed to do a milkround, I was dressed as I would be to take out a girl. Nice shirt and pants and my favourite suede shoes I'd bought in Ireland, this wasn't milkround kit but it wasn't dirty work, I think this amused Phil but he said nothing. I soon discovered that saying nothing, was one of Phil's strong points, loquacious he was not, he gave clear instructions and that was it.

For some reason, I turn up for my second night dressed just as I had the first night. After another night of running through the streets of East Fremantle and its surrounds, I discovered my favourite shoes were no more, the soles were gone. Phil of few words said a few.

"I've never seen a milkman yet, who wore long pants," he said, "And if you're going to keep doing this you'll need some decent shoes. These Volleys I wear are the best, Ken Rosewall wears 'em too so they can't be bad." Phil has a bit of a chuckle.

'Fuck, he's got a bit of humour,' I thought as we drove back to the depot in silence.

54 A MILKMAN IS BORN

Night three sees the real Tom Watson turn up to learn this milkround, shorts, volleys and a head in gear. I could see Phil was a little more impressed than he had been so far. I'd the idea of bottle for bottle (The customer left out the number of empty bottles they required that night.) cashies, they left out the right money each night, for the milk they required. "Never give 'em change," Phil told me the first time someone was a few cents over and I was going to find change for them. Then I returned to the truck with the milk that I'd left with and reported, "They didn't want any milk tonight." "Where's the note?" an angry-sounding Phil asks. "I just threw it away," I answered. "You always keep the note and put it on the spike, now go and find it," Phil grumbles, "I'll show you why later," he continues.

This third night we're putting out bills, Phil has them in his top pocket and hands me one every time I go into the darkness to deliver the milk. I start to get used to this and put out my hand each time I leave the truck. "Two in there for cash," says Phil, I pause and no bill appears, "Where's the bill?" I ask. "It's a fucking cashie, they don't get bills, do they?" Phil sighs and probably thinks I'm not as bright as I was starting to look.

Saturday comes around, it was Friday when I left home. Double delivery tonight and the bills start to get paid, I pick up my first payment and return to the truck with the money and the bill. "You leave the big piece of the bill under the bottles and tear off the small piece and put it on the spike," Phil tells me. This unassuming spike seems to be the place you put every bit of litter you find, I didn't know Phil cared so much. This double delivery is a little confusing for the new boy, who was just getting used to how much milk went where even though, he was totally lost from the moment he left the depot.

It was alright for Phil, he had this exercise book open on the seat of the truck, I'd been sneaking a look at this book from time to time. I began to realise that this exercise book had the pages divided down the middle and the lefthand street numbers down the lefthand side of the page and vice-a-versa for the righthand side numbers and how much each house got. Phil caught me looking at the book, "That's the round book," Phil tells me. I start to get the hang of the round book but I'm lost as far as knowing where I am.

We do two loads of milk for double delivery and daylight is starting to show as we finish. I now realise I can see where I am and some of the places look slightly familiar. It dawns on me that if I did this milkround in daylight, I'd pick it up much quicker and have some idea where I'd been. Before we parted I asked Phil if I could have the round book for the weekend. "Yeh, that's alright, and can you meet me at my place on Sunday night and leave your ute there? They're complaining about where you park, you know where I live don't you?" Phil ends.

"Corner of South Street," I answer, I'd seen the little truck parked there during the day.

"That's right, see you Sunday."

Saturday night is Canterbury Court night, I'd met this gorgeous shelia there and her rather cute friend. Bugger the cute friend, I wanted the gorgeous one and hit it off with her. I was quite sure the gorgeous one worked in a glamourous boutique in Perth. The gorgeous shelia, I discovered was called Julie and her friend, the little cutey was Dunka. Dunka, I discovered worked in Tom the Cheap in Belmont, she was a checkout chick.

I'd made the mistake of telling Julie I thought she worked in a glam-ourous boutique, there was no way she was going to reveal where she really worked. It wasn't long before I suspected that she worked for a vet and took great joy in seeing animals being castrated. Besotted though I was with Julie, and she enjoyed my company, there were rules, no slow dances and no taking her home. Perhaps you can understand why I thought she worked for a vet.

Sunday morning I drive down to the Sunnywest Dairy and all there was there, was a highly polished stainless steel tanker unloading milk, a rather eerie sight after the hustle and bustle of my nighttime visits. I get Phil's round book and my bearing and off I go, right into Samson Street, this is a little confusing as Phil has spelt Samson with a 'p' Sampson. As I follow the round book it gets a little scary, the streets in Whitegum Valley are divided and the round book has me going down the wrong side of the road. This causes me to take a broader view and just imagine where I should be, rather than meeting the traffic head-on.

I follow the whole round and discover I've been miles and covered three or four suburbs. Anyone who knew what they were doing, would have known this wasn't a very good milkround, I didn't know what I was doing. What I had achieved from this exercise was, I now knew where the round went and would be able to re-enact it in the dark, I could also understand Phil's round book.

From the moment I set out to apply for this milkround, I knew it was what I was going to do. I was halfway there, as I had my ute, no need to spend money on a vehicle. Phyllis was the first to know what I was doing as I always confided in her. "You'll be right love," was about all she said.

When Phylis said 'love', it always filled me with confidence. Her husband Don, was all gung-ho and encouraging, as was his style. It hadn't gotten him far, he now seemed to drift from one dead-end project to another and was less involved in the panel-beating business.

Sunday afternoon I visit Robyn at her share house in Subiaco, how I would have loved to live there, I dreamt a lot sometimes. I broke the news of my decision to take on the milkround to Robyn, "You're bloody mad," was all she said, the subject was closed and my confidence shattered.

"Can I come out with you one night, Tom?" Robyn's housemate Kerry pipes up.

"Sure, when I get started you can," I answered, thrilled that a girl had asked to go out with me, albeit on a milkround.

Phil must have seen the improvement in me on Sunday night, I no longer needed to be told, how many and where. My Sunday morning with the round book had paid off, as I could now tell where I was, as I'd been there in daylight. I could now understand and read the round book with only a fleeting glance. Phil arranged for me to meet up at Sunnywest on Monday afternoon to sign up and pay my eight hundred dollars.

Monday afternoon and I met Phil at Sunnywest, I hardly recognised him, he looked quite dapper in his civvies. I now meet the famous Jim Onderwater, a big bloke in a suit, dangerously smooth, I shake hands and find he has a worthy handshake. I rather like the bloke, he assures me I'm going to make good money at this milkround caper by growing the round, no promises are made. I still had a week or so to go with Phil learning the round thoroughly. Phil assures Jim I was going well, I leave them both, eight hundred lighter in the pocket.

55 WOOLCLASSING EXAM

Once signed up for the milkround, things seemed to fly. Phil felt I was ready to go on my own after my improvement on Monday continued. I had to learn how to work the ledger, an afternoon with Phil at his place. The ledger work was just basic arithmetic and now I see why we keep the notes on the spike, and it wasn't to keep East Fremantle litter free as I had first suspected. You worked through the notes and payment tabs backwards through the ledger marking them off as you went. Although the ledger looked ominous at first sight because of its size, it was just simple bookkeeping and the obvious heart of the business.

I had a big week as my woolclassing exams came up this week. Even though I was no longer pursuing a career in the shearing industry I felt compelled to do the exams as it would give me a trade if the milkround turned bad. I think that is just a feeble excuse for doing the exams, I had no intention of returning to the shearing industry. In real terms, I was doing the exams to prove that I could do them and pass them.

Off I went to South Fremantle Technical College that morning for the exams, theory in the morning and practical in the afternoon. I waltzed through the theory but the afternoon was another matter. We were presented with several wool samples, 'What the fuck is this?' I thought. It had only been a couple of weeks earlier that, I'd been working in shearing sheds and pressing wool. It was almost twelve months since I'd handled wool, in the sense of feeling and understanding it. For the last eleven months, I'd just grabbed armfuls and hurled them into a wool press and trampled on it. I was lost at sea without a lifeboat and whatever I wrote about this wool was rubbish, I knew then that these exams were a waste of time.

Back to the milkround account keeping on Thursday afternoon, I'd be doing the milkround on my own that night. Phil shows me how to keep the bills in order and peel them off one by one from a top pocket as I'd seen him do. Each week Sunnywest printed out the names and addresses on the bills in order, it was far from a perfect system. To me, they looked like crap, with the names and addresses sometimes not in the right place, too far to the right or the left. They used some sort of archaic printing device and the print was awful and a touch splotchy with ink overload. Phil seemed to write almost half out by hand.

I struggled through my first night, it was a real struggle. My ute was useless, the handbrake wouldn't hold on steep hills and the milk crates were almost impossible to move around in the back of the ute, this wasn't the right vehicle for the job. The front wheels of the ute were almost airborne when I left the depot. Others used utes but it seems they didn't carry as much milk as I was. I couldn't do another night using the ute, I had to get a tray back one tonner and fast, double delivery on Friday night.

I had to buy a new one-ton tray back, I needed a reliable vehicle and never even dreamt of buying secondhand. This was an easy process for someone as cashed-up as me, thought and research were never my strong suits. I drove into Ray Kelt Motors with a Falcon ute and left with a Datsun one-ton truck and a chequebook seriously damaged. At least I could get through my first double delivery without killing myself.

Proud as punch with my latest purchase, I arranged to pick Robyn's friend Kerry up to take her out on the milkround as she'd requested. Kerry was up for this night on the town of East Fremantle and I picked her up around eleven-thirty, not even getting home time on a Friday night. It could be said neither of us knew what we were putting ourselves into and 'it could be,' was dead right.

Reversing up to the loading ramp at Sunnywest Dairies with a brand new truck and an attractive girl in the cab, raised eyebrows. It probably got me an instant 'Flash Harry' reputation, I certainly wasn't going to last at this milkround caper. Little did I know at the time, that the streets of Fremantle were, metaphorically speaking, littered with the bodies of failed Sunnywest milkmen. If I'd done my research I would have known this and still done, what I was now doing.

Let's say Kerry was company, yes, she could carry a couple of bottles of milk but the help she gave was absorbed by the time I spent giving her instructions. By about three in the morning, reality was coming home to me, I was managing but only by the skin of my teeth. I'd spent too much on this enterprise to fail, but failing I was, my head was a blur and my eyes were constantly looking at the round book, that I knew by heart. I became as weak as a kitten, and then it started, I threw up, I almost collapsed and I threw up some more. I felt I couldn't go on, I felt I was failing, after throwing up my toenails I must have been reeking of vomit, I paused, and I saw Kerry looking helpless in the cab, 'What must she be thinking?' I thought and carried on. The rest of the round was a breeze, for me at least, I have a feeling that Kerry wasn't too keen on the breeze she was getting as it was full of the smell of vomit.

I returned Kerry to Subiaco and returned to Phyllis' place and just slept. When I woke, I did my ledger and sorted my money, and yes, I had the energy to front at Canterbury Court for a night of dancing and failing to win the heart of my beloved Julie.

Monday was my first day of 'collecting' the day I had to go and collect the milk money from those who didn't leave it out for me. Phil had organised me to get a collection bag from "A bloke who has a place in Carrington Street near where you live, he makes 'em." I think that was how he put it. I was only a little nervous as I left 9 Adrian in my shorts and long socks and new collection bag which looked far too new.

I was terrified as I knocked on the first door, 'What the fuck am I going to say?' My mind was asking me, "Milkman," was about all I could come up with, it seemed to work, I got their money. There were a few conversations, none of them encouraging, "I hope you're better than the last bloke," was the average comment. I tried my best to convince my new customers that I was a nice bloke and would do my best to be 'Better than the last bloke,' but none seemed convinced. Let's face it I was speaking to women and my record wasn't good on that front.

56 IT'S GOT TO GET BETTER

I was right into this milkround caper, just had to organise my sleep pattern. As Christmas came around I thought I was getting into a pattern. Double delivery for Christmas so I was ready for a good sleep, I rose in the afternoon and retired to bed after tea, I was still tired. I was woken by some long-haired lout leaning over me, it almost scared me but I realised it was my shearing team mate Henry Jones, "Come on Tom, we're going to a party," Henry let out in his raucous manner. The other half of 'we' was Davy Rutherford, the roustabout who had hung around at cut-out at Yathroo.

How could I tell them I was tired? I couldn't, I just had to join in the fun. Off we went to someone's place in East Fremantle to party on. I may well have been tired but I was also lost, it was only a few months since I'd been working with these guys and I discovered we now had nothing in common. My body attended that party but my brain wasn't there.

During the party I was obliged to attend, I must have mentioned to little Davy that the milkround wasn't that lucrative. Because once New Year had passed, I got another visit from Davy. He had got himself a job at the wool stores, "Hey Tom, they're looking for a presser down at the wool stores, you'd piss it in, hydraulic press, couple of hours a day," spouts Davy, full of enthusiasm.

"Yah reckon you're not making much with the milkround, what yer reckon?" Davy adds. I agreed to give it a go and got the details from Davy.

Monday morning after finishing the milkround I headed down to the wool stores in Phoenix Road and saw the boss, who was less enthusiastic than Davy. I guess that he'd seen my frame and thought I wasn't the real deal, being so light. I pressed my ration of wool and knocked off, I hadn't put in a top performance. I returned home exhausted, as I walked to the front steps, I stopped and threw my guts up. Five pints of milk don't taste very nice after processing in a stomach for four or five hours. About this time I made the decision, that there would be no more wool pressing for me.

My social life now consisted of a night out at Canterbury Court on Saturday night and perhaps a visit to Robyn's place on Sunday afternoon. My interaction with other humans was limited to, the ladies I was collecting milk money from and perhaps a chat with Phil Tucker if I saw him at the depot. The mere thought of speaking to the other milkmen at the depot was ridiculous. Never had I seen a more miserable group of people, and my new milk truck and cheerful disposition didn't seem to inspire friendliness. Quite the opposite, I could tell they disliked me.

I started to get into the milkround and was finding it pretty easy and had made changes by swopping customers with other milkmen. I now wrote out all my bills ignoring the old Sunnywest system, I'm guessing that the other Sunnywest milkmen would have died if they knew I'd strayed from the system. No, they wouldn't, they would have thought I was mad. I could now start to understand why so many of them failed.

One night I arrived at the depot and saw a stack of milk at the very end of the loading ramp, well away from where we loaded. Well, I couldn't resist a sticky beak, it was Browne's milk, from a competing dairy. The stack was not made up of only milk as all the Sunnywest ones were, there was yoghurt, flavoured milk and orange juice. I was filled with envy, 'Why aren't I selling that shit?' the envy asked me. This mystery stack of milk was there every night and seemed to belong to nobody. Then one night I sprung the owner, "G'day," I call out. This bloke smiled at me, "G'day," he replied. The only other bloke who smiled at Sunnywest was Gerry the storeman, oh, and Phil Tucker if he saw me.

The new man in town was highly suspicious, I would hazard a guess no one else had spoken to him while he loaded his milk. I got that, 'Who does this bloke think he is?' look.

"Why are you getting Browne's milk here?" I ask, rather brazenly.

"I live in Mosman Park and have a milkround in South Perth so this is convenient for me," comes the reply.

"You, been at this caper long?" Asks the new man.

"No, I'm pretty new to it," I answer.

"Norm MacNamara," says the new man, "Tom Watson," I return.

"We've got a meeting of the association of milk vendors on Sunday, would you like to come along?" Norm asks me.

"I'll be in that," I reply.

Norm gives me the details and I forget to ask him about all the yoghurt and orange juice, I've got a milkround to do. I load my milk and take off in a state of shock, no one else loading at this ramp had spoken to me until this night. Now it's happened the person is a blow-in, who shouldn't even be there.

I go to my first meeting of the West Australian Retail Milk Vendors Union at a small milk depot in Manning, it's also a squash court. Yes, I was confused but liked what I saw and heard, wasn't sure about Union being in the name of the organisation but still. I was talking with people who had made big money out of milkrounds (Hence the squash court.) and there was a bloke my age there, but most were over thirty. The bloke my age, Norm introduced him to me, Mike Feeney also had a milkround in the Fremantle area but owned his round and got his milk from another dairy, Masters. What a great experience it was for me to learn that other milkmen spoke to each other and were willing to share ideas.

I returned to my milkround that night inspired, even though the milkround was just the same. I had, of course, joined the West Australian Retail Milk Vendors Union and as I got more confident, I asked my fellow milk vendors at Sunnywest if they would like to join, to a man they refused. I was starting to accept I didn't fit in but liked what I was doing and my customers were starting to warm to me. There was a nice shelia in Moss Street, I could really warm to, a customer's daughter. Life was looking good.

I get a visit from Phil Tucker, he knows when I should be doing the bills and will be home. There are the usual pleasantries, I can't go over the top as there is only a bed in my room, a sleepout on the verandah.

"We've got this round coming up in Hamilton Hill, the guy that's got it is a wanker and has to get out," Phil tells me.

Before thought comes into the equation, Phil adds, "We'll take your round, the one in Hamilton Hill is bigger and more compact. What Yah reckon?"

I didn't give this much thought, it sounded like a fait accompi to me. Of course, I said, "Yes." I didn't ask 'Why me?' I had a fair idea it was me because I was doing a good job with my current round, and perhaps because I got on with Phil.

57 MEETING HAMILTON HILL

No sooner had I said, "Yes," to Phil's proposal for me to take over the bigger milkround in Hamilton Hill than the wheels were in motion. I was to teach my round to another Sunnywest employee and Phil would learn the round in Hamilton Hill. This was their way of doing things, the bloke who they had lined up for my milkround couldn't learn it from me and I couldn't learn from my predecessor with the Hamilton Hill round. I think they may have done that at one time and found the new chums took to the hills when the old chums told them what a terrible thing they were putting themselves into. Let's face it, few milkmen left Sunnywest on good terms, the records would show most had gone broke or couldn't cope with the lifestyle.

The Sunnywest man I had to teach my milkround to, was not like Phil Tucker had been with me, parsimonious with words, he was loquacious to the extreme. This bloke had had dozens of milkrounds it seemed, just a few less than the conquests he'd made while doing these milkrounds. His interest in learning the milkround amounted to zero, how this bloke would go after only a week with me was beyond me.

After that time he was going to teach the next man, this didn't look as if it was going to work. On our second last night on my now, old milkround my newfound friend Ray, produced a stick of chalk and at every house chalked on the kerb the number of bottles they got. A cunning plan if it didn't rain, I would have much rather he'd quietly learnt the round and spoken much less. The change over of milkrounds was seamless and I learned the round in Hamilton Hill from Phil in relative silence compared to the previous week of prate.

I went out for my first money collection in Hamilton Hill, full of confidence, after all, I'd been chosen for this milkround because I was capable. It took the dear ladies of Hamilton Hill no time at all to cut me down to size. They were a scary bunch of ladies if ever one was produced, the 'last bloke' as he is always referred to, was as Phil had chosen to tell me early in the piece, a wanker. And it seems that I, like him was young and was going to be just as useless. "We'll give you a month," was the usual remark, as I swore I'd look after them. I got through the first month and didn't lose a customer and was starting to make friends. The kids of Hamilton Hill, and there seemed to be swarms of them, liked my milk truck and the rides I'd give them on it as I collected money.

It wasn't long before I'd recruited a couple of the milk truck riders to help me on Friday nights with double delivery. After what I thought was a disastrous start to the milkround in Hamilton Hill things were starting to turn around and I was gathering a fan base, albeit small fans.

I was getting involved in milkrounds, going to milk vendor meetings and now looking at upping my by-product sales, yoghurt, cream, flavoured milk and orange juice being the main ones. I got together with the guy I met at that first milk vendor meeting Mike Feeney and we decided to put a flyer together promoting the by-product side of things.

The flyer worked and soon I was selling a lot more by-products than anyone else at Sunnywest, not a great achievement as the others sold bugger all. It was obvious that I was selling quite a few by-products as my load showed it as I left the depot, not one of my fellow milkmen ever mentioned it to me or questioned me. Let's face it they hadn't plucked up the courage to speak to me yet.

Word was out, Masters Dairy was going to buy Sunnywest Dairy and they didn't want the milkround component of Sunnywest. Was I the first to hear? I'm not sure, probably not but there again I was the golden boy, the teacher's pet, the one no one spoke to, the one who got that good milkround, so perhaps I was. I liked what I did and saw an opportunity to get hold of some security, off I went up those stairs a

- 238 -

Sunnywest and went to see the big man, Jim Onderwater. Could I buy my milkround? Jim was pretty straight with me and told me that a few months earlier the answer would have been no. Things had changed and yes I could, the deposit I'd given when I started was enough to get me into the milkround with vendor finance provided by Sunnywest.

The wheels were soon in motion, I was to become the holder of a Milk Vendors Licence. I knew a bit about the licencing system but not much. Each Milk Vendors Licence covered a certain area, this had never been a problem before as I operated under the licenses held by Sunnywest and they had everywhere covered under their licenses.

Buying my milkround meant that I took over their licence in my area, and their licence became mine. This was simple enough, except that a couple of other milkmen from Sunnywest also delivered within my now licensed area, and I had to buy their customers too. If they had gotten something for what they felt I stole from them, all would have been well, they didn't. My already rock bottom popularity rating went through the floor at the Sunnywest loading ramp, care, I didn't.

When those first milk bills went out with 'Tom H. Watson, Milk Vendor' printed on them, there was barely room in my top pocket to put them, my chest was pushed out so far. Proud as I was, it didn't seem to make much difference to the customers, I don't think they believed it was me when I went to collect the money. I got the odd question, "Tom Watson, is that you?" I was proud as punch and said, "Yes." And in no time at all, I was famous throughout Hamilton Hill or the bit on the eastern side of Carrington Street.

It seemed that it wasn't long after I bought my milkround, that I got one of those visits from Phil Tucker, a bit like when he wanted me to take on the milkround that was now mine. If I saw Phil, it was usually at his place and lager was involved. Seeing him at my salubrious sleepout was unusual. "That bloke who took your East Fremantle round on has fucked up." Starts Phil.

"I thought he was a star," I smile.

"He was a fuckwit," continues Phil, "and I've been left with his round and I've got enough on without that shit. I was wondering if you could take it back on?"

"Nah, I couldn't do that and my round too, it'd be too much." I quickly reply.

"You wouldn't have to do the Melville bit, I'd do that and if you had a runner you could do it, I know you'd manage." Phil is trying his best to sugarcoat this setup. "I know this kid in Mosman Park who might do the running for you, let's go and see him, he was working for another bloke and went well with him."

Off we go to Mosman Park, 'How does Phil know all these people?' I question myself as Phil drives recklessly over the Fremantle traffic bridge.

"You won't have to pay any rent on this round you know and if you can do it, and I know you can, it'll be an earner for you, pretty much set you up." Phillip the universal salesman I know he isn't tells me as we pull up outside an asbestos house in Mosman Park. 'This house looks less salubrious than 9 Adrian Street,' I'm thinking as Phil goes in to find my new runner. Yes, within minutes I have employed my first employee and it's on, I'm to become one of, if not the largest personal milk vendor in Perth.

58 THE GOOD TIMES ROLL

The next six months seem to fly but why wouldn't they? All I seemed to be doing was working and sleeping. I'd been welcomed back to the East Fremantle milkround with open arms, it seemed they didn't need to 'hope I was better than the last bloke.' That was very reassuring, it seemed we were old friends. There was one bloke in particular who liked a chat when I went to pick up his cheque, Bert Glazinti, he'd been a milkman in his day and retired when he was forty. He now had his own concreting business and told me you couldn't retire at forty. This sort of took the wind out of my sails as the forty-retirement was my plan.

I remember one night he scared the hell out of me, "Leave ten extra pints, will yah Tom," came this voice out of the darkness. It was a hot night and the whole family (There were about six kids.) was sleeping on the front lawn, luckily I'd stuck to the path or would have run over the top of them. East Fremantle was the only place I came across people sleeping on the front lawn, Bert wasn't the only one.

I was only the largest personal milk vendor in Perth for those six months, but as Phil had promised me, it 'set me up.' My income was at last healthy and I was aware of my capabilities so when my run came to an end I wasn't disappointed. Yes, Sunnywest had found another mug to take on the East Fremantle milkround and I was left with the round in Hamilton Hill and a little free time. It wasn't long before the drop in income and the spare time started to catch up with each other and I now had a couple of school kids to help me on Friday night. I wanted more and was looking for opportunities.

One such opportunity arose, a bloke I knew had a small milkround in Bicton he wanted someone to lease. We spoke and everything seemed rosy, his wife came to visit me in my sleepout and wasn't impressed. That opportunity was lost, I can smile as I look back on it, I was judged on my lodgings not, on my ability.

Living in Palmyra, I sort of knew the milkman there, he'd been Phyllis' milkman before I started the milkround, a Sunnywest milkman. I knew these rounds were for sale and this was ideal for me, an extra fifty gallons, it would just make my milkround very profitable.

Back up the stairs at Sunnywest, "Can I buy Jacko's round in Palmyra?" I ask Jim Onderwater. Of course, the answer was "Yes" and the wheels were again in motion, there was a little bit of juggling to be done but I soon had the milkround I wanted. Jacko Hutchings was popular down at Sunnywest so when I 'stole' his milkround, my popularity dropped a few more notches. My purchase of the round in Palmyra coincided with the Masters Dairy takeover of Sunnywest and the move to the Master's depot in East Fremantle.

After losing an opportunity due to my lodgings I decided to move out and get my own place, Phyllis was heartbroken when I told her. Don her husband wasn't happy either, why? Because I was income and he liked income, although he wasn't fond of work.

I got a flat in East Fremantle, not far from the milk depot so it was handy for me. I asked the caretakers, an old couple who were very welcoming if I could get the phone put on. "No need for that," they announced, "You're in flat three and the redphone is at the door, we'll give you the number, you can use that," they excitedly tell me. I wasn't so sure but went along with their idea and had the number printed on my bills. I just had to be alert and get to the phone when it rang.

Moving into the flat was great, the food was great, the cook was great and the company was fantastic, all that and I was on my own. There's no end to the delicious meals you can get out of a can, steak and kidney pie was my favourite, steak and onions with new potatoes, wow, I was in heaven.

59 A SOCIAL LIFE

My social life at this time wasn't exactly on a high note, my one night out each week was still spent wasting my time chasing Julie at Canterbury Court. The Sunday afternoons I'd spent at Robyn's place had come to an end as she had taken off up north with her friend Kerry.

I did meet a couple of girls from Hamilton Hill at Canterbury Court one night, one was a customer's daughter, I thought I was made, until the following Monday when I knocked on their door to collect the milk money. She answered the door and ran away to get her mother, but she never answered the door again. The heart I thought I'd won, was lost. From that Saturday night, every time I met a girl at Canterbury Court, my now good friend Julie, would call them Hamilton Hill girls.

I was to go on and meet another 'Hamilton Hill' girl as Julie insisted on calling her, only she lived in Balga at the other end of the city. Was this love? We started going steady, with my lifestyle that meant Saturday night at Canterbury Court and a Sunday afternoon drive. Brenda was my first 'steady' girlfriend, (I couldn't call Karen steady as I wasn't around enough.) as opposed to a girl who was a friend, they seemed to haunt me.

Brenda and I got on very well and she didn't seem to mind my work schedule, although she didn't seem to have any idea what I did. She was proper Scottish working class, as were her parents who it seemed, rather liked me. Her mother did once mention that my activities were ruining Brenda's clothes, I tried to ignore the remark but blushed.

Things seemed to be going well with Brenda, was she the one? I was starting to think so. As another winter started to bite, I got myself a touch of influenza. It was the sort of touch that would kill a lesser being, for a week I thought it was coming close for me. For that week I worked as best I could, slept and ate very little. It was a relief when the weekend came and I had the boys to help me on Friday night. I hit my bed on Saturday morning and slept and slept and slept, I awoke at around eight-thirty on Saturday night.

Brenda didn't know any of this, (No phone.) so when I arrived to pick her up at around nine-thirty, it could be said she wasn't happy to see me. I, of course, apologised profusely and explained I'd been near death for a week. We hopped in the milk truck and headed into town, there was silence for the complete journey.

When I pulled up in the carpark close to Canterbury Court, I broke the silence, "If you're not going to talk to me you may as well go home," I let out.

"Alright then," she replied.

I now knew this wasn't the girl for me. When I finally got to Canterbury Court, my question from Julie was, "Where's the Hamilton Hill girl?" I think I told her I was free, didn't make any difference, she didn't throw herself at my feet and ask for a lift home.

60 MY LIFE NEEDED TO CHANGE

My milkround was going well, I now had a reliable group of runners who helped me on Friday night during school term and all week on school holidays. While these kids were having school holidays I was effectively having a holiday too, it was damn hard when they went back to school. This group worked one at a time mostly. The best was Garry Tucker, Phil's eldest son, he came to the job already trained by his father. If he wasn't available there'd be his brother Stuart, same story but he lacked the interest that Garry had and was just going through the process. The other two I had were the O'Sullivan boys, David and John. Their mother was a customer on the milkround and I felt she could have gone for beatification. She dragged these little buggers out of bed, either at midnight or three in the morning without fail.

As a result of the school holidays, my social life could be stepped up a little during this time, most notably during the Christmas holidays when the kids had six weeks off school. I now went in person, to pay my weekly milk bill at Masters Dairy in Bentley and I was treated to lunch by Julie. Yes, my friend from Canterbury Court, who worked in a chemist's shop in Carlisle. She still hadn't gotten rid of me and was now treating me to a hamburger every Wednesday. I, in turn, allowed her to drive the milk truck along the straight streets of Carlisle without any sort of licence. We were getting along fine, provided there was no physical contact.

Just before Christmas 1973, I met this shelia at Canterbury Court, I felt I'd met her before but wasn't sure. We got on well but she was with a friend or something like that and had transport home. I didn't want to let her go too easily and suggested we catch up at Canterbury Court on New Year's Eve, "It's a great night here, you don't want to miss it." I try to convince her and she, in turn, promises to think about it. I reckoned that was as close to a yes as I was likely to get with my record.

New Year's Eve 1973 arrived and I head off to Canterbury Court full of expectations, that shelia from Roleystone would be there and we'd pash at midnight and my life would change forever. I wandered around that ballroom for almost two hours, looking into the eyes of every girl present. I got some strange looks back and was starting to feel like a creep when I slunk back to Julie's table and joined Michael and Charlie. Michael was one of my competitors in the conquest of Julie competition, we had become friends after realising that neither of us was going to win. I think he may have got the pash at midnight, slimy bastard.

My heart had been broken, but not for the first time, there would be other shelias who would swoon at my feet I felt sure. I didn't give up on my favourite haunt and it was just as well, as a couple of weeks into the New Year my girl reappeared. This time she was with another girl who had enough red hair to start a fire, she looked hot. Enter my friend Michael, he could have the redhead, I had the cutey in my sights.

The old 'divide and conquer' strategy was put into place and it worked, Michael got the redhead and I got my quarry. She no longer lived at Roleystone she told me as I was driving her home, she now lived in a place called Gosnells. She directed me or I would never have found the place, I had to remember where this place was as I was going to pick her up later today. It was well into Sunday when I left her.

This must have been the real thing because the next Saturday night I picked her up around six-thirty, I never went out that early on Saturday night. We went into Perth and I knew of this restaurant in Hay Street, (I'd taken Robyn there for lunch once and it was in her lunch hour and it wasn't suitable.) it was called the Heidelberg. We managed to get in without a booking, Anne was lost, she'd never been to a place like this (I had but only briefly.) she was overwhelmed. I remained cool and asked her what she'd like, "What are you having?" she asks me.

"I'm having the T-bone," I answer.

"I'll have the same," she replies rather flustered.

She didn't really want the T-bone but that is the easiest option when you're flustered.

The sommelier at this place was brilliant and picked us as a couple of new chums at this eating-out caper, he had me with a Lowenbrau beer and Anne with her Bacardi and coke, then the Ben Ean Moselle. This was living, and I was sweeping a woman off her feet for the first time in my life, I couldn't believe I was doing this, but I was.

Back to the milk truck and the short drive to Canterbury Court, we just cruised in and took our seats with the rest of the crew. I'm pretty sure we didn't tell anyone where we'd been for dinner and to Julie, Anne was never a Hamilton Hill girl, she was the real deal.

On Sunday I picked Anne up and we went for a drive in the hills, I didn't know her second name, she wrote it down for me, Dell Borrello, I had no idea she was Italian. She wasn't Italian, she was born in Australia to an Australian mother and an Italian father she explained. I told her I wanted to marry her, I guess that was a proposal, but it was rather blunt. She had a load of excuses, she didn't know me very well and did I have any money? God this woman was so bloody practical. She refused to give me an answer straight away, finally, she said. "Give me a week and I'll tell you then."

Before my week was up I rang Anne, it was her birthday she told me and she couldn't go out with me on Saturday night. Anne was to be a bridesmaid at her friend's wedding, she'd asked if I could go but the answer was 'no.' Arrangements had been made and they didn't allow for Anne meeting someone and then wanting him to accompany her.

"What about marrying me?" I asked not caring about her friend's wedding.

"Your week's not up yet," she answered.

"Well, I'll see you Sunday, will I?" I asked, "And you'll give me an answer?"

"Yes," she replied. And now I had to get her a birthday present. I'm guessing here, but perhaps a romantic would have got an engagement ring, it never crossed my mind.

That Saturday night I did my usual thing, got the freshly pressed pants out from under the mattress and dressed up for Canterbury Court. I was surrounded by my usual group of friends, and Anne barely got a mention. Everything seemed the same, I had my normal (If you can call it that.) touch-free dances with Julie and left a little early. As I drove home I realised I'd had the loneliest night of my life and I'd been surrounded by friends.

61 NOT AS EASY AS I THOUGHT

Anne's week was up, would she marry me or not? It was Sunday afternoon because even for this shelia, who wasn't sure if she wanted to marry me or not, I didn't do Sunday mornings. Anne was her lovely self with that eternal smile when I got to her lodgings in Gosnells. She came running out to the truck and said "Hello."

It seemed she was just as infuriating as all the other girls I'd met. She clambered into the truck, we kissed and I waited.

"Well, what is it?" I asked somewhat gruffly.

"It's yes," she replied.

"That's great," I said, "when?"

"In about a year I suppose, we've got things to organise you know."

"Bullshit, I was thinking next week or something like that, I'm not waiting a year."

This wasn't going as well as I'd hoped, it was slowly heading toward an argument. We drove off and settled ourselves down and started to talk sensibly, well at least Anne did, seems she knew a bit about weddings. I knew nothing.

Well, I'd have to meet her parents, they didn't know anything about this wedding yet. Everyone Anne had spoken to thought she'd be mad to say yes and I was mad to have even asked her. I didn't care about people thinking I was mad, but I wasn't impressed that they thought Anne was mad to say yes. By evening time we both realised this was bigger than it was last week and I, for one had to think about things more constructively.

"See you next Saturday morning and we can go shopping together." Seems the best way out of this for me and we parted with the worries of the world on our shoulders.

Anne had to tell her parents her news, I on the other hand had nobody to tell. I might write and tell Robyn, drop in and tell Phyllis but that would be about it, 'I'll tell Mum next time I write,' I thought as I drove home happily. This was going to be a big week.

Anne rang on Wednesday, she'd broken the news to her parents and they weren't that happy. Her brother, who she idolised, said she must be pregnant. It was obvious to me that he didn't know much about the birds and the bees and even less about Anne and me. We knew that Anne's pregnancy was impossible but didn't tell him that and had a good laugh. I was to meet Anne's parents on Sunday afternoon at their place, there was something for me to look forward to.

Saturday came around and as soon as I'd had breakfast I took off to pick up Anne for our shopping expedition. I had started shopping Saturday mornings, rather than sleeping as it seemed the easiest day to shop for my modest groceries, sleep came later. Anne smiled when I picked her up and smiled through the tales of woe from all she told about our yet-to-be-made plans. She now knew we were both completely mad and it seems she didn't care much.

The jewellers came first, "We want an engagement ring," I boldly declared as we strode up to the counter. The next bit for me was writing out the cheque, I rather hope the price wasn't spoken about, something needless as we didn't look rich. Had I pulled out my chequebook earlier I suspect we would have ended up with a more expensive ring.

I immediately got Anne to put the ring on her finger, it turned out it was the right finger but on the wrong hand, we were new at this caper. Then over to Coles New World supermarket to do my grocery shopping, Anne wasn't impressed with my purchases, bananas being the only thing that related to fresh in my trolley. I took her home and returned to my flat and got some sleep.

I remembered to book the Heidelberg, as I'd seen people being turned away two weeks earlier. I picked Anne up around seven and we had dinner, Anne was more daring with her food choice and picked something she wanted. She insisted we start with a prawn cocktail, all the thing, back then. Canterbury Court, the big announcement, hugs and congratulations all around and someone discretely told Anne her ring was on the wrong hand. We had a great night and ended up at Bernie's burger place on Mounts Bay Road, I still had to take Anne to her lodgings, and I had an early morning journey home.

Sunday, meet the parents day. I was completely unfazed by this, I must confess I was now a cocky, arrogant, young buck. I was a successful milk vendor, independent, a twenty-four-year-old businessman, I feared nothing. Anne on the other hand was nervous, she hadn't seen much of her parents since she left home after too many disagreements with her mother. Her brother thought she was pregnant and she was doing something, totally unorthodox in the eyes of her parents.

Anne's parents lived on a small orchard on Brookton Highway in Roleystone. For me, this place was on another planet, I'd never been anywhere quite like this. I was used to the city and open country and this was neither, it was country but in a confined place, it was rather nice. I pulled up and Anne jumps out of the truck and grabbed me and says "Come on." This middle-aged man is walking out of the orchard and heading for the house, he stops; Anne drags me up to him and announces, "Dad, Joe, this is Tom."

"Glad to meet you, Joe," I confidently say, as I put out my hand.

My hand is dwarfed in this giant's claw and Joe mutters, "I hope so."

And he shakes my hand, never did I imagine my confidence could be crushed so easily.

We go into the house to meet 'mum,' a dragon of a woman it seemed, it turns out she's not that bad but has ideas about weddings which don't match mine. It's got to be a Catholic Church, and it's got to be done just right, and you're not a Catholic, well that's the end of that. I reluctantly agree to convert to another religion and we part on good terms. Anne is on good terms with her parents again after some angst in the past.

As we drive down the hill back to Gosnells, Anne confesses that she didn't think things would go so well.

"You don't have to convert to a Catholic if you don't want to," Anne tells me.

I tell her I'll do it, "It'll keep your mum happy and it can't be that hard," I say without conviction. We've got to start working on a date and it sure as shit isn't going to be twelve months away.

62 PLANNING, NOT MY STRONG SUIT

The date for the wedding is set, 1st of June, unbeknown to me it's a public holiday weekend, milkmen don't have long weekends so they aren't marked on the calendar. I now have to front the local Priest and ask him about my 'conversion,' to Catholicism. This bloke isn't really the local Priest but he's the only one I know of, and then I only know that I deliver milk to the presbytery and that's where the Priest lives. Without splitting hairs he is the Palmyra Parish Priest and I live in East Fremantle the adjoining suburb, close enough for me. This miserable dirty looking excuse for a man isn't that keen on me becoming a Catholic, just to marry some decent Catholic girl but agrees to give me 'lessons.'

Finding a time for my 'lessons' was going to be hard it seemed, but the Priest and I worked our busy schedules around and agreed to a time that wasn't suitable for me but suited the Priest begrudgingly badly. This man's heart wasn't in the conversion of Tom Watson and Tom Watson's heart wasn't in this conversion. I went to my first 'lesson' and left convinced I was never to be a Catholic, I sure as shit wasn't going back to this dirty room with this grotty being, I have intentionally left out the word 'human.' I now had to break the news to Anne and break the promise I'd made.

Was I the one who baulked at the first hurdle? Perhaps I was, Anne wasn't going well on her course either. After what seemed like a rec-onciliation with her mother things were rapidly turning to excrement there too. The date was too soon, where was the reception to be held?

And the list went on, guests, how many? Who? Or who not? I'd laid down my hard-earned on a reception venue, in terms of a deposit and had one lesson to become a Catholic, admittedly that had failed but I put it in the credit column. On Anne's mother's side all there had been was negativity, somehow I managed to hold my tongue and roll with the verbal punches.

It wasn't long before Anne's patience broke and she threw caution to the wind and declared that they could all go and get lost. We were to get married our way and her parents could do and think whatever they liked. Any brownie points I'd amassed after first meeting Anne's parents were now thrown out the window. I didn't have a car, I didn't have a block of land and I lived in a flat and I'd seduced their daughter and this wouldn't last more than a few weeks and they'd have to pick up the pieces when the shit hit the fan. A likely scenario, and one shared by some of the people I knew, at least the bit about it not lasting.

Bollocks to the lot of them was our thought, and I was now in charge of wedding plans or the practical stuff. I set out to find out how you got married without all the pomp and circumstance, I knew it could be done and headed into Perth to the then registry office. From memory, I think we needed to get a licence first, then we had to book the registry office and make a time. As the date had already been set the booking of the wedding wasn't hard, thank goodness the registry office was open Saturday afternoon, two o'clock sounded fine to me.

Anne got her side of things in order, she wasn't wearing white, she wanted to have Ina as a bridesmaid and that was pretty much it. Somewhere in the frenzy of non-arrangements, the reception got lost along with my deposit. Life for Anne and me was going swimmingly, we spent our weeks apart and our weekends together. We went to the Heidelberg every Saturday night and then on to Canterbury Court and Bernies or the Sheridan for late-night coffee, it was however always the early morning. For someone who worked nights, I was at my best in the early hours of the morning and rarely in a hurry to get home, regardless of the rewards on offer.

Garry Tucker who worked for me on the milkround became my cleaning lady and cleaned my flat while Sunday lunch got cooked, his payment if I remember rightly. Phil had taught him to run on the milkround and his mother, Nancy had taught him how to clean the house, a well-trained lad.

Life was good, but these were the times of the Whitlam government and times of change and times of strikes. The dairy industry was one of the innocent victims of the strikes, mostly by the Transport Workers Union. The TWU loved a good strike and stopped work at the drop of a hat, there were the fuel strikes when the tanker drivers stopped work and the service stations ran out of fuel. That wasn't handy as I used around a tank of fuel every couple of nights. And there were the other tanker drivers who went on strike the milk tanker drivers, they were the hardest as it stopped the whole industry when that happened. Some milkmen got untreated milk direct from the farmers and ladled it out to their customers, I never went that far and took the nights off.

The 1st of June was drawing closer, I needed a best man, I didn't have many close mates so it wasn't as easy as it sounds. I decided on my Canterbury Court friend Michael, after all, he'd been there from the very beginning. It was Michael who had got the redhead out of the way and allowed me to sweep Anne off her feet.

Now, I'm quite sure that Michael was assigned to pick me up and drive me to Perth on the day. It was Michael who promise to take the photographs and he was very good in the city, he knew every corner and it was he who introduced us to Bernies and the Sheridan. I didn't hold the fact that he'd got in the way of my failed conquest of Julie, against him. He wasn't a bad bloke for a Slav.

Friday night I did the milkround as usual, with the help of the boys and managed to do a triple delivery for the Palmyra section of the round so that I could have some extra time with Anne after our wedding. No shopping on Saturday morning, straight to bed, I had an early afternoon to rise for.

I must have woken up at around one, showered shaved and smelt like a pox doctor's clerk. 'Where the fuck's Michael?' I think to myself as I pace the flat floor to a pulp. It was now too late to wait, I got in the milk truck and headed into Perth with a degree of haste and desperation. I wasn't late but I was one of the later ones to arrive for the big day.

Anne shone like a beacon in her hot pink dress, her message to her mother and the world of white weddings she found so hypocritical, a brave gesture in her world. I didn't brush up quite so well, the jacket I had bought wasn't the best fit and it showed. Everyone I wanted there was there, at least that's how I felt. Anne couldn't hold her head still as she looked around for her parents, but they weren't there. Things had to go on and the room was full of love and joy and people who we cared about, but Anne's parents weren't there and she still loved and cared about them, I think it put her on edge.

The ceremony over Michael with camera clicking leads us all up to the Palace Hotel, I empty my pockets buying drinks. Anne and I head back to the milk truck and our new home, Flat 3. 161 Holland Street, East Fremantle. We hear on the news that evening that the milk tanker drivers have gone on strike and there will be no milk deliveries on Monday. That was our honeymoon, courtesy of the TWU.

63 THE HONEYMOON IS OVER

Our honeymoon was over, the milk tanker drivers were back at work and I had milk to deliver, I also had a wife to join my business. Anne had holidays from work and something had changed around the flat. Anne had visited and most weekends lived in the flat, my flat, everything was fine back then, remembering back then was one week earlier. This week everything was different.

"Where do you keep your iron?" was the first question, "Haven't you got an ironing board?" and so it went on.

I was at great pains to explain that these things had never been necessary in the past and we didn't need them now, "Surely."

Well, surely we did and they had to be purchased posthaste or even yesterday would have done. What had I done? Just as I had plans for Anne to join my business, she had plans of running the household.

Yes, she got the iron and ironing board and after dragging her along to the bank, the accountants and the solicitor I got my business partner. I'm guessing that most twenty-year-old women would be thrilled to be business partners, Anne wasn't the least bit interested in being a business partner but went along with it.

This disinterest worked both ways, I wasn't interested in any changes to the flat which had served me well in my time there. "These curtains are filthy," was the next cab off the rank.

"Well wash 'em," is my rapid reply.

"Can we?"

"Course we can, you just bung 'em in the washing machine," I tell Anne.

I'd made the simple mistake of uttering that fateful word 'we,' Anne didn't much like the look of the community washing machine and hadn't yet used it. I must confess it was something of a monster of industrial proportions.

"I'll take the curtains down if you wash them," Anne tells me.

"You'll have to use the washing machine sooner or later," I tell her.

"You'll have to show me," she tells me.

All the curtains down I dump them in the washing machine, noting that Anne had been right, they were filthy. I take care of some bookwork in full view of the neighbourhood and allow the washing machine to do its thing, in truth I forget all about the curtains as I look out to see everything unfold in the street.

Anne reminds me of my duty and I go and check the washing machine, it has done its thing and I lift the lid, but there are no curtains to be found. 'Somebody must have stolen them,' is my first thought, 'What for?' is my second thought. I return to the flat to tell Anne, we return to the laundry and look into the empty washing machine.

"I told you," is all I could come up with.

"What are we going to do?" was Anne's effort.

We both noticed a small piece of purple material in the bottom of the washing machine and realised that the curtains must have disintegrated and gone down the drain.

In my time at the flat, I'd got to know the owner, a station owner from Norseman and I got on with him pretty well. The owner used the flat upstairs as his Perth base when in town, some may have called it the penthouse, but I prefer, the flat upstairs even though it was twice the size of mine and a bit fancy. This weekend the owner was in residence so I traipsed upstairs and knocked on his door and apologetically explained our dilemma, I had a feeling this was going to cost us.

"That's alright," he says.

"Just go and see the caretakers they have spare curtains in the storeroom."

Relieved, I return to Anne with the good news and then went and picked up replacement curtains from the caretaker. Anne didn't seem impressed when I tried to explain the moral of this story was to leave things alone in my flat. How long were we going to use the words, yours and mine, when we should have been saying ours?

Anne had to return to work after her holiday/honeymoon. It was a long trip for her each day as she worked in a shirt factory in Perth, we weren't close to the bus route and it was a good walk to Canning Highway where she caught the bus. We now saw each other mostly on weekends as I was in bed early and hadn't got home when she left for work in the morning.

This didn't last long as her employer was one of a dying race, he owned a shirt factory and things were not looking good in the ragtrade. Anne was put off and looked like being out of work, she felt she was letting me down by not working. Every day I passed a food factory and thought that perhaps Anne could get a job there, not being the shy boy I once was, I fronted the office and asked for a job for her. Now all she had to do was go to the office and get the job which the nice man had promised me.

This new job suited Anne as it was an easy walk from the flat and some evenings at least, she got to share with me. In reality, we only got the weekends together as we had before we married, and that timetable hadn't changed. Saturday morning shopping, that had changed, it now included vegetables, I got the meat on my way home from the milkround but all else remained the same. Dinner at the Heidelberg, dancing at Canterbury Court, Bernies or the Sheridan for afters, a totally irresponsible lifestyle for a young married couple who should be saving for a house. We weren't saving for a house or even a block of land, we weren't saving, we were having a good time with the time we had together.

There had been something of a 'mending of the ways' with Anne's parents but things weren't special, we visited but it was barely cordial. Anne hadn't forgiven their absence at our wedding and their trust in me needed work, add to that, we didn't have plans and weren't saving for that block of land or house. You could throw in that we lived in a den of iniquity, a flat and we still didn't have a respectable car. The more they thought this way the better I liked it but it was hard on Anne.

Our first Christmas together was fast approaching and I was a Christmas lover, Anne tended to be a little 'bah humbug.' Of course, Christmas, as it was for normal people couldn't happen that way for Anne and me. I got a day off, as you could get away with a double delivery on Christmas eve, but in real terms, the day off was Boxing Day. Christmas day lunch was in the middle of my sleep time and out of the question.

I had my usual joyous milk delivery for the customers' Christmas morning, helped by my able staff, Garry Tucker for half the round and John or David O'Sullivan for the other. It was fun as the boys returned to the truck with the spoils of our endeavours over the year, the beer which had been gifted to the customer and declared unpalatable. Fosters seemed to lead the pack, and how handy it was that stubbies and cans were now in vogue. Regardless, it's the thought that counts and I loved the thought.

Anne and I shared a rather bland Christmas and when I arose from my bed in the early afternoon we hear on the radio that Darwin had been all but destroyed by a tropical cyclone. We sat on the edge of the bed and realised how lucky we were to be having an uneventful Christmas.

64 VALENTINE'S DAY

Anne never seemed to complain about my working hours but it must have been trying for her sometimes. Working midnight to dawn six days a week had now become second nature to me, the other milkmen worked similar hours, although I did more than the others at Masters Fremantle. I had the biggest milkround and an ego to match, which didn't make me the most popular. Being popular didn't matter much when you worked from midnight to dawn alone, as I was doing once the kids were back at school.

I had one companion on that dreaded shift, my radio. I had sought solace from the radio since childhood and loved music. The disc jockeys on the graveyard shift seemed to have an affinity with the other workers who worked this shift, we became friends without even meeting. These guys played all the right music from melancholy to rock and roll and the plain eery with the cello on Harry Chapin's Taxi leading the pack, I became a mad Harry Chapin fan. The eery sound of the cello at three in the morning should have made you worry about what was out there in the darkness, but it was the right sound for that time of the morning.

My favourite disc jockey, or the one I heard the most was, Graham Bowra on Radio 6PM, the radio station of the day. Graham had a timetable that suited mine, about three-thirty he had a toilet break, I presume and played a comedy tape, Bill Cosby or Bob Newhart fitted my bill fine. I took my break then and sipped on a Masters iced coffee, it was awful stuff but a change from plain milk.

From time to time, Graham ran a phone-in competition for some prize or other. As a general rule, I ignored these competitions as I was never near a phone box and the prize was most unspectacular. Valentine's Day 1975 was different, I wanted to win this prize.

In 1975 Valentine's Day was not widely celebrated in Western Australia, I remembered it from my time in England where it was quite big. It can't have been that big as I never got a card or had the intestinal fortitude to send one. Graham's prize this night was a red rose and a box of Red Tulip chocolates delivered to your Valentine.

I now have a feeling that Graham gave away more than one of these prizes as I was delivering milk in Palmyra when I won mine and that was in the latter part of the milkround. And the first time I'd been close enough to a phone box to ring and even then it involved speeding, but I won the prize and gave Graham, Anne's work details. This was the most romantic thing I'd done in our seven and a half months of marriage.

I was so chuffed with my effort, I could hardly sleep when I got home to bed. When I rose from my eventual slumber, ate and did my bookwork, it was with the deepest restraint on my part that I didn't jump in the truck and pick Anne up from work. I just sat patiently and waited for my reward to come to me. When Anne eventually got home, she must have come the long way home because she was late. I, sitting and smiling at the table was confronted by an angry woman, "Don't you ever do that to me again," I was convincing told.

"What's all this about anyway?" The rose and chocolates are now hurled on the table, "I was so embarrassed at work when this bloke turned up with these."

I'd stuffed up good and proper. Anne had never heard of Valentine's Day and I hadn't softened the blow by presenting her with anything the previous year. Poor Anne had been teased all afternoon about what lay instore for her when she got home. My time as a romantic was brief.

Anne and I never made plans, we did things, and bought what we wanted when we wanted and we didn't consciously save for anything. I was making good money and Anne was bringing in a wage, we lived well and knew one day we would look at buying a house, but there was no plan. We had one day, looked at a house in Stock Road Palmyra but for some reason or other not gone any further, it was on a busy road so that may have scuttered that deal. Anne's parents couldn't understand how we lived and hints of house buying came thick and fast. I was getting bored with the game I'd been playing with them and they had slowed down on the house buying front. It was perhaps time to show I could ameliorate and make the move they so wanted us to make.

The weather was plain and winter was with us and I sat down with the Sunday Times and looked at the real estate classified advertisements. Well, we wanted to live somewhere handy, for Anne's work and the milkround, Palmyra, East Fremantle, both a little pricy I thought. There was a house in South Fremantle at a reasonable price and one in Hamilton Hill, I knew that one, it was on the milkround. It had once housed a gorgeous blonde who'd invited me in to talk about being in business a couple of years earlier, it was a nice house, in my eyes anyway. The talk about going into business was quite innocent, her husband was and she wanted to know if it was a good idea, me being in business and all, I was twenty-three. Well, that ended in divorce and the house was up for sale.

We checked out the South Fremantle house first, it was cheaper. I didn't even get out of the milk truck, "I'm not living in this hole," I put on record to Anne, as we took off to Hamilton Hill. I hadn't been referring to the house in South Fremantle but the closed-in nature of the place. We both liked the house in Hamilton Hill, I returned to the truck and got my cheque book and put down a deposit, signed the papers and left the cretin selling the house somewhat confused.

I now had to get finance from my building society, I knew the bank was a no go as I'd tried there a couple of years earlier. I was with the Commonwealth Bank and they had the best interest rates but strict conditions, twelve hundred in a savings account or twenty-four hundred in a cheque account over twelve months. I had our money in the Home Building Society as they paid better interest. I remember when I'd gone to the bank for money and the bank-johnny had come back to tell me in a rather embarrassed state that I didn't qualify, but he was amazed at how much I turned over.

I got the finance from the building society and a cheque to top up my deposit, we had a house and even though we had the finance the process of it going through was over a month. We were both impatient but never thought of looking at furniture or anything like that, we lived in a furnished flat, why on earth would we need furniture?

65 MOVING TO NUMBER 42

I got the phone call from the real estate agent telling me we could move into the house even though it wasn't officially finalised. This worked out just right for me as our rent arrears and our bond were around on equal footing. I paid the rent monthly and ran into arrears before the next monthly payment, unconventional but as a long-standing tenant accepted by the agent. I quickly gave notice of my impending departure from flat 3 and got new milk bills printed with the new phone number and address, I was ready to go.

We were to move into the house on Friday, we had the keys and we were ready to go. It was about now that I realised we didn't have a fridge or a bed or any furniture at all. Now, was Friday morning, I'd seen this place in South Perth that sold secondhand furniture and when I awoke from my slumber on Friday afternoon, I headed out there.

This place that sold secondhand furniture was strangely called South Perth Supermarket, to me, a supermarket sold groceries but not this one. This emporium sold everything I needed: bed, sideboard, wardrobe, table and chairs, fridge and a twin tub washing machine, a whole house full of furniture and accessories as far as I could see and we managed to get it on the back of the milk truck in one load.

This was my lucky day, as Briggsy who lived on the corner and had done a couple of shifts on the milkround, was around to welcome me into Hamilton Hill and gave me a hand to unload and get the furniture into the house. Anne came home to the flat and we cleaned up there and moved house. I usually collected money on Friday afternoon but this week it had to wait till Monday. Anne was quite happy with the furniture I'd bought, perhaps not thrilled, but happy to be in our own house.

Usual double delivery Friday night, the boys excited that I was now a Hamilton Hill resident. I dropped them off when we finished the round and I had to remind myself that I didn't have to go back to East Fremantle, just round the corner and I was home. Anne now went shopping on her own on Saturday mornings, she didn't drive so must have taken the bus into Fremantle and a taxi home. I was knackered after the excitement of the move and the effort it took so ate and hit the hay ready for a good sleep.

No sooner had I laid my head on the pillow, the phone rang, 'Who the hell can that be?' I thought. 'I haven't put out the bills with the new number yet, must be somebody for the old owner.'

"Hello," I said as I picked up the phone.

"This is Gordon Howman from thirty-nine Helen Street, Hamilton Hill, you left me one pint of milk short this morning."

"Oh I'm sorry about that," I lie, and going through my head is the thought that I'm going to have to take one bottle of milk all the way to Hamilton Hill for this fucking moron.

"Do you want me to drop that bottle off for you?" I politely reply.

"Yeah, if you don't mind," he answers.

Yeah, well I did mind but the customer comes first, the death of David O'Sullivan can wait but I'll get to him later, David had delivered the wrong order.

I was in something of a haze as I put the phone down, how did this bloke I'd never heard of get my phone number? Where's thirty-nine Helen Street? I now used names for customers not, street numbers. My head is a blur as I dress and stagger to the fridge for that one bottle of milk, and then it dawns on me, I'm in Hamilton Hill and I'm at forty-two Helen Street and this moron is in the house across the road and he's rung me on the bloody telephone because he's one bottle of milk short.

I laughed to myself and wandered across the road to meet my new neighbour. I think this bloke wrote the script for this adventure because he seemed to like a chat and was in no hurry to let me go home to bed. I was still scratching my head as I walked back over the road, I couldn't believe that someone had used the telephone to communicate over thirty yards.

When we had settled into our new house, well, been there a week, we got a phone call from the previous owner's, let's say 'woman.' She was looking for our rent, I'd been warned we may be expected to pay rent until the settlement was finalised but thought little of it. I knew this good woman, as I was her milkman too and collected her milk money from her hairdresser's shop. I'd always thought she was quite nice, and perhaps she was, but she liked a dollar too. We had to begrudgingly pay rent until the settlement was through.

I think it took three weeks for the settlement day to come around, this may have been the result of us having finance from a building society or just the way things were done. Obviously, things were done at a very high level for this transaction, because I was asked to attend a solicitors office in Fremantle and 'bring your chequebook.' The office I attended with my chequebook was that of Unmack, Frank and Cullen, I think in that order, it was one of the grottiest offices I had ever visited. I was even less impressed when they had taken a page from my chequebook, but at least, no more rent for the nice lady.

I now had my own garden to play in, I was rather looking forward to that, a Sunday morning job. Some of the trees had to go, what could I grow? Well, I knew I could grow anything but I had to work things out, the seasons and such. There wasn't much in the way of a vegetable garden, a piece fenced off at the bottom of the block that had been a chook yard with grapevines and citrus trees and of course heaps of fennel (Which I then thought was a weed.) and a cape lilac tree that had to go. Here I was with a garden and no time to spend in it, I made time and slowly got rid of the trees I disliked, most of them.

I got rid of the trees how I'd seen them got rid of in the country, simply cut them down and stacked the branches around the stump and burn them. This was not always to the delight of our neighbours who started to think I was mad. Briggsy, the lad on the corner cut my lawn, he was better at that than he was at delivering milk, he'd cut his hand one night and that was the end of him for milk delivery.

Life was looking good in Hamilton Hill, we maintained our frivolous lifestyle even though we were now serious homeowners. I was starting to be a little dissatisfied with what I was doing, I seemed to be working hard and making good money but I was locked into long hours and no growth in my business. I was seeing my business stagnate and along with it me, I was tired and looking for more, I was looking for something else but I didn't know what. To get that something else I'd have to sell the milkround.

66 TIME TO MOVE ON

Our first Christmas in our new house was looming, Anne had her holidays and life went on as normal for me, work sleep, work and Saturday nights on the town with Anne. Holiday life for Anne must have been pretty boring, with me coming home in the morning and going to bed alone, leaving her with the day to herself. One of these lonely days she just took off, unbeknown to sleeping beauty.

When I rose from my slumber around two, I found myself alone, well that was normal but Anne should have been there, she was on holiday. Anne eventually returned from her travels, all smiles and happiness.

"Where the hell have you been?" a disgruntled husband asks.

"Oh I've been to Vic Park and bought us some furniture," she replies.

"But we've got furniture," I reply.

"Yeah, but I wanted something nice," well that was a putdown, as I thought what we had was nice.

The next day a truck turns up and unloads; a lounge suite, table and chairs, a bed and a china cabinet. I had no idea what we were going to do with the lounge suite and china cabinet as we'd never needed them before, we sat at the kitchen table and didn't have anything to put in the china cabinet. I had to confess I was very impressed with Anne's purchases but kept it to myself. It was now my turn to buy, I bought a fridge, a big modern Kelvinator, we now had a whole new house full of furniture that our lifestyle didn't need.

This Christmas we put ourselves out and had lunch with Anne's family, things were starting to warm and I got on with Anne's dad at least. I discovered that Anne's mother wasn't the best cook and in years to come, we should avoid having Christmas lunch there. This was one of those occasions when both Anne's brother and sister were at the same table, it was a bloody 'boast fest' who had done more than the other and who knew something better than the other and poor Anne tried to throw her two bobs worth in too.

I could cope with Michelle, Anne's sister, but her brother, John (Who Anne idolised.) was too much for me. Anne was most disappointed when on the way home, I told her I thought her brother was, "A fucking idiot." I thought it was pretty fair that I could cast aspersions on a member of her family as none of them rated me, or so it appeared to me.

Life strode on into 1976 and my dissatisfaction with my milkround life was starting to get to me, but what would I do if and when I sold? Well, the consequences of making a move without a plan had never worried me before, I advertised my milkround in the Sunday Times at what I'd paid for it, the going rate at the time.

I sat by the phone on Sunday morning waiting for it to ring, it didn't. I was disappointed, as I was expecting to be taking a prospective buyer for my milkround out with me that night. This was a time of pretty high employment, so there weren't many mugs like me looking to buy a job, as I had done a few years before. I buckled back down to work and accepted that I'd be a milk vendor for some time yet.

I'd set my mind to moving on, to where, I knew not, but I knew I had to move on. Milkrounds were dying, I was the only milkman delivering to households six days a week, I couldn't physically do a mid-week double delivery on my own and it was a school day for my workforce. There was no cheap labour for easing my workload and no buyer for my milkround. I bit the bullet and advertised my milkround for a third of the going rate, no instant takers, that told me, the price was too low or it was not a salable business. I backed both theories and became a little despondent, till Tuesday came around, I got the call I'd been waiting for, a young bloke who seemed as keen as mustard.

"Oh, I can't make it tonight, I've promised my girlfriend…" he tells me as I offer him the chance of a lifetime, that of going out on the milkround with me tonight.

"How about Thursday?"

I put some bills out on Thursdays now so it isn't that convenient, but I agree. I know this bloke is a dud, for a start he's promised his girlfriend and everybody knows they're no good to an aspiring milkman.

And Thursday comes around, I'm the best judge of a man ever. A rather too well dressed bloke introduces himself as I load up the truck, he doesn't look like work. If I'd had any sense of reflection, I would have remembered that was how I presented myself on my first night with Phil Tucker, I should have been more forgiving.

This scrawny looking specimen in his long pants, with his loquacious nature, didn't seem right for the job. It was pretty obvious that this bloke was no slouch because he told me he wasn't. Night one over, and I'm pretty sure I'm not going to see this bloke again, but I can't shake him off. As the nights drift by and I learn more, this bloke should have been a teacher, he has so much knowledge to impart on the unsuspecting, I learn that a bloke in the office at Masters Dairy is a family friend and put his father onto this milkround. "Perfect for that lad of yours if he can't get a job," I imagine is how the conversation went.

I can't believe my luck, I can't get rid of this bloke, I've got a buyer. I take abit longer than Phil did with me, to mention the long pants and how I'd been told, "I've never seen a milkman yet who wore long pants."

"Oh, I've got to wear long pants because I've got nobbly knees." He must have had the words lined up for me they came out so quickly.

"Nobody sees your knees in the middle of the night," I counter, but left it at that. As the days of learning roll on he drives to the depot in a brand new Holden one tonner, 'Wow he's got the kit,' I rather enviously think to myself. And then along comes his mate, employee, to learn the ropes, this bloke can afford a full-time employee and a new truck, how dumb was I?

Change-over day comes and it was normal practice for the buyer of the milkround to buy the debt, or the monies owing to the former owner, not this cretin, he digs his heels in there, I've got to collect my own debts. At this stage, I'm only too glad to be rid of the milkround but it means I have to squeeze into the new milk truck every night for a week to collect the money and he gets my free labour and advice. The only money he gets is cash sales, this bloke was far too smart for me, he's got wages to pay at the end of this week and will have to draw them from the bank and his pay too.

I now moved into semi-holiday mode, I went round and collected from my usual collection customers and said my sorrowful goodbyes, I was going to be missed I was told by many, what was I going to do? That was a question I couldn't answer, I had no idea. The biggest farewell was to the mother of the O'Sullivan boys, my loyal staff over the years now growing up. Mrs O'Sullivan had been a good customer in her home, but it extended further, she was the canteen lady at Saint Brendan's School and introduced the kids to chocolate flavoured milk and orange juice delivered by her milkman.

67 MORE CAREFUL PLANNING

On my collection round up of money, I got talking to one of my lesser customers, lesser as not noteworthy in any way. He was an Italian, who seemed to dominate his wife, but didn't they all? This bloke sells real estate and suggests it may be the life for me, "Would I like to give it the try?" He asks me in his disjointed English. I'm doing nothing so agree to spend a morning with him, "Seeing what it about."

Well, one morning with an Italian real estate salesman tells me that it's about sleaze, but I go along in discomfort. I'm told I should get my hair 'done' at the best hairdressers, I should own a nice car, I should wear a nice suit and the coup de gras, I should canvas all the people I know, especially friends. It took me no time at all to see that this wasn't the job for me. I retreated without much grace and went on my merry way, I wasn't much closer to my new life, but one option had been crossed off the list of none.

I guess the crunch had to come, I had to visit my accountant to get our tax done. I told him that I had sold the milkround and was looking for something else, "Perhaps I could open a shop somewhere, selling jeans or something like that," I may have blurted out in a rather casual manner. As I uttered the words, the idea seemed a good one, people were making a squillion selling jeans and everyone wore them, well, I didn't have a pair but what the hell. "You could go up to Phoenix Shopping Centre there seem to be plenty of empty shops there," the accountant suggests.

I knew nothing about jeans, other than they were made of denim and everybody but me wore them, but I decided I'd open a jeans shop somewhere. On my accountant's advice, I went to Phoenix Shopping Centre to look for a shop. I'd never set foot in this shopping centre in my life, even though it was just a couple of miles from our house, we shopped in Fremantle or anywhere but Phoenix Park.

Well, the accountant had one thing right, there were plenty of empty shops. There were also some shops that were open or had lights on and what appeared to be someone sitting in them, it could have been a dummy of some kind, but no, that would have looked too lifelike. It was mid-morning and no one stirred, I ventured to ask someone where the centre manager's office was, I was given rather strange directions and almost gave up on my search.

I did find the office, it was conveniently located just beyond the rubbish bins and gave Unmack, Frank and Cullen a run for their money in the grotty office stakes. The office smelt of inexpensive perfume and housed a lady in her late thirties, dressed to seduce. I explained I was looking to open a jeans shop and would one be available there. She told me there was already a jean shop there, I hadn't seen it but I hadn't seen much. The shopping centre manager wasn't in at the moment but would I like to make an appointment to see him. Well, I ventured to say, "Yes," isn't it strange how people wrestle with one-word answers? An appointment was made.

I keep my appointment and the centre manager is late. The lady, the centre manager's secretary, is a Pom and obviously likes Poms and tries to get me into a pommy conversation and finds it's a waste of time. She tells me how busy the centre manager is and, and he walks in the door, "Tom, is it?" he says, "Ian Armstrong," he introduces himself and shakes a good hand. Ian gets right into things, they've got a jean shop of sorts, what do I know of the industry? How much money do I have? I give all the wrong answers, except for the money one, I had a quid to invest in this reckless venture. That was all that mattered, but perhaps this bloke gave a damn. He told me he had a shop, he had four or five, but I should really look into things. He directed me to a bloke in one of the other centres he managed, I should talk to him he told me. The ball was rolling.

I went to see Ian's recommended jean shop owner and had my blinkered eyes opened, he sells ladies clothes and he isn't gay. I then realised I too was going to sell ladies clothes and I wasn't gay, I discover that selling womens' clothes is what this business is about. At this stage, it had never dawned on me that women wore more clothes than men. I was heading into this venture knowing nothing of consequence. Des, the bloke Ian had sent me to was a full bottle, like me he had got into this business without much knowledge of it, albeit more than me. He had learnt by mistake and knew all the pitfalls and was willing to impart his knowledge to me.

I now got serious and was soon signed up for the shop, it had been a ladies clothing shop before, a chain operation, they couldn't afford to keep it going and had pulled out, as had a few other chains. As such it had lights, carpet, a backroom and two display windows. There was the framework for changerooms and bloody awful floral wallpaper. When you rent a shop in a shopping centre, you get the walls and a sink, so I was getting a pretty good deal, not that it had been given to me by the shopping centre, it had been left by the previous tenant.

I had to cover the gaudy wallpaper with an upbeat colour, I'd seen that Jeans West in Fremantle had bright blue walls. As my shop was to be something of a knock-off of theirs I went with that sort of colour, Peak-a-Blue it was called. Wow, did that shop start to change? And now I had people looking to see what I was up to. The lady who owned the 'sort of jeans shop,' was not happy, my arrogance and bravado came to the fore and I cared not. The façade of the shop was tiled with orangey-yellow tiles, to match the awful wallpaper I guessed. I painted them a gloss navy blue, I was breaking all the rules, you couldn't paint tiles, I knew what I wanted and I worked accordingly.

While I was painting and generally been noticed, I set out to stock this new shop. To my amazement, I discovered you can't just go out and stock a jeans shop. The first thing I discovered was that nobody wanted to sell you anything, the second was if they did, they didn't have anything to sell you. Thirdly, if they did have something to sell you, chances are it wasn't worth having. In amongst this confusion I was learning that the clothing business is not all glamour and men dominate the business and are very much men, their profanity was up there with mine, I could get on with these blokes.

Jeans and accessories aren't just pulled off a shelf, in most cases, they needed to be ordered six months in advance, and credit, you didn't get any of that. With my persistence and my chequebook, I managed to drag enough stock together to open the shop, but it wasn't easy.

I knocked together some changeroom walls with plywood, bought some new rotunda stands, a secondhand counter and a cash register. I bought a few metres of denim material, it was much easier to buy than jeans. With the material, Anne sewed up change room curtains. I got stick-on mirrors for the changerooms from Alco we were all ready to go.

I have used 'we' there and perhaps I shouldn't, the lady who had been keeping me the last few months, Anne, had very little to do with this project. Anne had made the changeroom curtains but other than that this had been my baby and Anne had little interest in it. She was, however, the support around which I worked and continued to keep the household going whilst I chased dreams.

68 THE BEST LAID PLANS OF MICE AND MEN

The sign was on the façade, polystyrene letters, to which I'd glued aluminium foil and glued up there. Tom Stones Jeans it whispered, it could have been bigger, it was inexpensive. I'd put what I thought were the finishing touches to the shop on Friday afternoon, adding a denim coloured bean bag for me to sit in. Sitting in this bean bag would be a new experience for me, I'd never felt the urge to sit in a bean bag before. The whole thing about this shop was to be, that it was cool and hip, two things I knew nothing about.

Monday the 8th November 1976, I got to the shopping centre early and opened the doors and flicked on the lights. To my horror, the first thing I saw was, two of the changeroom mirrors had somehow fallen off the wall and lay broken on the floor. I was devastated but got over the devastation by cleaning up the mess and high tailing it over the hill to Alco for two new mirrors. It seems that these stick-on mirrors weren't designed to be stuck on painted wallpaper.

With the new mirrors in place, I opened the shop a second time, just before nine o'clock the official opening time. The first person to enter the shop wasn't a customer, but the manager of the ANZ bank that was situated opposite my shop. He introduced himself and wished me luck, chances were he was touting for business. I take to my bean bag as there doesn't seem to be any customers around. I immediately realised that the purchase of the bean bag was a bad idea, it didn't present comfort and I may as well have laid on the floor as I couldn't see over the counter.

As the day wore on, I started to get uneasy, not only had I not had a customer, no one had set foot in the shop except for the ANZ bank manager. It was around four o'clock when a young blonde girl came into the shop and looked at some jeans, was I excited? Well, I shouldn't have been, as she didn't even try on the jeans, she did however ask me for a job, just Saturday mornings. I gave her the job without hesitation, as she was pretty and would fit the image I wanted to portray. Not long after she returned with her father and I was the one being checked out, I passed.

It was now four-thirty and I had an employee but was yet to have a customer. And then it happened, two ladies, and I use the term to be polite, entered my shop. I must admit they didn't look like likely customers and they had been drinking. There was one, older than the other and she was the leader, going through the shop with gay abandon, they unloaded a fusillade on me verbally tearing me apart.

I thought I was a man of the world and had seen abit, but these ladies ripped me to shreds, I was a blithering idiot by the time they turned to leave the shop. And as she did reach the door, the older woman picked up a pair of jeans I was selling cheap to attract customers, (That hadn't worked.) 'They're never going to fit her.' I thought. She held them up gave them an examination (These ladies wore Fremantle Hospital uniforms so I'm sure I've used the right word there.) and said, "I'll have these." I didn't want to sell them to her after what they'd put me through and knowing they wouldn't fit her, but I did, my first customer. I think she knew, as I had trouble working the cash register, as I handed over the bag, she smiled. 'God I hope she never comes back,' I thought. I may have managed another customer before five-thirty but it wasn't a day for celebration.

My dreams may not have been in tatters but they had been sorely tested on my first day. I had to go home and tell Anne about my disastrous day. I gave Anne the bad news and she took it well, perhaps she was thinking that I'd give up on this dream and get a 'proper job.'

We'd had the news some time ago that we were to have visitors from England. Dad was now retired and Mum and Dad had made the monumental decision to come and visit their son and his new wife in Australia. I say monumental, as Mum and Dad had never been very far in their lives, they had certainly never left the British Isles. I think this visit had got lost in my shop dreams and I'd thought no more of it. The end of November was the designated time and that was now two weeks away.

I was still driving around in my milk truck, it had been handy for carrying things for the shop, but I couldn't see Mum and Dad riding on the back of it. I had to get a car and I was now tied to the shop, for some reason I had to buy a new car, easiest I guess. The bloke in the shop across the way said he knew someone who would give me a good deal. And so a new car was purchased sight unseen and the bloke across the way got his cut.

I'd written to Mum from the moment I got my first job in Australia, weekly for a start and later the weeks went out probably to monthly, but I wrote regularly. We got the odd photograph and to me, Mum always seemed the same she had been when I left home. You've sprung me, I was a 'Mummy's Boy,' I hadn't got on with Dad since Cox Bank was sold. In my eyes, Mum was the stronger of the two. When I picked them up from the airport, I was taken aback to see Dad taking the lead role, Mum had aged much more than I expected. Dad, who always seemed to be sick when I was young, looked hale and hearty. Mum and Dad were no longer the couple I'd left in England and I was no longer the boy they'd farewelled eight years earlier.

I was at the shop all day and Anne continued to work so Mum and Dad had to survive on their own during the day. They loved Anne, I was a different proposition, I was no longer a Mummy's Boy, I no longer fitted into Mum's mould. I got on with Dad, I showed him my garden and he was as proud as punch that I had a vegetable garden. Dad even went as far as saying that he couldn't grow cauliflowers like mine, this is a man who had never paid me a compliment in my life. But yes he did, I remember the day I left England he said, "Tha's doing right thing lad."

Saturday came and we had Mum and Dad with us, Saturday was Anne's shopping day and now we went to the shops together, me to work and Anne to shop. Mum and Dad tagged along, they hadn't seen my shop yet, and to be honest I don't think they were in any great hurry to see it. When they cast eyes on my pride and joy they thought I had done alright. There was something wrong with these old buggers and for the life of me I couldn't work out what.

Anne took them through the supermarket and had to fight them off at the checkout as they wanted to pay. That done Mum, Dad and Anne disappeared, this had me somewhat perplexed as in those days there weren't many places to disappear to in Phoenix Shopping Centre. They were gone for what seemed like an age, when they finally return they were led by Anne with a shopping trolley loaded with a television. My first response was, "What's that fucking thing for?"

"It's a television, your Dad bought it."

"What for?" is my reply.

Anne goes on to tell me that Mum and Dad have been missing the television. So that's what was wrong with them, it had never dawned on me.

We didn't have television, it wasn't that we couldn't afford it, we just never had one. I had worked nights and went to bed early so what would we have a television for? This telly was a black and white job, in 1976 colour televisions were coming into vogue and you could pick up a cheap black and white one at the Phoenix record shop, which Dad did. I couldn't believe that my parents found it difficult to live without a television set, I'd had to spend my childhood looking at other people's televisions. It wasn't until Marion's husband, Fred had come on the scene (He was a television salesman.) that there was a television at Ivy Garth.

How humble my parents were, I felt a twinge of shame that I hadn't thought that when I left England they had spent their leisure time in front of a shiny new television set, the only luxury I ever saw them indulge in. Now they were visiting their son in Australia and had to go out and buy a shabby secondhand telly to entertain themselves.

69 UNTO US

Having Mum and Dad was great, I took them for long country drives and showed them our countryside, they were in awe. They got to meet Anne's parents and thought they were nice and simply loved Joe's orchard and the fresh fruit, they'd never seen anything like it. We had Christmas with them and it was time for them to leave. Although they missed my sisters and their grandchildren, I felt sure they weren't ready to go but the flights were booked. There were no promises of a return visit and I was sad to see them go.

After Mum and Dad had left it was time for Anne and me to get back to what was a new normal, with the upheaval of having my parents around we hadn't got into a routine with the shop. The shop was struggling and we were living off Anne's wage. I was putting all my effort into the shop and getting, very little reward, it would be fair to say that I'd made a misjudgement when I took on the shop. It wasn't in my nature to give up on my dream so I persevered trying everything I could think of, most of the other shopkeepers just sat and waited for customers.

It was around now that Anne felt she may be pregnant, a visit to the doctor confirmed her suspicions. We were happy about this, albeit it was going to be a strain on our finances when Anne gave up work. True to our usual form, we didn't care, we kept quiet and carried on with our irresponsible lives. We still went to Canterbury Court and enjoyed ourselves while we could, knowing a new child in our lives would change things. I think Anne was three months pregnant when we let the cat out of the bag and we remained the most excited of anyone.

All was going well, I thought, I was no expert on matters of pregnancy. At about six months, Anne's visit to the doctor revealed that she was suffering from high blood pressure, she was forced to give up work. Not the best news for our finances but something we'd have to live with. I'd changed banks sometime earlier than this and was afforded a loan which allowed us some freedom from financial worry. The shop still laboured.

Anne's blood pressure became a problem and towards the end of August, she was placed in Woodside Maternity Hospital in East Fremantle. After a time at Woodside, she was taken by ambulance to King Edward Maternity Hospital in Subiaco. Apart from hospital visits I'd had no part in any of this, having babies was womens' work as far as I was concerned and Anne was very capable of looking after things.

On the 1st September 1977, Thomas James Watson was born, although I wasn't much in the childbirth department, I was sure as hell going to be the best dad in the world to our new son. As soon as I finished at the shop I raced to King Edward Hospital and went to see Anne and our new son. Anne first, I went into the ward and almost fainted, Anne had tubes going everywhere and looked like shit. I was shattered, somewhere through all those tubes Anne managed to smile and say, "Have you seen him? He's beautiful."

"Bugger him, how are you? You look like shit," was the best I could do.

Anne assured me she was alright, but for the life of me, I couldn't believe her. I eventually went into another ward and saw our son, he was beautiful, Anne was right.

It hadn't been an easy birth, epidural and all the sordid details I didn't want to hear. Anne had to stay in hospital awhile, I took advantage of this and got into decorating the kitchen, a surprise for when she got home. I leant how to change nappies and how to bring up wind and general mothercraft while visiting Anne and Thomas in hospital, I wanted to be part of that sort of thing. Just before Anne came home I got this strange call from a doctor, a psychologist, saying he was a little worried about Anne and I should get in touch with him if she had any problems after she left the hospital. I couldn't understand this call, what sort of problems was Anne going to have? She was going to be a great mum.

The day finally came and Anne was to come home with Thomas, we had nappies, a cot and bedding but little else. The journey home involved topping up on what we needed from after-hours chemists shops. On our arrival home I was met with a fusillade of abuse. The place was a mess, the decorating I'd started was still in its infancy, with a ladder surrounded by stripped wallpaper the most obvious flaw. Tears were called in, and I had to make things right in double-quick time. After a hastily prepared meal and some rapid clearing up by me, we retired to bed. Anne was breastfeeding Thomas and so had no relief from nighttime feeding duties but I could at least change the odd nappy.

In business, nothing stops for babies and so I had to attend to business, this was something that Anne and I had agreed on when we married, or perhaps I'd pointed out when we got married. I had a shop to run and a living to make, I wasn't making a very good job at either at that time. This meant that Anne was left at home to fend for herself if there was a problem, I was stuck at the shop and Anne would have to sort it out herself. This didn't worry me as she had always shown she was very capable. Things went fine, in my eyes at least.

I felt a day at New Norcia would be good for Anne and me and give me a chance to show off my newborn son to the Halligans. Since I'd got the shop, I'd had more chances to escape the city and visit Dennis and Vivienne. I could work with Dennis and Anne could be entertained by Vivienne and I could return to the city refreshed.

It was a great day showing off Thomas, Anne was a little coy about breastfeeding Thomas in front of Gavin, now a growing boy. To my amazement, Vivienne (Often on the prudish side.) stated quite openly, "He'll have to get used to it one day, may as well be now." I did get a bollocking from Vivienne when she heard about the state of the house on Anne's return from hospital.

Everything seemed to be going swimmingly, showing off our handsome son gave Anne almost as much joy as it gave me. Anne was driven by this showing off and determined to take Thomas and show him off to her old workmates at Anchor Foods. It's a fair walk from our place to Anchor Foods but Anne took it on with Thomas in a pram and pulled it off. I found out about this when I got home, I thought she may have done a bit much and told her so. That night wasn't good, Thomas cried and Anne couldn't sleep and I tried to appease both wife and child without much success, none of us slept.

By the next evening, Anne was in Heathcote Psychiatric Hospital and I had a baby to look after, we were on our own. I was lost, I had a baby to look after and a shop to run and nowhere to go. To say I felt a little down would have been an understatement. Anne had this good friend who had helped her when she was younger, Dot Ponton, an older woman, but a really good friend to Anne and a motherly figure to her too. Anne was closer to her than her mother, not a big call in those times. Dot was the only person I could turn to, the only person close that I could trust with Thomas. I bundled up all his things and dumped him on Dot.

I now had to face Anne in the Psychiatric Hospital, she was a fucking mess, soaked in breast milk and decidedly untidy for a woman who had pride in her appearance. I spoke to a blank face, a hollow face, someone I'd never met before, a total stranger. Anything Anne said was meaningless, anything I said was pointless, I held my nerve but I soon had to leave, but I had nowhere to go. Home would no longer be home without Anne and Thomas. I left that place of coldness and terror, sat in my car and cried and cried, I didn't dry my eyes, I stopped crying and drove to an empty house. I rang her parents and told them what was going on and I rang Vivienne and the tears returned and I went to bed.

I got up the next morning and went to the shop and faced the world knowing that I had that visit to make that evening. That visit, where someone would turn the giant key to what they called, a ward and let me in to see my wife who was now a total stranger.

70 LIFE GOES ON, FOR SOME

I thought I had Thomas' care in hand after dumping him with Dot. Although I'd set out to be the best dad, I had no idea about babies and their needs. Thomas now had to go from breast milk to baby formula, this wasn't as easy as it may sound to a simple new father. He didn't fare well in this process and Dot took him to Princess Margaret Children's Hospital. I think she told the staff there that she wasn't equipped to look after a baby, as her child-rearing days were behind her. The upshot of this was that Thomas was taken to Lady Lawley Cottage in Mosman Park and cared for there.

This was something of a weight off my now sagging shoulders and convenient for the continuing father-son relationship. I was now a full-time visitor, I saw Thomas in the morning, sometimes was allowed to give him a bottle and always a cuddle, it was such a positive way to start the day. I spent the days in, what can only be described as an existence, going through the motions of being a shopkeeper.

The evenings were spent with Anne, a few minutes of serious talk that went nowhere and meeting her new friends who were as mad as her. It would be wrong to say it was cold because Anne could never be cold, not even on her worst days, and these were they. After a few days, I got used to going through that locked door and into another world, of men and women walking around in a zombie pose. This walk was to become, what I called the 'nutcase walk,' they all had it and it showed the patients from the staff.

Leaving Anne, was sadly too easy, we hugged, a pathetic hug and I called a nurse to be released. Once back in the real world it took up to five minutes to regain your sanity, you couldn't just drive off because it wasn't safe. Going home was hollow, my bed was empty, my head was a blur. I had to write to Mum and report how things were going, but I couldn't. Our frivolous lifestyle was coming back to bite me on the arse.

The friends we had, had been casual weekend acquaintances and frittered away as our lives changed. The Tuckers who had been stalwarts in my milkround days had bought a pub in Laverton, Phyllis had been deserted by her husband Don and taken off with someone else. Life without Anne, because I no longer had her, was unbearably lonely. And we had done the wrong thing when we married, Anne's parents were nowhere to be seen. I can only imagine that this was our own doing.

I got a phone call early on Wednesday 16th November 1977, I answered with my usual "Hello."

"Mr Watson?" the caller queried.

"Yes," I replied. I could have put the phone down then, I knew what this was.

"We're terribly sorry but your son Thomas died early this morning."

There was a pause and the voice continued to explain that Thomas had died of a cot death, Sudden Infant Death Syndrome. It was now my turn to be cold, not that the caller had been, but I'd somehow guessed what this phone call was about so the shock was gone. What did I have to do?

"If you come down here, someone will be here to help you with things," I was told.

I now went through the motions with the social worker, I suppose she was, a visit to the mortuary, given the name of an understanding funeral director, and left to it. I went to work in the shop and my existence that day was somewhat feebler than the other days that had been merely existences.

That evening I had to break the news to Anne, she was her, now usual non-plus self but read my face and said, "Has somebody died? It isn't Dad, is it?"

I assured her it wasn't her father and went on to tell her it was Thomas. She cried, but they weren't real tears and I cried because they weren't real tears from the real Anne. This visit didn't last as long as it probably should have, but it was long enough.

Life can be a bitch, I now had to tell Anne's parents, it was so easy to pick up the phone and dial the number. But speaking the words was almost too much, I don't know how long it took me to get the words out but there was hollow emotion on the other end of the phone. Well, there was nothing they could do, and it's what they did.

I had more of these phone calls to make, I got more emotion from these calls. When I got to Dennis and Vivienne Halligan, it was still just as hard to say the words "Thomas died this morning." Vivienne was the first person of those I called to ask, "Are you alright?" Of course, through my tears, I said "Yes." I don't know how long it took me to write the letter to Mum and Dad, but it was on a wet aerogramme.

The day of the funeral came around, I had to get someone to mind the shop as business goes on, Bev who helped Saturday morning had a sister who fitted the bill. I had to pick Anne up from Heathcote and take her home and dress her in something reasonable, the easiest of my duties. It was then on to Subiaco and the funeral directors and on again to Karrakatta Cemetery. No limo, just the trusty Gemini. At the gates, I saw only Dennis and Vivienne Halligan, the service was cold and sombre, the tiny white casket should have brought a tear to every eye. I think some eyes remained dry, not mine.

After the service when everyone gathers, Anne and I were surrounded by what I considered strangers, mostly Anne's relations, whom I'd never met. Thank God Dennis and Vivienne were there, I took them aside and invited them home for lunch with Anne and me. This was a smart plan as I had no idea what we were going to feed them. Between Vivienne and Anne, something was organised and we had good company in our hour of need.

I now had to return Anne to Heathcote with more clean clothes and get myself back to my shop and my mind off the events of the day.

I think Dennis and Vivienne were surprised by how I was able to do this and show so little emotion after what had been such an emotional morning.

71 I GET ANNE BACK

I was left in no man's land, I'd lost my son and my wife was a person in a mental institution, polite people would call it a hospital and strangely I would when talking to others. My social life revolved around visiting Anne and talking to her newfound friends, which of course, they weren't. I then had to wind down after the visits before I drove home, how people worked in these places was beyond me. At times I wondered if I'd ever get Anne back, she'd now been in Heathcote for two months and I saw no progress.

Christmas was closing in on us, the one time of the year there was a chance of making a quid in the shop. The shop was now starting to pick up a little but was no great earner, my heart, head and pocket were pretty much locked in with the business so I gave it all I could. My head was a can of worms and I was constantly changing things around in the shop. I think there was a belief that perhaps I belonged with Anne, in the nuthouse, no one else changed their shops around, at least, not at Phoenix Shopping Centre.

Just before Christmas, I asked the staff at Heathcote if I could have Anne home for Christmas day. It seems strange having to ask if I can spend a day with my wife, but that's how it was, they had control of her life and I had no say in the matter. Anne was legally committed to the care of the State and I was blithely accepting it. I was thrilled when the staff said yes, I could have her home with me from nine in the morning till four in the afternoon. This would be the first time she had been home since Thomas' funeral.

The day arrived and I picked Anne up and we came home and cooked lunch, Anne doing most of the work, it seemed there wasn't much wrong with her and she was being kept under false pretences. After lunch, there was an emptiness and neither of us knew what to say, this was the longest time we had spent together in almost three months.

There was a knock on the door, it was Mrs Baker from next door, we knew the Bakers, I'd been their milkman, but didn't have much to do with them.

"Would you like to come over for a drink?" asks Mrs Baker.

Our void had been filled, we went over to the Baker's place and spent a joyous hour or so there. A kind thought by someone we hardly knew made what should have been our worst Christmas, one of our most memorable. Then I had to take Anne back to Heathcote, armed with more clothes, my heart felt lighter and I now wanted Anne home where she belonged.

I had to wait to get Anne home, electro-therapy (Shock treatment.) was employed and it worked, Anne started to return to being Anne but without the gusto I'd hoped for, and it would be a while before I got the whole Anne back. Even when I got her home Anne was on a lot of drugs and still retained the zombie walk. I now had to become a better husband and be there for her. I determined to attend psychiatrist appointments with her and try to understand this awful affliction. I never will.

The Phoenix Shopping Centre was being expanded, to this time I hadn't had a proper lease on my shop, just a rental agreement. I must have been going well enough for Ian Armstrong, the centre manager to think I should be signed up to a proper lease. I signed up for a three-year lease, trusting in Ian and his apparent faith in me. As I was going through this process the words of Phil Tucker were whispering in my ear, "Never sign up to a shopping centre lease," but I had, for better or worse.

As things turned out it was for the average, the shop was starting to make headway, the shopping centre was expanded and included a

Coles supermarket and around ten more small shops. The expansion was a dismal failure, but my end of the shopping centre was trading reasonably well and changes were being made there, with a butcher and fruit and vegetable shop added.

On the home front, I was regaining my wife, her drugs were reduced to lithium, a poison supposed to stabilise the brain, I was happy with the results so far. I was not happy it was poisonous and Anne had to have her levels checked quite often by a blood test.

On our psychiatrist visits, Anne started to ask about having children again, we were told it was too risky while she was taking the lithium. Of course, I wanted children but this was Anne's decision, her body, but I couldn't go through what I'd been through before. I didn't say anything and was then currently happy as we were, for a while at least. I got home one evening and Anne proudly announced, "I've flushed my tablets down the toilet."

I was so happy, but I was so scared, I held her and cried and said, "Are you sure?"

"Yes," she answered with confidence, that was enough for me. I had my Anne back and it made me so happy.

Our lives seemed to be undergoing a vicissitude, the shop was rolling along quite well and Anne's health was in much better shape, and we were getting on with Anne's parents. Perhaps the shop wasn't as big a mistake as I thought it had been, I was getting some sort of grip on this ragtrade caper, not an easy task. Due to the changes made in the shopping centre my shop was now in a prime location. Somewhere in this euphoria, Anne got pregnant, I'm still not sure how those things happen, I think it's some sort of women's business.

I was now around two years into my lease with the shopping centre, we had a new shopping centre manager and he wasn't a patch on Ian Armstrong. The new centre manager sent me a letter advising me that they wanted me to move shop, from my now prime location to the old pet shop which had gone broke. To say the least, I wasn't happy, I'd just repainted my shop and got a new sign on the front, and the wheels were starting to move forward. The only concession I was offered was a new shop front, if I didn't comply, my lease would not be renewed. I had been given the pointy end of the pineapple.

I made my feeling quite plain, and reeled in agony when I discovered my neighbour who was asked (I'd pretty much been ordered to relocate.) to relocate was to get a completely new shop fit-out, he had a few years left on his lease. Phil Tucker's words could be heard loud and clear now, I was finding out that I was dealing with ruthless people. I wrote my first letter to the shopping centre owner, or at least to the head man but got no reply. I was left with little option, I could sit tight and lose my business or I could comply and keep my business. I opted for the latter.

I had plenty of time and so started to plan my move, all the time feeling I'd been done over, I think that spurred me on. I now had a shop to fit out from scratch, and we also had a child to bring into the world.

72 STILL MISSING THE ACTION

The 1979 Melbourne Cup was run on Tuesday 6th November, nothing unusual about that, it has always been run on the first Tuesday in November. I believe it was won by a horse called Hyperno but the real winners were Anne and Tom Watson. On Tuesday 6th November Anne Watson gave birth to a beautiful baby girl, we called her Julie-Anne after the two most beautiful women I'd had in my life. Well to be honest I'd never had Julie, but she was beautiful and around when I met Anne.

All had gone well with this pregnancy, apart from Anne's high blood pressure which had come back to haunt her. There was, however, one thing missing at the birth, the child's father. He was still firmly of the belief that childbirth was the domain of women and so it is. What he didn't seem to grasp was the fact that those women giving birth need support during this gruelling process.

Although Anne seemed fine, she wasn't and the lack of support from her husband was probably the reason she was again, a patient in Heathcote Psychiatric Hospital. At least this time we knew more than we had two years earlier and our beautiful Julie-Anne was with her mother. Her arrogant father had learnt a little and he did make an effort to be a great dad, he could feed and clean the results of the feed, almost all a baby needs, oh, and love there was shitloads of that for her.

Back at the shop, there was the move to think of, I was to fit out this new shop on my own as I couldn't afford a shopfitter and felt able. I had learnt that you can do most things others can do, in my first job, working for Tom Sanderson, he could do anything. I had plenty of time to work things out, as there was no sign of the person who was to take over my shop. Much as I'd disliked the thought of this move, it had now become a challenge and my heart was in it. Sadly I wasn't always there on the home front but did the best I could.

It was one afternoon in January 1980, if you've kept shop, you know some summer afternoons can be long and dreary, this was one of those afternoons. A bloke about my age wandered into the shop and was looking at jeans, this was strange, as most blokes my age should be working in the afternoon. The penny dropped, I recognised this bloke, and he was my age, it was Dennis Cherry who I'd worked with in the shearing teams.

Well, there was a handshake that took some matching and life stories shared. Dennis now had a piggery, my eyes lit up at this news, pig shit for my garden was my first thought. We must have had something in common, as Dennis later told me, he was wondering how he'd get those jeans shortened. We could use each other or be useful to each other or we could just be good mates.

Cleaning out the soon-to-be new shop turned out to be one of the worst jobs I'd had in my life. The carpet needed to be taken up, more than once I was forced to wonder, who could have thought of putting carpet in a pet shop. It wasn't long before I realised it was the moron who allowed animals to wander over it and shit and piss on it, it was putrid. The painting was a breeze, got timber at cost from the lady at the shoe shop's husband who worked at Alco. The lights were moved from the old shop by an electrical apprentice who hung around the shops, one Saturday afternoon. The final move would happen on Sunday, my day with Anne and Julie-Anne.

I was discussing not much with a young lad I'd met when I had the milkround, Bomb. Bomb wasn't his real name, his real name was Mark Timewell, he'd forgiven me for not giving him a job on the milkround and we got on well. As our conversation went on, I told Bomb I had to move shop on Sunday and do it on my own.

"I'll help you, Tom," came the raucous cry from Bomb, "When you want me?"

I gave Bomb a time to meet me outside the shopping centre and the deal was done. Well, there was no mention of money so a deal hadn't been done.

I'd made a good choice of the person who was to help me move shop, he turned up on time and worked like a champion. It was well into the move and things were going great, I found this lad good to work with, I felt there was something familiar about the way he moved and his expressions.

"You remind me of a bloke I used to work with, Bomb," I finally got out.

"Who was that, Tom?" Bomb tended to be loquacious but could question and answer without stretching his limited vocabulary.

"Just a bloke," I answered.

"Who, who, what was he called." Rattled Bomb in a demanding manner.

"Just a bloke I worked with in the shearing teams."

"You worked in shearing teams, Tom? What was this bloke called?" This was getting almost aggressive from Bomb.

"Henry Jones," I relented, knowing the name would mean nothing to Bomb.

Well, seems I was wrong, "Henry Jones? He's related to me, don't know how but he is, what was he like?" I went on to tell Bomb, that Henry was a great roustabout, great bloke and good fun to be around.

"Just like me then," Bomb shoots out quick as a flash.

I never paid Bomb for his work and he never asked me for a reward, I was, however, to become his banker and accountant. He borrowed money from me and I did his tax return.

Loathed though I am to admit it, because it hadn't been instigated by me, this shop move was a good one and my business started to take off and become very worthwhile. I think the reason for this was that there was a bread shop almost adjacent and most days a queue formed for bread in front of my shop and it was full of thirty to forty-year-old women. It took me some time to realise that these women were my target market and I had to change the range of clothing I sold.

73 BIT OF A UNION MAN

My shop move meant that I was now surrounded by a different set of shopkeepers, there was Burnsy in the sports shop, Gordon in the hardware shop, a Pommie bloke in the ice cream kiosk, a florist, a barber, a menswear shop and a camera shop, and of course, the bread shop, my saving grace. I got on well with Burnsy in the sports shop, he had sought my counsel before he opened his shop, can't imagine why as I was merely a struggling jeans shop owner at the time.

Burnsy was a character and liked a drink, this made him a good communicator and he brought people into the shopping centre as he got sportspeople sponsorship from his suppliers. Gordon had been an accountant and was a wise and steadying head. My move was turning out to be beneficial, but I remained bitter towards my landlord.

I heard from somewhere that there was a group of shopping centre retailers setting up an organisation to fight for the rights of small retailers, I was on the phone and soon on my way to my first meeting of the W.A. Shopping Centre Retailers Association. Just like when I joined the Milk Vendors Union, my eyes were opened to a new world, the men setting up this organisation were go-getters and mostly successful retailers who didn't like being pushed around by their landlords.

The good part about that sort of organisation is you learn from others, not anarchy, but about retailing in general. Here I was again, the Messiah, spreading the word of this new organisation to deaf ears, just as it had been with the milk vendors. To a man, not one of the shopkeepers at Phoenix Shopping Centre joined the W.A. Shopping

Centre Retailers Association, obviously, none of them had a gripe with their landlord.

There was to be another visit from Mum And Dad, it was a great time for them to visit as Julie-Anne was growing up and they could enjoy their Antipodean grandchild. I was now more prepared for my changed relationship with my parents, Dad was like an old mate and we could share a beer, something we'd never done before. Mum could be a friend to Anne and help her in the kitchen and both Mum and Dad adored Julie-Anne. I think they brought out some Beatrix Potter books for Julie-Anne and I was now reading to her every night before bed.

This stay seemed to last forever, I think they stayed two months and we were able to do more with them this time. New Norcia was our first trip, they were delighted to meet Dennis and Vivienne and see where I'd lived when I first arrived in Australia. I remember Dennis driving us along Batty Bog Road, Dad and I were on the back of the ute and I said to Dad, "Where does this remind you of Dad?"

"Bloody middle of nowhere, that's where," was Dad's prompt reply.

I was expecting him to say, "Helgill Bridge." The road which ran over the top above Cox Bank and Camsgill in England, it's what it reminded me of, perhaps it showed me how much my life had changed.

High summer was something my parents hadn't experienced, at least high summer in Australia. Mum and Dad loved an afternoon walk and enjoyed their Antipodean granddaughter too, this didn't augur well for their wellbeing. They braved the afternoon walk with Julie-Anne in the pusher oblivious to the afternoon heat.

Anne came to the shop most afternoons to allow me to do the banking so didn't witness my parents stupidity. One afternoon she got home to find them exhausted, after their walk and reported back to me, I had to explain to them the afternoon walk wasn't a good idea. This must have been Mum and Dad's biggest holiday, they'd only ever had one before and it was to the same place. I think we all had a great time and Dad went home with the most hideous Hawaiian shirt you've ever seen, courtesy of my shop. His insistence, not mine.

In the shop, my boredom was always relieved by a change around. When I'd left the original shop I hadn't left much, the one thing I discovered was some floor-to-ceiling fitting that I felt had been underutilised. With help from my friend Dennis Cherry and his welding skills, I created a new style of shopfitting. Instead of being along a wall as these floor-to-ceiling fittings had been in my original shop, I had them angled all over the place and I moved them as the mood took me.

This was often looked upon as madness by my - I reluctantly call them peers. One day during one of my brainstorms, Burnsy came over, looked around rather perplexed and asked, "Didn't you have a Meccano set when you were a kid?"

Of course, not only was Burnsy attracted to my shop to see what I was doing customers were too.

It was around now I saw an advertisement for a ticket-writing course, available through the state government tertiary education system, via correspondence. My eyes lit up, I'd always written my own signs and wasn't that bad, better than most, here was a chance to learn how to do it more professionally.

A slip was filled out and a cheque in the mail, almost before I'd finished reading the advertisement. The idea of doing this course by correspondence held no fear for me, as I had done my woolclassing course by correspondence. I still hadn't had the results from my last exam, it was now ten years down the track and my life had moved on.

I got myself equipped for the ticket-writing with the paint and brushes, it took me some time to master the brush, but I got there. I soon had the best handwritten signs in the shopping centre which didn't put mine at any great level but made my shop at least professional-looking.

Having a friend like Dennis Cherry was great, Dennis was a bachelor and lived a bachelor life, he took me to the football, (Aussie Rules.) bucks parties and all the stuff I'd missed out on by being a milkman. Well, Dennis must have made a New Year's resolution to improve his intellect, one afternoon I get a phone call from Dennis, "Hey Tom, we should do something this year, you know, try and improve ourselves."

'Sounds alright to me,' I'm thinking.

"There's this men's thing called Rostrum or something, we should check it out," Dennis drawls out.

When Dennis had said "we," I knew he meant you, and I was right as his next words were, "Can you check it out and get back to me?"

Getting back to Dennis, wasn't as easy as him getting back to me, as he was never at the end of the phone like me. I wasn't as enthusiastic as Dennis about this, improving ourselves but researched Rostrum.

Rostrum was a public speaking organisation for men and met weekly at the Booragoon Hotel. Dennis was good at getting me 'leave passes' as Anne worshipped him, when he dined at our place he always had 'seconds' and cleaned his plate, he could do no wrong. And so it was, I could go with Dennis to the Booragoon Hotel for a Rostrum meeting.

Dennis and I attended our first Rostrum meeting and I couldn't believe it. I was sure they were taking the piss - see why we needed to lift our intellect - the chairman of the meeting was Bob Willis, now I knew that Bob Willis was an English cricketer not some bloke in Booragoon. They'd had a letter from another Rostrum club that had been written by a bloke called Enzo Fantasia, 'I'm not dumb,' I thought.

'There's nobody in the world called Enzo Fantasia,' I concluded, 'and sure as shit if there is he doesn't live in Gosnells.'

Then came 'General Business,' my head was spinning by this time and I knew I was in some kind of fairyland. Before we left, we'd been converted and discovered that the chairman was another Bob Willis who worked in the National Bank. There was a bloke from Gosnells called Enzo Fantasia and if we hung around long enough we too could speak at the drop of a hat on any topic.

I went on to win the novice speaker of the year and we both progressed to the speaker of the year competition the following year. I think we did so well because we were different and spoke more freely than the rather starchy normal members, we had fun, and the others took it seriously.

74 ALMOST A CATHOLIC

Anne and I tried to be the best parents we could be to Julie-Anne, I read to her each night and Anne always had her dressed in the best clothes. I have a feeling that I enjoyed reading to Julie-Anne more than she enjoyed being read to, and Anne enjoyed dressing her in the best clothes more than Julie-Anne liked being dressed in them. It was probably our way of showing our love for her and it was now time to think about her education.

Before Julie-Anne was born, Anne had developed a close friendship with my old milkround customer and employee parent, Saint Irene O'Sullivan. Irene wouldn't let up on being our good friend, the support she had afforded me when her sons worked for me on the milkround spilt over into her support to Anne as a mother. Irene became like a grandmother to Julie-Anne and an unpaid babysitter, Saturday mornings and whenever Anne and I ventured out. To Julie-Anne and later to us she became known as Aunty, I don't think we had much say in the matter. As Irene had been a canteen lady at Saint Brendan's Catholic school that my loyal employees had attended, Julie-Anne's education was leaning towards the side of being Catholic.

With my involvement in Rostrum, I sometimes had to go to children's public speaking competitions and adjudicate or act as chairman. I must say it was eye-opening listening to these girls speak, boys didn't seem to get a guernsey. I was most impressed by the girls from Catholic schools as they had just the right degree of maturity, thirteen-year-olds were thirteen, and at some of the other schools, thirteen-year-olds were twenty-five and downright scary. Both Anne and I determined that Julie-Anne should have a Catholic education.

Julie-Anne having a Catholic education, we discovered was a small problem, she wasn't Baptised, mostly my fault as I'd turned my back on religion at thirteen and hadn't made plans to return. Let's face it, I never made plans and here we are making plans for our daughter's education. The local Catholic primary school gave Anne a flat, no when she enquired about an enrolment, but there was a new school being built in Bateman, a good stride away and inconvenient. We still needed to get Julie-Anne Baptised to get her in there. And so Julie-Anne was Baptised at the ripe old age of five.

Our next problem was getting Julie-Anne to school every day, I would be working at the required times and Anne didn't drive. At one stage when I had the milkround, I looked like I may lose my licence and I'd made an attempt to teach Anne to drive, I had failed miserably. Anne's mothering instincts now came into play and she, not I, determined she'd learn to drive. It was a costly exercise as she had a load of lessons, but she eventually made it, as a much safer driver than me.

I now had to look around for a car for Anne, a nice small car, cheap to run and reliable. It would have to be a new car because I only bought new cars. I'd had a look around before Anne got her licence and thought a Suzuki Swift would fit the bill, if or when Anne got her licence. I had something of a dislike for car salesmen and so when the day came to buy the car I rang the dealer and did the deal over the phone.

"The only two-door we've got is red, is that alright?" asks the salesman.

"Yeah, red's fine," I answered.

"Can you drop it off at Phoenix Shopping Centre?" I asked.

"I don't believe this," mutters the salesman over the phone.

"Yeah, I can do that, this afternoon alright?"

A rather flustered salesman arrived at the shop for his cheque that afternoon.

"Don't you want to look at it?" he asks me as I take the keys.

"Nah, I know what a car looks like, where did you leave it?"

"Just up the side of the carpark," Gino tells me and leaves the shop muttering to himself, "I don't believe this, I don't…"

Dennis Cherry was coming to tea that night and met up with me beforehand at the shop, we wander out to the carpark and view the car and I relate the purchase story to Dennis and we enjoy a chuckle. Dennis sees the car and says, "You've done well Tom, it's red, red ones always go faster."

When Dennis and I arrive home and Anne isn't overly interested in the car and is more into concentrating on providing a good meal for Dennis. Julie-Anne, like her mother, adored Dennis and just as she had named Irene O'Sullivan 'Aunty,' she named Dennis, 'Cherry Dennis.' I think she almost got us saying, Cherry Dennis.

These seemed to be heady days in the shop, business was good and we were living in a time of inflation. The shops around me were changing hands and people were buying jobs in the form of businesses. My mate Burnsy had moved on, making a good profit selling his sports shop to a job buyer. This bloke had been a boat builder and knew very little about sport, so was hoping he'd bought an easier job, of course, he hadn't. Retailing in a shopping centre bore no resemblance to 'beer and skittles.'

The Pommie guy, Shaun in the ice cream kiosk had sold out, to of all things, a school teacher. It would be fair to say I didn't rate school teachers as business people and it was some time before this Yankie sounding bloke revealed his former profession. If ever I'd miss judged a bloke, it was the school teacher in the ice cream kiosk. Not only wasn't he a Yank, but he was a natural in the business of selling ice cream and doughnuts.

This bloke, it turned out, was a dinky-dye West Australian who had worked in Canada for twenty years or so and was tired of teaching. Vern Smithers and I became good friends and I saw a side of teaching I'd never seen before, the commitment.

One Friday evening as I was about to lock up the shop, Vern turned up with a couple of cans of beer and an Italian sausage, pepperoni, if my memory serves me right. And so was born the Friday night drinks, just Vern and me in those early days, however, we managed to solve most of the world's problems most Friday nights. A conversation with Vern was like an English lesson, I'd never had a lesson in my native tongue at school and here I was accidentally having them in casual conversation with a mate. The school teacher in Vern, would slip out and correct my English, it was just a natural reflex for him and I thrived on it.

Gordon from the hardware shop had moved on and been replaced by a video shop, I knew they'd never make a quid. I only knew they'd never make a quid because my childhood attraction to television was now a thing of the past. Of course, they sold 'life memberships' and rented out videos like there was no tomorrow. Was I losing track of the modern world that was what my business was about? I felt sure I wasn't and felt on top of my business, I was, after all, making a quid.

75 ONWARD AND ONE PRESUMES, UPWARD

Things were starting to happen in the shopping centre, the first of these was a change of owners, the second was that the centre was to be expanded. The idea of new owners didn't excite me much as the owner who had forced my move to a lowly position in the shopping centre, was, at least a beast I knew.

Stories I'd heard as a member of the W.A. Shopping Centre Retailers Association were not good, the common or garden leasing agent was a creature of dubious parentage, a bastard. These morons held your business in their hands and didn't seem to care whether you sank or swam, or this was what I'd been led to believe. Of course, they always told you that if you were a good tenant you had nothing to fear.

The expansion of the shopping centre was something I was excited about, I was outgrowing my little shop in a lonely corner of the shopping centre. I knew a new larger shop, in a prime position would see me on the path to prosperity, I was more than ready for the move. It seemed to take forever for the expansion to come to fruition, but it did. I wasn't the only one waiting excitedly for this expansion and one by one we had appointments with the new centre manager to negotiate a position in the new, expanded shopping centre.

There was little in the way of negotiation, or at least it seemed that way to me. I was one of the first to be called to the table of non-negotiation. I was shown a plan of the new shopping centre and asked to point out my preferred site, my first choice it seems was taken, and my second. I got my third choice, larger than I wanted but a prime position just the same, I'd just have to lift my sights a little. It must be said that every other tenants I spoke to got a much better deal than I did, something I doubted. I was close to the expiry of my lease so was in a vulnerable position, which had been pointed out to me in the non-negotiation meeting.

There were tenants who I hadn't spoken to as they hadn't yet been 'called to the table,' it seemed to me they had pretty good businesses and were safe where they were. I wasn't right, their call to the non-negotiation table, was less than satisfactory, when their leases expired they would lose everything as far as their business was concerned.

I should have felt for these tenants but I didn't, no one had been at my side when I'd been given the pointy end of the pineapple a few years earlier. I'd told these tenants about the W.A. Shopping Centre Retailers Association and offered them membership. It would be fair to say these people were sure they were smarter than, 'that galah in the jean shop,' they'd paid 'goodwill' for their soon-to-be defunct businesses.

My focus now was on how I was going to make a success of my new shop and how I would fit it out. I determined that I'd stick with my floor to ceiling poles and I'd need more and I'd have to get them chrome plated. The place I had got my fittings from when I started didn't have these poles and I had no idea where I could get them.

It was now I discovered the handiness of having a boatbuilder across the way. Graham MacDonald wasn't much in the retail world, but he knew his boatbuilding and cabinet making and was invaluable with his knowledge. Graham knew where I should go to get my shopfitting poles and when I explained my idea for changerooms and screens he advised me on what panels I could use. "Sixteen mill melamine would be perfect for that," he told me, and it was.

My biggest problem it seemed was getting my shopfitting poles chrome plated, the ones I'd been using were just steel and that wasn't good enough for my new shop. I now spent a good deal of my 'spare time' sorting these things out. I cleaned my first batch of poles and took them to a chrome plater in Whitegum Valley, close to Fremantle. As I unload them from the top of the car and deposit them in the workshop, I'm accosted by a bloke in a boilersuit, "What yah doing with them?" he questions.

"I've brought them to be chrome-plated, I spoke to someone on the phone," I answer.

"We can't do them our bath is only two metres long," the smartest bloke south of the river tells me.

'You could have told me that before I unloaded them,' I thought, but went for the, "What can I do then?"

"I dunno, find somebody else I suppose."

"Do you know anyone?"

"No."

I dejectedly reload the poles and that was most of my time away from the shop that day wasted.

On my return to the shop I searched the yellow pages for chrome platers, there wasn't many in the Perth area and so I start the ring-a-round. I find no one wants to chrome plate three-metre long poles, well that was my first impression after calling a couple and finding the mention of three-metres was above and beyond. I'm almost ready to give up when I call a company called City Platers in Cannington, I explain I have these three-metre poles to chrome plate and the rather layback voice on the other end of the phone says, "Can you bring them here?"

"They're three metres long," I reiterate.

"So fucking what?"

"Nobody else can do 'em," I say.

"Well we can," he tells me, "When can you have 'em here, we're a bit busy, probably take a week." I have myself a chrome plater and he speaks my language.

The changerooms and screens were my next project, I'd found a shop in Osborne Park that sold aluminium tubing and channel that could be fixed together with plastic fittings. I really should have been an inventor. I worked out that I could pop rivet the channel to the square tubing and if I cut the channel at forty-five degrees it fitted flush using the plastic jointers. This frame could then be filled with the sixteen-millimetre melamine as recommended by Graham MacDonald.

I set to making these changerooms in my double garage at home, it had never seen either of our cars so was now being put to good use. I had to do this job at night and in stages, as I wasn't sure it would work, it did. I now had a system of shopfitting that were both functional and portable, they looked the part too. I needed the portability as when I moved shop it wasn't a simple move from one shop to another, I was to have a temporary shop before I moved to my new super shop. Portability was also important to me as I now liked to move my shop around and change things all the time.

I planned to have a tiled floor in my new shop, I knew this was a stupid idea as no other shop in Phoenix shopping centre had a tiled floor, carpet was the only floor covering you could have in a shop. I'd seen tiled floors in other shops, not many but enough to win me over. I spent my time (Trading hour time that is.) away from the shop buying stock or looking at other shops, others may have chosen golf or fishing. With the tiled floor, I needed feet for my screens and changerooms and my pole fittings, I found these adjustable feet and I thought I was home.

The day of the first move in the big move was drawing closer, I had to organise signage for my temporary shop. This shop was on the outside of the shopping centre and had floor to ceiling glass frontage, I've always found that much glass confronting. I got a signwriter in and at about six feet from the ground he painted a strip right around the front of the shop and signed Tom Stones Casual Clothing as many times as he could within that strip. The result was Tom Stones Casual Clothing, Tom Stones Casual Clothing and again and again. And again I was mocked for this stupidity, no one made a sign like that.

A new shop, new name, I was moving on and there to help me was my mate Bomb, we had the move together in no time. There were only a few fittings to move, the new changerooms counter and screens came from home and just needed to be fitted together. The temporary shop was how a shop should be, or how the leasing agents thought it should be, it had white walls, a sink and bloody awful brown carpet on the floor.

I rather liked my temporary shop, being on the outside of the shopping centre I could see daylight and on Thursday nights (Late night trading.) it stood out like a shithouse on a desert. The thing I found most gratifying was that a month or so after I moved, the chemist moved into his temporary shop opposite mine. After being mocked for my temporary signage, the chemist's shop had the same style of signage, albeit not quite as dramatic as mine.

My temporary shop was a success and traded well for the short time I was there. We now had our house paid off and a bank manager offering me money so that our house would still, be in part theirs. I may need the bank's money for my next move and so I kept my powder dry.

I wasn't altogether suited to being a shopkeeper in that I liked the outdoors and being a shopkeeper kept me indoors. I enjoyed the challenge the ragtrade gave me but missed the outdoors and as a result, my garden got a serious workout most weekends. Odd Sundays we would go to New Norcia and see Dennis and Vivienne Halligan, I'd be armed with a change of clothes and Dennis and I took off and did some work, usually sheep related. It was great to go out and get covered in dust and dirt after sitting in a shop all week and staying clean. One of my other recreations was helping Dennis Cherry on his pig farm, another pleasantly dirty pastime.

Julie-Anne was at her Catholic primary school and as good parents, we involved ourselves there, it was expected of us. As it was a new school there was much work to be done on the grounds, I was a willing worker and could use both a wheelbarrow and a shovel without having to consult the instruction manual.

Needless to say, I was one of a few and there was a plethora of chief executive officers, upper management, middle management, supervisors and foremen, none of whom owned or could operate a wheelbarrow or shovel. I found helping at the school was quite an amusing way to while away a Sunday morning. Anne became a member of the uniform committee and found that too was made up of many superior beings. We both became redundant after the first year or so.

At long last my new shop was ready for fit-out, that is to say, there were three walls and a tap and a sink, I had to supply the shopfront and everything else. In this case that was floor to ceiling glass frontage and roller doors, about half and half. There had to be a bulkhead over the roller doors and a neon sign, the neon sign was compulsory. Centre management were mad on neon signs, they helped light up their shopping centre, the appearance of your shopfront also added value to their shopping centre.

As everyone else was going through this process it was fairly easy to find the right people to do the work and most of the tradesmen got the work via word of mouth. Things seemed to slot together quite smoothly. The tiler seemed as if he could be a problem as I was to be the only shop with a tiled floor, not a tiled entrance it seemed. I caught a tiler tiling the entrance of a shop one day and pounced on him.

My enthusiasm for the move to my new permanent shop was waining as I knew my rent would be high and the shopping centre extensions weren't finished yet the super re-opening was a while away. I'd got away with reasonable rent in my temporary shop after they'd tried to hike it up to my new level but knew I couldn't pull that stunt again. In real terms, the fit-out of the new shop had gone too well and I was pressured to move in too early.

The weekend of the move arrived, my trusty servant Bomb would be there Sunday to help and I was now a consummate shop mover. I got everything moved into the new shop on Saturday afternoon with a bit of help from Bomb, but it was just a heap of clothes and fittings. Sunday morning, no Bomb as promised, I rang his mum, she had no idea where he was. I was pissed off, I'd have to do this on my own. Then there was a banging on the shopping centre doors, it was Wombat, Bomb's mate.

"Where's Bomb?" I ask.

"I dunno," answers Wombat, "I'll give you a hand anyway, Tom."

And bless his little cotton socks he did, a good worker the Wombat.

It was a couple of days before I saw Bomb and when I did, he was all smiles, "I see you got moved alright, Tom."

"Where the fuck were you?" I quickly cut in.

"Aw shit, I forgot all about you, did Wombat give you a hand?"

I could have questioned Bomb for a month and never found out where he'd been, it was years before the secret came out. I was disgusted, I thought she was such a nice girl too.

This move ticked all the boxes, it was the right thing to do, more space, a clean bright shop, a move away from just jeans to a wider range of clothing and financed from our pockets. Everyone I spoke to thought I was on the right track and this shop was going to be a success. It didn't seem that way in the first few weeks as I was on my own, none of the other new shops had opened yet. I bade my time and just had to grin and bear it till the 'Grand Opening' of the shopping centre, then I'd see the fruits of my labour and forethought.

When the big day came the crowds came too, for the opening of the Big W store. I knew it was going to be big and so I'd asked Kaylene, my Thursday night girl to come in and help. Well, I think it was Robbie Burns who uttered those fateful words, "The best-laid schemes o' mice an' men, Gang aft agley, An lea'e us nought but grief an' pain, For promis'd joy!" Ironically, he wrote those words in an apology to the mouse for ploughing up its nest. Yes, I had gone beyond the status quo and broken fresh ground and it was obvious that my plans had 'Gang aft agley.' It was an awful day, the crowds marched past my beautiful new shop as if it wasn't there.

I could, I would, I should have cried, but I didn't. I can't promise I slept well that night, I know I wouldn't have, I would have tossed and turned and dreamt up something for the next day and fought on, it's what I did and how I coped. I had a ten-year lease and the rent would go up every year so I had to soldier on and make this thing work. I hadn't failed yet and one bad day wasn't the end of the world.

I was now steering the Titanic across the Atlantic Ocean, barely a day went by and the deckchairs weren't been moved and I didn't man the ice cream container to bail some water. I must have known I was going to sink sooner or later, but I couldn't accept the facts. This was the start of an adventure of epic proportions and I was up for it.

76 NO LONGER A MUMMY'S BOY

I kept the shop afloat through struggle and toil, thinking up something new to maintain my sanity. I think the one that rocked everyone was my Christmas in July. Traditionally, in the rag trade, July was sale time, I felt I could pull off this Christmas in July and maintain some margin. I dragged out my Christmas decorations and decorated the shop as if it was December. I had Australian Christmas posters with koalas and kangaroos and banksias on them, for all the world it looked like Christmas.

I was ridiculed for this outrageous move – nothing new for me - I think my customers were embarrassed by it, they kept away in droves. It was a disaster, by the third week of July the decorations came down and the sale signs went up.

Christmas in July didn't maintain my sanity and sometime in the second week, I was expecting two men in white coats to wander into the shop carrying a straightjacket. My Christmas decorations would never again see the light of day in July. Restaurants seemed to be able to pull it off, but I certainly didn't and I'm now of the belief that Christmas is in December.

It was the 10th July 1987 Dennis Cherry and I went to the football, Anne had been left to babysit, Dennis' mother Dawn. Dennis now had a pig farm in Baldivis and if he'd left her there it would have been very lonely for her, I'm not sure why she was staying with him but, Anne enjoyed her company. Dennis and I arrived home in good spirits, I'm guessing the Eagles won and we were laughing about something. Anne came to the door before we set foot in the house and turned on me, "I don't know what you're laughing about your mother has died."

Anne has a subtle way of breaking bad news and it floored me. Mum had died the day before but the news had only just arrived via a phone call from Marion's husband, Fred. I didn't know what to say or what to do, of course, neither did Dennis or Dawn, I think they made a discreet exit.

I had no idea Mum was close to death and I don't think she did either, I know we'd had a letter at Christmas saying she only had forty more Christmas pudding to make for the Women's Institute Market. The thought of Mum being dead left me hollow and empty, she was my only real connection with England. Yes, I got Christmas letters and birthday cards from Barbara and Marion but Mum was the only true connection.

When I first came to Australia, Mum wrote every week, as did I, we didn't write as often now but we still wrote. The worst and saddest thing here was that I couldn't write to Dad, I don't, even think I tried, I knew if I did write he wouldn't reply, Dad wasn't a writer, but I still couldn't excuse myself. The last time Mum and Dad came to Australia I had got on with him, really well, we'd developed a relationship we'd never had in England and here I was unable to write to him. I still feel the guilt.

I was now disconnected from England, I had been since those first few days after my arrival in Australia, but Mum had maintained the only thread I had, I had no intention of ever returning. I considered myself an Australian, albeit a Pommie Australian. Every Australia Day (26th January) I now dressed up my shop with Australian bunting, posters, flags and anything else I could find Australian.

In 1988 it was the Australian bicentennial year so I got more stuff and went over the top as the shopping centre had a competition for the best-dressed shop. I was pretty sure I had this in the bag, there were only two entries of consequence, Fudgie the butcher and my shop. I think there was money in this, I'm sure there was money in it.

Give him his due, Fudgie got a ticket writer to tart up his shop and I did my own. I had the prize money spent and I came second, the second prize was a crystal vase, you can't spend them. I was not a happy camper, not because Fudgie had won, he was a mate and his shop looked alright but mine was the clear winner. The judge for this competition was none other than Fudgie's ticket writer, and knowing Fudgie, the ticket writer got the prize. Knowing the ticket writer, I know that was the deal, I had never held him in high esteem.

It must have been late 1988 that I got this strange phone call at home, those telemarketers know just when to call. Just after seven, tea's out of the way they're just sitting down to watch telly, we've got 'em they think. Well, to me this was one of those calls and I must have been in the mood for it, I was armed to the teeth with vitriol and venom.

"Is that Thomas Watson?" the Pommie sounding voice asks.

I'm weakening I feel as I reply through gritted teeth, "Yes."

"Thomas Watson from Goose Green?"

'You've got two questions out sweetheart and the second one has floored me.' I'm thinking. Not even the savviest telemarketer could know I came from Goose Green.

"I'm Ada Robinson from Black Yeates," this Pommie voice tells me, "do you remember me?"

Well, I did but not well. The last time I'd seen Ada Robinson was at a dance at Preston Patrick Memorial Hall, I was probably a little under the influence at the time but always remembered it, as she and her sister Sandra, had been dressed up for the occasion and looked identical. Sandra was about my age, no she was a year younger and there was her baby sister ruining my chances. I probably related the story to her, which I'm sure would have made her feel comfortable.

This Ada Robinson goes on to tell me, she's no longer Ada Robinson, but Robbie Maxwell. She had migrated to Australia and met the man of her dreams and married him. This was after the first man of her dreams had proved to be a dud, a working-class lad from Preston Patrick just like me. Now she tells the tale of how she found me, not knowing I didn't want to be found and had no interest in Preston Patrick.

Ada's mum, Ivy posted her letters to Ada at the Endmoor Post Office where my Aunty Margaret was Post Mistress, a little nosey and liked a chat, two things she had in common with Ivy.

"Our Thomas is in Australia, I'll get his address and your Ada can get in touch with him," Aunty Margaret would have piped up and Ivy would have thrived on it, and so I get this phone call.

The news comes thick and fast, Ada takes after her mum in the chat department, soon I hear that Ada's sister Sandra had married my old schoolmate Dennis Atkinson and it just went on. For someone who wasn't interested in Preston Patrick, I was taking a deep interest and the gossip was something that Mum never told me, her talk had been about family and their people. This stuff from Ada was about the people I went to school with, the people I drank with and rarely danced with, my Preston Patrick generation. I eventually got her number and said I may ring her back one day, I didn't think I would.

Sitting in the shop the next day, I found myself on an emotional roller coaster, a life I'd left behind years ago had come back to haunt me. I was lost as to how I felt, I didn't want to go back to England, my home was here in Australia, but this woman had sparked something in me and I felt I had to at least meet her.

By that afternoon I was on the phone and talking to not, Ada Robinson, but Robbie Maxwell and arranging a time we could meet up. She lived in Hamersley, so that was a fair way away, she worked as a rep for a travel company and got around a bit. I only had Tuesday morning to myself for buying and checking out other shops. We agreed to meet at Mirrabooka Shopping Centre, I'd never been there so could check out some shops there.

I recognised Ada straight away, well she had the same hairdo she had when I'd last seen her at Preston Patrick Memorial Hall. We had a coffee and just chatted about old times in Preston Patrick and the people we knew, we both had to go, we agreed that we should meet up with our spouses, we'd organise that another time. What amazed me, was that if we both still lived in Preston Patrick we could never have spoken as we did that day if we had still lived there.

77 A NEW CORRESPONDENT

Well, I couldn't leave this woman alone, catching up with someone I'd had nothing to do with after twenty-four years, was the strangest thing. Apart from having mutual acquaintances, the only other thing we had in common was that we had lived inside the same little dot on the map, on the other side of the world. The meeting with the spouses was arranged, lunch at Chris and Robbie's place one Sunday – my only day off.

When I pulled into the driveway of our newfound friend's home, I knew we had little in common. Their house was newer than ours, the perfect suburban home with a pool and brick paving forever, to some, this may have seemed common or garden. Our place was a whole lot more commoner and gardener, but best not to be too judgemental. I had discovered that Chris was a Kiwi so I'd arrived armed with a six-pack of light lager, to be sociable with a Kiwi, he didn't drink.

Chris had been a mobile mechanic but was now working from a unit down the road and was into all things petrol. Pleasant enough bloke but we had nothing in common, Robbie had been in touch with the only other person I knew with links to Preston Patrick, Lesley Young. I hadn't seen Lesley for years so she was one up on me. Finding people from Westmorland seemed to be a passion of Robbie's, hence I was sitting in their house. Anne seemed to get on with Robbie so our friendship was maintained. We had days out with them and did things we wouldn't normally do, probably because we had nothing in common.

Robbie and Chris had lived in Sydney and sold their house there and moved to Western Australia where the houses were much cheaper, one reason for the nice house. Robbie's parents had visited them in Sydney a few times and were planning a visit to Western Australia, Robbie told us. I suppose Anne said, "That's lovely," and I would have said similar and thought no more about it. One afternoon I got a call from Robbie, advising me that her mum and dad were at her place and would like to come and visit us.

"Is tonight alright?" asks Robbie.

"Fine by me," I answer, not realising it may cause a panic on the home front, which of course, it did.

Must have been about half-seven when the knock on the door was heard, I opened the door and there was Robbie in the light and her parents behind her in the darkness. Robbie bursts into the house with her parents in tow, "I've brought mum and dad," announces Robbie.

There was no need for introductions, I recognised Harry and Ivy, I didn't know Harry and Ivy, I knew of them but I'm pretty sure I'd never spoken to them before. There was no need to talk to people in Preston Patrick as everyone knew who everyone was, a nod of acknowledgement was all that was needed. If I had still lived in Preston Patrick and had a house, there is a very good chance these people would never have crossed the threshold. And here I was, welcoming Harry and Ivy Robinson into my house in Australia.

What happen next, should have been a strained silence, it wasn't. These people I barely knew, sat in our house as if they belonged in it, they slotted into our furniture as if into the comfy chairs they sat in at home, they seemed at home. Robbie, who was by nature a cynosure was cast aside and became part of the audience.

Two old people I barely knew were now our best friends, it was the strangest feeling, but a beautiful one. Harry remembered me from my days working at Camsgill – their farm was next door – and it seems, rated me. Ivy too remembered me and had been a member of the Women's Institute with Mum. It was as if I'd been best friends with these people, or they were desperate for friends, neither was the case.

Robbie finally got the floor and rounded up her parents for the trip home, I had my photo taken with Robbie. Before she left, Ivy came out with the question, "When are you going to come and see us?" I fobbed it off as it was last on my list of things to do, after all, why would I want to fly halfway across the world to see a couple of strangers. Anne was besotted with Ivy and I liked Harry, in an evening we had made firm friends with people I'd hardly known. Ivy wrote to thank us for the evening, when she got home to England and a firm friendship was cemented by correspondence.

These years of my life are years I will call the lost years, the shop had gone from a reasonably good business to a failing business. There was only one person to blame for its demise, me, I was locked into a ten-year lease, I misguidedly felt I could turn things around and refused to acknowledge that I couldn't. I no longer had Mum to write home to, but I had started writing to Marion's eldest daughter Anna-Marie, she wasn't as consistent as Mum but wrote a nice letter. I felt this writing to Anna-Marie was keeping a family tradition alive, as Marion had written to one of Dad's cousins in America for years.

I now had Ivy Robinson to write to, Ivy wrote a good letter and kept me up to date with Preston Patrick's news, not that it meant much to me anymore. I also started writing to another of Dad's American cousins, Adella. Adella's husband had written a family history and either Marion or Barbara sent me a copy, I got a guernsey in the book, albeit a short-sleeved guernsey. Hence that line of correspondence started.

My best writing work was reserved for the shopping centre management, that was when the typewriter came in handy. They must have disliked me with a passion, as I now sent a carbon copy to their superiors, a trick I'd learnt from my school teacher mate Vern. I think, learning how to write a business letter in primary school was one of the best lessons you could learn. Sadly the writing I should have been reading was on the wall and it said, "Get the hell out of this mess," but I couldn't or wouldn't read it and stumbled from day to day getting nowhere.

78 WISE WORDS FROM THE WALRUS

Although the shop was going in reverse, it didn't mean that I had given up and was forever looking for ways I could make it better. My Tuesday morning in Perth when I was looking at stock to order for the shop, usually ended with me wandering around the city looking at shops to give me new ideas. One of these mornings I wandered into the R. M. William's shop, they sold over-priced clothing and boots for squatters and wannabe squatters. This place didn't seem to do much business, but I noticed something on the counter, a visitor's book, inspiration is cheap, even in R. M. Williams.

By Tuesday afternoon I became the first shop in Phoenix Shopping Centre to have a visitor's book. It knocked my clientele side-ways when I asked them to sign my visitor's book, and needless to say, they and my fellow retailers were yet again doubting my sanity. It goes without saying, that the visitor's book was not a great success, but it was a nice touch and it made people feel good and I got feedback from their comments.

As I was hanging on with the business, my fellow retailers were starting to fall by the wayside, it was rather depressing. My mate Vern from the ice cream kiosk was having marriage problems and sold out. Most were going broke and just disappeared or sold out at a loss, there were only a few of us diehards left, Joe the hairdresser and Fudgie the butcher, being the oldest hands. With Vern gone my Friday night beers landed me at Fudgie's butchers' shop, where there were often guests –

not shopping centre tenants – this meant a broader conversation than just shopping centre talk.

I should have known the end was nigh when the shopping centre welcomed a new tenant in Just Jeans, Australia's largest jeans retailer but I continued to battle on. Amongst the moves within the shopping centre was a tenant on the outside of the centre who moved inside and no one filled their old shop. I'd liked my time in that temporary shop on the outside of the centre and saw an opportunity to lower my rent and perhaps start to see daylight again. I approached the management and they agreed to let me surrender my lease and move outside. I was in arrears with my rent, so why they agreed to this move is beyond me but agree they did.

Another move, this would be my fifth shop in the shopping centre and I had the fittings that moved easily. All I needed was the floor covering, I couldn't afford tiles again so went for lino. Bomb and I had everything moved on Saturday night, yes, good old Bomb was in on this move too. Fudgie came on Sunday and helped and I had an electrician lined up to move the lights on Monday morning. All was going smoothly by mid-Monday morning.

The rent reduction felt pleasant, but there was no way I was going to kill the arrears I'd built up, but on I struggled. The new shop traded as the old one so there was some relief, it hadn't been as silly a move as most thought, but it was a pointless one.

Just as I moved, the shopping centre was sold and my arrears went to the new owners, that scared me a bit, but nothing happened. My mate Fudgie sold out and left clutching his underpants, his rental arrears were on par with mine. The bloke who bought Fudgie's shop changed it completely and didn't last long before he too was moving on, selling at a loss I believe.

I moved with Fudgie, my Friday night drinks that is. Fudgie had got a job with, and sold his smoke oven to Denis Ryan in Hamilton Hill. Denis had a long-established Friday night drinks session going and I was welcomed into the fold, not that I was the most cheerful soul in those days. I was however mixing with a couple of successful business people, Denis and his brother-in-law Murray Buchan.

Almost every Friday night I'd roll up and pour out my tales of woe, before cheering up after a few beers. This must have got on everyone's nerves, as one night I'm walking out with Denis and Murray and they turned on me and told me I had to get out of the shopping centre as I was going nowhere. They must have thought I was better than what I was doing. I couldn't say much but realised they were right, I was trapped in a lease, had a load of debt and had nothing to turn to if I got out of the shop.

I'd been at this retailing caper for almost sixteen years and had nothing to show for it and no escape, at least as I could see it now. All I had was a turnover that kept bread on the table and Julie-Anne in a Catholic school. There was no one queuing at my door with job offers or wonderful business opportunities. Denis and Murray had sown a seed, it was up to me to grow it. I was at least a gardener so I guess the seed had some chance, but I couldn't see it germinating.

It must have been mid-January, Christmas was out of the way and had given my turnover a boost and I was pretending that there may be light at the end of the tunnel. I bumped into the centre manager as I was about to open my shop. This bloke was new and had a reputation for kicking heads and throwing livelihoods to the crows, but I found him pretty straight.

"Would you come to the office for a minute, Tom?" he asked.

'Awe fuck, he's going to put the bite on me for money,' I thought as I followed to the centre manager's office.

When we were both sitting comfortably - he more so than me – he started to speak, "I think the owners want to evict you."

"The other option," he continues, "Is they'll give you three months free rent and you will leave."

It wasn't a long conversation but for me a life-changing one, I'd seen an eviction notice and noticed that they aren't a pretty document.

'Three months,' I thought, that would let me sell up my stock and give me some breathing space.

"I'll take the three months free rent," I replied without a second thought.

The chair I was sitting in, in that office, suddenly felt comfortable, I felt a load lifted from my shoulders, we shook hands and I floated out to my shop, a new man. It was only as I opened the door of my shop for the ninetieth last time and looked around me that I thought, 'What the fuck have I just done?' But I thought about it, with a smile on my face.

I'd have to tell Anne, how was she going to take the news, she didn't know the dire state our finances were in, the business had always been my business. I rang my mate Burnsy and told him, he was excited for me and wanted me to buy a newsagency post haste. Burnsy was always a keen supporter of mine and he was just the man to tell first.

It must have been one of those days when nothing can go wrong, I wandered out of the shop to get some air and there was another old mate, Gordon Crane. Gordon had had the hardware shop at Phoenix when I made my first move there and knew a thing or two about winding shops down, he'd closed his years ago.

I told Gordon my news, he then spoke very quietly – as he always did – and said, "Whatever you do, don't put up an 'everything half price sign,' because they'll come along and pick the eyes out of your stock and leave you with the rubbish, the unsaleable stuff." These words stopped me from doing what he had just told me not to do. A simple piece of advice, spoken so quietly, I think the way Gordon spoke, was what let it sink into the rash brain of Tom Watson.

Anne didn't take my news well, especially as I'd told Burnsy before her, but as usual, she accepted my decision and was behind me all the way. I was mostly busy going through my stock and filling up the 'please take one,' rack and carefully moving my good stock to a less conspicuous position in the shop.

79 THE INHERITANCE

Dad had died in 1991 and it's just come into my mind now. I'm sure I reported these years in my life as the lost years, Dad's death didn't get lost in those years, it was just another empty time. Dad must have had his last holiday in Ireland with my sister Barbara about Easter that year. I remember it clearly as she rang me and got Dad to speak to me, he sounded out of breath but otherwise fine. He'd just had his eightieth birthday and I remember saying to him that, I remembered when he didn't look like making fifty, he'd had terrible health in his forties, brucellosis and an ulcer.

Since Mum's death, I'd been a terrible son to him, never writing or making a phone call, surely he got a Christmas card. Gavin Halligan – Dennis and Vivienne's son – had gone to England and called in on him, he would have liked that. On his return, Gavin and his then-girl-friend Katrina came to visit me in the shop and said I should write to Dad, but I still didn't. I remember Katrina being quite strong about me writing to Dad, I may have sat down and found I simply couldn't write, but I still can't explain why I didn't write.

Dad's death had a profound effect on me, not a life-changing effect, just a profound effect. I can honestly say I was a mummy's boy and my relationship with Mum was always close, she spoilt me. As a child, I worshipped Dad as all boys do and of course, wanted to be just like him, that is until I found out that other boys had bigger stronger dads. The mind of a child isn't much of a mind at all and when I thought my way, Dad's mind thought another. By my teens, we spent most of our time together at loggerheads, we agreed on nothing, but I was allowed to go my own way and make my own mistakes.

As I've said before when Mum and Dad visited Australia, that relationship changed and I got on well with Dad. And due to that change, I was no longer a mummy's boy, but a mate of Dad's. My lone supporter, I had had at home in England, Mum, found me rather hard and heartless, not the lovely boy she'd brought up.

Back when we got the phone call reporting Dad's death - I'm sure it would have been from Fred, sister Marion's husband – I was seriously rattled. Not because it was a shock, reality and hearing his breathless voice a month earlier had told me he was on the way out. Dad was dead, the man who led my family, who went without so that my sisters could have the best education. He would have gone without more if I too, had wanted the best education, he was a great believer in education. He allowed me to make my own choices and never criticised my decision to avoid education and choose a career as a labourer.

No, Dad's death was not lost in those lost years, but I was lost. The rudder that had steered my life in the early years was gone and it was gone without me acknowledging it had been there, there was the guilt and then there was the shame to come.

With Dad's death, there was an inheritance to collect, I knew I'd get my cut, the inheritance would go three ways. It was never spoken of, but we all knew that's what would happen, all being Marion, Barbara and myself. I had no idea how much Mum and Dad had, I did know they had bugger-all when we were kids. Turns out they had a house and not much else.

In 1991 an inheritance would have come in handy as we were in pretty dire straits so you can see where the guilt came in. I had my inheritance spent long before I knew its value, it would pay down my debts and give us some breathing space. Good fortune jumped in and stopped my inheritance, the wheels of law move slowly at the best of times. The wheels of law barely turn in country towns in England and when they do, the cost to the practitioner must be kept to a minimum.

The solicitors corresponded with me by surface mail (It still existed in those days.) so it was super slow.

I've used the words good fortune for a purpose because it was good fortune, the money didn't land when I wanted it most. I would have just thrown it in the hole of debt trying to fill it and there was no way it could. The money finally made it when we were starting on the journey to close the shop and I didn't need it to keep afloat.

The closing of the shop was to take the full three months the landlord had given me, although I had a heap of debt, I wasn't short of stock. I started to sell the rubbish off and reduced the good stock slowly, thankyou Gordon. The response to the news I was closing down was amazing, best wishes from the customers and offers to take stock back from suppliers and that question. 'What are you going when you finish here?' Well, I didn't know, and when I told the customers this they just said, "You'll be alright."

Of the best responses from customers was one from a Serbian lady, who spoke little or no English. She always came into the shop with a friend who advised her and translated for her and her son about four years old, I babysat the brat and guided her selection as best I could. After her last purchase, her friend translated for her after she had said something I didn't understand. "She said she is never buying jeans again because you won't be here any longer," her translator told me.

And who could forget that awful woman who had been my first customer all those years ago, we were now good friends as she continued to buy clothes for her now grown-up family. Dear Lesley Pitman came into the shop and said so genuinely, "We're all going to miss you, enjoy this, it's a good drop." And presented me with a bottle of Happ's Fuchsia, she was right about the wine, but there again I'd say she was something of a connoisseur.

My fellow traders in the shopping centre, via the centre Manager's secretary, had a whip-round and bought me a plastic gold clock and a card. In real terms, those at the shopping centre then weren't my fellow traders, as most of my fellow traders had moved on long ago, not many to bigger and better things. Most moved on bruised and battered with little to show from their experience.

It was now my turn to move on, I had no idea what I was going to do. I was handy, I could be a handyman, I loved gardening, I could be a lawnmowing man. As I drew a line through menial tasks that were simply someone else's, but they were too lazy to do them, it dawned on me. I had been doing my signs in the shop for years and was pretty accomplished at it, I could do the same for others. I'd progressed from cardboard and paint to blackboards and chalk and was the only person doing it and for it to look good. I'd found a way of getting blackboards clean, everyone else wiped their blackboards and was left with a foggy mess, I got mine clean.

Enter my first client, the butcher at Phoenix shopping centre, he had a dirty scribbly blackboard in the mall and got me to change it each week. He was thrilled with the results and got me to do some boards for his shop too. I now knew I could do this work and hopefully make a quid at it but it would take time as I currently had one client. I would need something to keep bread on the table while I built up this new business dream.

80 FOLLOWING A DREAM

The last few weeks in the shop saw my stock dwindling healthily, I'd got rid of the rubbish and what was left was salable. I advertised my fittings and got a bite straight away, someone who was opening a shop in Newman or some other mining town. I wasn't sure he'd understand my floor to ceiling posts but he didn't seem worried and bought everything, but the changerooms and counter sight unseen and transferred the money into my bank account. I didn't realise you could do that but times were changing.

I was still taking my Tuesday morning off and rather than searching for more stock for the shop, I was looking out for people with crappy looking blackboards that needed my magic touch. I found a couple and added them to the butcher at Phoenix as clients, this was filling my Tuesday mornings but things didn't look strong enough to make a living. I was now also searching for that little job that would tide me over as I built up the blackboard job. I had my sights set on a window cleaning round as I'd cleaned my shop windows for years. It was dead easy and looked just the thing for me.

I found just the window cleaning round advertised in the paper, ten thousand dollars and supposedly earning twenty-two thousand. I was sold on this round before I even spoke to the seller, the price was just right and the earnings would be fair enough. When I got the blackboards going I could sell off the window cleaning. Everything was falling into place. I rang the window cleaning man and asked if he could hold the round for a couple of weeks, he reluctantly agreed and I was happy I'd have that income guarantee.

I finally closed the shop just before Easter and had someone lined up to buy the changerooms, that went smoothly. I was now out of work and income, I did have a little mattress money and my inheritance from Dad had been deposited into our savings account. I got on well with the young bloke who had the trolley collection contract at Pheonix Shopping Centre and Easter, being a busy time, he asked me if I would do a couple of days of trolley collecting. Being a man of little pride and fresh out of employment, I agreed and did my couple of days. There was no future in the trolley pushing, the money was pitiful, but it kept me off the streets.

I finally got to meet my window cleaning man, it would be fair to say he didn't impress me. He lived in a unit in Belmont, drove an old Valiant station wagon with a couple of ladders on the roof and – the winning blow – a Pro-Ma sticker in the back window. I wasn't sure exactly what Pro-Ma was but felt confident that it was some dodgy soap powder company that sold directly to the public via my window cleaning man. A direct invisible distrust was built between us, or at least I hope it was invisible.

Off we went on my, soon-to-be window cleaning round, we drove for miles and pulled into the driveway of a private house, "I've been cleaning this lady's windows for years," the Pro-Ma man announces.

"You do the outside and I'll do the inside," he continues.

Well, we got that house done and off we drove again, through heaven knows how many suburbs to yet another private house. I had envisaged a window cleaning round to be shop windows and office windows, not household windows. We got back to the Pro-Ma man's unit and he shows me his window cleaning round, it was a small box of cards with names and addresses on the cards. I left the Pro-Ma man's unit and the deal was still on.

As I drove home, I thought about what Dad had left me, a third of his life's work and I was going to hand it over to a Pro-Ma man for a box of cards. Twenty-two years in business told me this was a bad idea, I'd go out and see if I could drum up a bit of business with the blackboard idea. I quickly picked up a couple of clients with very little effort and I gave the Pro-Ma man the call he didn't want.

I scraped around building a few clients together and was worse off than if I'd gone with the Pro-Ma man. I got a couple of window cleaning clients, not household but commercial and struggled along.

It was tough going, trying to sell something new to an unreceptive audience but I dragged together enough clients to keep alive and Dad's money had paid off the house, I'd already paid it off once but got it back in hock with the shop. The shopping centre hadn't pursued our debt and within a few weeks I was getting cheques from the managing agent for work I was doing at another shopping centre, I saw irony in that.

It was during those, arse dragging weeks that our daughter, Julie-Anne got a bit sick, she rarely got sick, she once got a touch of chickenpox and Anne washed the spots off her. Anne was a very hard mum and getting sick was one thing she didn't like Julie-Anne doing, a pride thing I think it was. This was serious stuff, this sickness and Julie-Anne was taken to the doctor.

"Just keep doing what you're doing Mrs Watson, I'm sure it's just a stomach bug she's got at school," was the doctor's reaction.

Anne doubled what she was doing and it wasn't working, back to the doctor, an anti-biotic needle and if she got worse, "You'd better get her off to Fremantle hospital." She got worse.

Julie-Anne had never been a big child she had, over the last few months it seemed, stopped growing and after being sick and not eating she was rapidly fading away to very little. The decision to take her to the hospital was an easy one and I picked up a very light and feeble child and drove down to Fremantle hospital. I rushed into the emergency department and they asked what was wrong with her, and all I could say was, "She's crook." It must have been pretty obvious she was, as they rushed her straight in with no messing around.

Anne and I were beside ourselves, we had lost one child, we couldn't lose Julie-Anne, she was too precious to us. That was how crook she had gotten in the few hours since she'd seen the doctor, we felt as if we were going to lose her. Anne was far more capable than I in this sort of situation and could talk, what I would describe as 'doctor talk.' Not that 'doctor talk,' was much good in this case, it was doctor action we needed.

When Julie-Anne was examined by a doctor she was still breathing but weak as a kitten – thank goodness cats have nine lives – and the young doctor ask her symptoms and smelt her breath. The young doctor should have been in general practice in Hamilton Hill, he immediately diagnosed diabetes as the problem, the weight loss and an almond smell to Julie-Anne's breath being the giveaways. Julie-Anne was in a coma for two days and we were lost but assured she would be fine.

I had trouble with Julie-Anne's diagnosis, thinking she'd be lumbered with injecting herself every day and all the problems that would throw up. Anne, on the other hand, was a full bottle on diabetes as her father had been diagnosed a couple of years earlier, she had made it her business to know all she could. Julie-Anne and years of Anne and me proving our worth had reconciled us with her parents and we were reasonably close with them now. It's fair to say Anne coped with this situation better than I and she moved back into research mode. She immediately found out that Julie-Anne's diabetes was different to her father's.

Diabetes has two categories, type one and type two, Julie-Anne had type one and Anne's father Joe, had type two. Anne now became a full bottle on all diabetes. Julie-Anne eventually came round and who was there to welcome her back? It was none other than our dear friend and adopted grandmother to Julie-Anne, Irene O'Sullivan, Julie-Anne was happier to see her than us. It was a very happy moment for us all.

81 SEEING MY LITTLE SISTER AGAIN

We got Julie-Anne home and Anne was in control with her superior knowledge of type one diabetes, we weren't needed as Julie-Anne had been filled in by the hospital staff, she had a diabetes educator assigned to her. We were amazed at the available support and grateful for it and the way Julie-Anne managed the four injections a day, the constant blood testing and it all seemed to be natural for her. I guess it had to be natural for her as she would have it for the rest of her life.

I'm not sure when we got the news, but it was delightful news. My younger sister Barbara, her husband and two children were coming to visit us. Barbara, like me, had used Dad's money to pay off their house in Northern Ireland and obviously, it left them flush enough to visit us. I hadn't seen my little sister (She was actually, the bigger of my sisters.) for twenty-five years, so this was exciting news.

I'd always been a little worried about Barbara living in Northern Ireland with all the troubles there, but she'd always sounded happy in her letters. Mum and Dad had visited Barbara many times in Northern Ireland and when they'd been here assured us it wasn't as bad as it sounded. "You got used to being searched when you went into shops," they casually told us on their visits here. Not something I could easily get used to, with our simple lifestyle.

The day arrived, I took off to the airport alone as there was, only room in the car for me and Barbara's family. As I hadn't seen Barbara for twenty-five years and had only seen a photograph of her husband

David and the kids and it wasn't a recent photograph, I thought I may have trouble spotting them in the crowd.

I did know that David was reasonably tall and bald and wore horn-rimmed glasses because I'd seen the photo. I worked on spotting David first as the passengers came out of customs, as I was sure there would only be one tall, bald bloke with hornrimmed glasses on the plane. I was wrong, there were none, I spotted Barbara first and her husband wasn't much taller than her. I was in a haze for a little while and then realised that David must have been standing on a box for the photo, it was a studio shot and the photographer must have felt David needed more height.

It was great to see my little sister again and hug her and meet David and the kids, Jo-anna and Bryan. The kids were noisy and lively, contrasting with Barbara and David who seemed quiet in comparison. Our household more than doubled in size but we managed, I think the biggest problem was feeding Bryan, it seemed he could live on a diet of fish fingers, and it was hard to convince him that Australian fish don't have fingers.

I still had to make some sort of living so could not be the guide I should have been, I gave David the keys to Anne's car and let them go. They were better organised than I would have been and had a Northern Territory tour booked, this put me to shame as I'd been in this country twenty-five years and never left the state of Western Australia.

I think we all took a deep breath when the Craig family took off to the Northern Territory for a week, Anne threatened to buy some fish fingers so she could feed Bryan better when they returned but was warned off by her husband. Anne had a passionate dislike of being unable to satisfy people's dietary requirements, but I felt buying fish fingers was beyond the pale.

The Craigs returned full of the Northern Territory and our house was again thrown into chaos, but something wasn't right. Barbara wasn't her usual self, she was on the sickly side. I'd never seen my sister sick, she was like me and never got sick so it took a big dose of whatever it was to make her sick. First to the doctor, then to Fremantle Hospital, it wasn't looking good as the Craigs were due to fly home the next week. Barbara had some mysterious illness and wasn't going to be able to fly home with the rest of the family. David had to get back to his job and the bookings were firm, David made the hard decision to fly home with Bryan and leave Barbara and Jo-anna with us till Barbara was fit to fly.

Barbara left the hospital after David and Bryan had left for Northern Ireland but still wasn't that well and her illness was still a mystery. She told us she would need further tests when she returned home, I had a feeling she wasn't being straight with us and she knew more than she was letting on. I didn't push things and soaked up the time I had with my sister to myself, a lovely time. Barbara took us out to dinner before she returned home as a thank you for having them, it was unnecessary as the pleasure had been all ours.

It was a good time later we were told by letter that Barbara had M.S. -multiple sclerosis – I was shocked but knew my feeling had been right, and she had been hiding the truth from us. I had visions of my sister in a wheelchair and turning into a vegetable, but still, I knew that if anyone could fight this dreadful disease my sister could. I still had sore shins from our childhood battles.

As if I didn't have enough to worry about, business in the black-board writing wasn't exactly going from strength to strength, it was hobbling and in survival mode at best. I took up the West Australian newspaper one Saturday morning and found, in the centre a two-page spread of part-time tertiary education courses. And there it was down nearly at the bottom of the second page, Signwriting, this was what I'd been looking for and didn't know it. I had a cheque in the mail and was attending my first class within a fortnight. Yes, I'd done the ticket writing course by correspondence all those years ago but this was the real thing, this could add to my blackboard writing.

In all honesty, it wasn't the real thing, it was a part-time course for sad people with nothing to do with their lives and thought that learning to paint signs would enrich their lives. I didn't fit into the mould, I went to these classes to learn how to write signs, I wanted another string to my bow and knew it fitted perfectly into what I was already doing. I got on, really well with the tutor who knew without me telling him that I was working in the field in some way. He was young and enthusiastic and doing this tutoring as an income boost, I was much older, equally as enthusiastic and doing this to boost my income.

I was a model student, I bought the right brushes, I bought the right paints and I went home and practised and practised. I made a maul stick - I knew Anne's knickers would come in handy for something one day. You're wondering what a maul stick is, aren't you? It's that stick that signwriters use that appears to have a boxing glove on the end of it, it's to keep your hand steady. I bought a chalkline and practised with it, I'd found my niche.

82 AND SO THIS IS CHRISTMAS

By Christmas, I was painting my first signs, well they weren't mine, they were the signs paid for by my clients. I wasn't very good but had now done two terms at tech, albeit one night a week. I went on to do a third term but it had become a waste of time, I'd learnt all I could learn in the classroom and doing work in the field was the best learning I could do.

Even with another string in my bow, things weren't going the best. I was earning enough to keep our heads above water but got knocked around when Julie-Anne's school fees came due or the rates had to be paid. Anne, from time to time mentioned getting a 'proper job,' it was something that got up my nose but I knew she had a point. By July 1994 things had gotten pretty bad, we had twenty-seven dollars in the bank and no mattress money left. I had more work than I'd had at the same time the previous year but lacked that mattress money.

With twenty-seven dollars in the bank, I couldn't draw a cheque to give Anne the housekeeping, I couldn't tell her how broke we were, but I'd just done a reasonably good job and got the cheque for it. I banked the cheque and drew the housekeeping, if that cheque had bounced we would have been overdrawn and in trouble with the bank. That was how my mind worked back then, in real terms we would have got by on our credit cards, but the thought of a credit card debt scared me.

This was the last time I would get so low, from that day on things took a turn for the better. For almost eighteen months I'd been out every day touting for business and now it seemed to be coming to me.

All the business cards I'd put out now appeared to be getting read, I was also getting business by word of mouth and being seen working. My signwriting was improving with every job and I was doing blackboard menu boards at a constant rate. It was time to get our tax returns up to date.

I hadn't lodged a tax return for two years, mostly because I didn't want to pay our accountant his exorbitant fees. I presented myself at the accountant's office and was treated – I thought at least – like some dirt off the street. I'd been with this accountant for over twenty years and didn't like my treatment or his bill. I was pleasantly surprised to discover I had to pay tax, that seems a strange statement but I knew if you were paying tax, you were making money.

It would be the last tax return, that accountant would do for us, my mate Brian Goodall had set up his own accountancy business a couple of years earlier and was going to get our business in future. Not that we were going to make him rich, but we would at least have an accountant who cared. I'd put off moving over to Brian as he was fifty and going out on his own for the first time, I felt fifty was a bit old to be going into business for the first time. Brian was to prove me wrong.

By Christmas 1994 I was doing lots of signs, Christmas signs were good business, especially with butchers. I got on well with butchers and enjoyed working for them, we spoke the same language and were equally course. The other good source of business was liquor stores and drive-through liquor stores attached to pubs. These businesses changed their signs either weekly or monthly advertising their liquor specials. Pubs, in general, were not thriving businesses back then, but their drive-through liquor shops were and so most of their business was focused on the drive-throughs.

What had started as a very scratchy operation was now showing signs of success, the regular work that I started with remained intact and I was growing that side of things too. I'd known that without regular work what I was doing wouldn't be viable and always pursued that avenue. The one-off jobs were usually good money but without regular work, it would be all stop-start. It was around now that my business cards were kept in my pocket and people had to ask me for one.

Each Christmas, my business seemed to grow, since my first days on the milkround I'd found Christmas to be a magic time of the year. There's goodwill in the air and people are prepared to spend, in business people are prepared to spend to make money and that's where I came in.

It was the Christmas of 1996 that I got a call from Joel Grossman, a butcher client who had sold his business and was now working for a butcher in the Herdsman Fresh Essentials building The butcher wanted a Christmas sign Joel told me, I paid a visit and got the work. I was very impressed with the Herdsman Fresh Essentials set-up and the blackboards they had there, I could see my scribble on them the moment I saw them.

A week later I got a call from Dennis Cerenich asking if I could paint the windows at the Herdsman Fresh Essentials for Christmas, the answer was, "Yes." Although I was painting the windows I was besotted with their blackboards, they had a picture of the trader on one side and an unused blackboard on the other, these blackboards had been waiting for me. As I was being parsimonious with my business cards I didn't pursue the issue, I just dreamed.

When I'd finished painting the windows I was asked if I'd return in January to clean them off, I always factored the cleaning of the windows into my price so it was no chore. During my time painting the windows, I met the marketing girl at Herdsman Fresh Essentials (What a mouthful.) she had recognised me from Phoenix Shopping Centre, where I still did work for the butcher and knew I did blackboard work, she'd worked at Phoenix after my time as a tenant there. This girl was waiting for me in January and asked if I'd like to write up their blackboards every week, again the answer was, "Yes."

83 BLOODY MOBILE PHONES

By the late nineties, mobile phones were the toy to have, I saw no need for me to have one, I could attribute this to my parsimonious nature. Since I'd started writing blackboard menus I always signed them 'Chalky 93373473,' my only advertising apart from those tedious tramps from business to business in the early years. Somewhere between having to write two extra numbers and the high cost of mobile phone calls, I resisted having a mobile phone much to the dislike of the odd client here and there.

Anne was my mobile phone, she must have covered miles, running to answer the phone for me. I must add, that Anne had a terrible telephone manner she simply picked up the phone and said, "Hello," as if it was her mother on the other end of the phone. Those sometimes breathless, "Hellos," seemed to work magic. I'd get home and cast an eye over the telephone messages and then be told exactly what they meant and exactly what the person who rang wanted. How Anne managed to get all the information out of clients I'll never know, but she did.

I think there was one exception, I got home this night in early 1998 and all Anne had was a mobile number and very scratchy information. For once she sounded a little disinterested, "This bloke rang about some blackboards, he didn't say much, only he's got a shop in Kalgoorlie," Anne related to me. The idea of having work in Kalgoorlie excited me a little, I'd done some for The Star and Garter, a pub up there but that bloke always contacted me from his home in Cottesloe, why was he calling from Kalgoorlie?

"It's a fucking mobile number, it better be good," I told Anne, we must both have gotten out the wrong side of the bed that morning.

"Hi, this is Tom Watson you rang my wife today about some blackboards," I spiel out.

"Do you make blackboards as well as write on them?"

"Yes," I reply – my telephone manner wasn't much better than Anne's.

"I'm in Kalgoorlie at the moment and we've got two shops up here we want blackboards in," the voice tells me.

'Who the fuck has two shops in Kalgoorlie?' I'm thinking.

"Look, I'll get the measurements tomorrow and call you back, is about this time alright with you?"

"Yeah, that'll be fine," I said, thinking at least I wouldn't have to ring him on his mobile again, I'd done enough money on this call already.

The next evening the phone rang, right at six our agreed time.

'Must be that bloke from Kalgoorlie,' I think to myself as I go to answer the phone.

"Hi, Tom Watson," I say as I picked up the phone.

"G'day, this is Eric from Coles, I spoke to you yesterday."

"Yeah, that's right," I stagger out.

'He was from Coles as in Coles supermarkets?' I think and I'd almost brushed him off.

"I've got those measurements I promised you, you got a pen ready?"

"Yeah, no worries," he goes on to give me the blackboard sizes.

"I'll get a bloke to ring you and you can meet up and work out what we want on them."

"Do you want a written quote?" I ask.

"Not really, but you can do one if you want, just tell us what they're going to cost, you've got my number haven't you?"

I spent the next day wondering what the hell was going on, a two-bit signwriter/blackboard writer working out his back shed in Hamilton Hill was getting a call from Coles supermarkets to do blackboards for them. I convinced myself that I wouldn't get the job, but at least I could give it a go. I got the call from the 'bloke' to meet up, "Can we meet at Southlands Shopping Centre?" the bloke suggested.

"Yeah, that's fine with me."

"Tomorrow morning alright?"

"Yeah, I can do that, there's a coffee shop there that I did some work for, we could meet there. Espresso, it's called."

'Well at least I was getting a free coffee out of this,' I thought to myself as I sat down to wait for this 'bloke.' Got to hand it to these people, they're on time. My man goes on to tell me what they want my blackboards for, they're developing a new concept deli department with chicken, fish and coffee added to the older style deli departments. He talks and I write and grasp the concept, thanks to my retail experience I was able to talk a bit about retail and show that I understood what he was talking about. All I had to do now was do those first few boards for the Kalgoorlie stores and "we'll see how they go." He winds up.

I couldn't let him go without asking where they'd got my number from, "I think it was from that chicken shop over there," he indicated with a nod to Fenesse Chicken.

All I did there was a quick change board each week, nothing like the work I was being hired for with Coles.

I got my quote into Coles and it was accepted without question. I now had to make the boards they ordered and write and draw them up. The sizes of these boards were stupid and were, obviously designed to fill empty wall space or something like that. Even though I'd had words from 'my man,' I still had to do some research for this job, mostly it was looking through the brochures they left in our letterbox each week.

I got those first few blackboards done and rang Eric.

"I'll send someone around to check them out and see how we go from there," Eric told me.

Another on-time appointment was kept, the man Eric sent around was the man I'd met in Southlands. I dragged the blackboards out of the shed one by one, I could hardly show them to him in the shed, it was a bloody mess and not showroom material. He seemed impressed, he took photos and told me, "The state manager is in California at the moment, I'll have to send these photos over to him and see what he thinks."

I wasn't sure what he'd think but I knew that I had a couple of weeks up my sleeve, as getting the photos developed and posted to America would take that long.

Just as I'd avoided mobile phones I'd also turned off my brain to any form of technology, after all, most technologies within the sign business competed with what I did. I didn't know about digital cameras, or heaven forbid the worldwide web. The boys at Coles did, two days later I was asked to drop the boards I'd done off at the Coles complex in Canning Vale and they'd put them on the truck for Kalgoorlie.

84 THIRTY YEARS IN AUSTRALIA

From the first few blackboards for the Coles Kalgoorlie stores work exploded, first was a new store in Forrestfield and then I just got calls from store managers around the state. I had to get into the system and find out how to get paid and then it was sweet. As far as I knew I was the only person doing this work for Coles and it was very easy going with no contracts or further quotes required. They seemed as easygoing as me, not a good sign for a business that controlled almost fifty per cent of the supermarket trade in Australia.

Although the work with Coles had become a major part of my business, I continued to service my established clients and worked into the night at times. Life was good and although I'd been self-employed since I was twenty-two, I'd never felt the freedom I was feeling in 1998. If I wanted a day off I took it and perhaps one day I'd be able to take a holiday. I had been working for myself for twenty-seven years and we'd had a long weekend in Busselton one Easter. Of my quick-change blackboard clients, a few were travel agents so I was reminded of holidays a few times every week, not that I knew much about them.

Since we met Harry and Ivy Robinson from Preston Patrick through their daughter Ada. I'd been writing to Ivy regularly and she kept me up to date with life in Preston Patrick. Every time they came to Australia to visit their daughter and their grandchildren we stole them for a day and took them out into the country somewhere. We had a ball, they seemed to like doing things with us and we got on really well.

Of course, after those days out we were asked that eternal question,

"When are you coming to see us in Preston Patrick?" I'd had no desire to return in my thirty years in Australia, Australia was my home. I had no excuse now, as I was free to do such things, Julie-Anne was all grown-up and yes we were free to go if we wanted. I always managed to think of some excuse and got off the hook till the next visit.

1998 was my thirtieth year in Australia and I felt it was some sort of milestone in my life, it was certainly proving to be a fruitful year. I decided to have a party to celebrate, at that time I'd never heard of anyone celebrating their time in Australia. When I put the invitations out announcing 'Tom's Thirtieth,' I got some strange responses and had to explain it was for my thirtieth year in Australia. It was a huge day for me, an emotional day, as Australia had been so good to me and who should be there but Harry and Ivy Robinson, to remind me of where I'd come from. And, of course, Harry and Ivy had that eternal question, "When are you coming to see us?"

After Christmas, that year Anne and I took a holiday, a week in Broome. We were both excited as we waited at the airport, we can see the planes on the tarmac. It's fair to say these planes aren't the latest model, Anne is looking to see our plane, "It's probably that one there," I tell her pointing to just any plane.

"I'm not going on that thing," an indignant Anne tells me.

I assure her it'll be fine and in no time we were off. Anne's first flight, my second, not sure who was the most nervous, neither of us openly admitted to their nerves but we held hands at take-off and landing.

As I said earlier, I didn't know much about holidays and here lies the truth, it's the wet season in Broome in our southern summer, luckily it didn't rain. Broome is not a compact little town, it spreads over miles and you need a car. To hire a car you need a credit card for a deposit, I had one but never hardly used it and didn't have enough credit on it to hire a car, I'd only got it to pacify a bank manager years earlier.

Here we were in Broome in the car hire office and unable to hire a car as my credit card wouldn't stretch that far. From memory, the deposit was a thousand dollars on your credit card or five hundred dollars in cash, I had the cash but they weren't getting their claws on that.

To say I was pissed off would be an understatement, no mobile phone either. It was back to the motel room for Mr Moodyman, 'I'll ring the bank and get this sorted,' I thought, Anne knew to remain silent. This must have been when you could still speak to a human at the bank, albeit a distant human, my bank no longer had a listed phone number.

The 'distant human' told me I would have to register for 'telephone banking,' a simple process if you could remember your mother's maiden name it seems. What they don't tell you is, that your mother's maiden name is your 'code word,' that you used when you opened your account some hundred and fifty years earlier. I juggled a few bucks and we got the car and we were able to holiday.

We had Broome to ourselves as nobody goes to Broome in the wet season, it was hot and muggy and you could create a litre of water with one cold beer. We did touristy things and even went to the outdoor cinema, the oldest in the whole world - I think. I wasn't sure going to the movies was a good idea as the movies on offer were less than spectacular. For once in my life, I had made a judgement that proved to be incorrect. We took our seats, they're deckchairy things - canvas over a steel frame – 'I've seen this frame before,' I thought, and yes, it's the same as the one we inherited when we bought the house. I'd put boards on ours and sit on it while having an evening lager. That was the first point of excitement for the evening.

The movie we were having to endure was crap and I was battling to keep awake, and then as I was thinking I should perhaps have draped our inherited outdoor movie chair with canvas as this one was very comfortable, it happened. QF something or other came in to land at Broome airport, lights ablaze and landing gear down. Broome airport is just over the back fence of the outdoor movie theatre. I reckon the landing gear of QF something or other missed the movie screen by a matter of inches. The movie I could have missed, but not that, that was spectacular.

Anne and I had enjoyed our first holiday together, we'd bathed on

Cable Beach and seen the mud flats of Town Beach, bought a tiny pearl and learnt about telephone banking. Best of all we'd watched a plane landing in the world's oldest outdoor movie theatre and we were ready to holiday again.

85 BECOMING AN AUSTRALIAN CITIZEN

After our Broome holiday, I determined to take the big step and return to England for a holiday, one day. Anne wasn't all that enthusiastic, but liked Harry and Ivy and thought if all Poms were like them it would be fine. I was in no hurry to return so no plans were made and the idea remained an embryo.

If Anne and I were to make the trip to England we would both need passports, Australian passports naturally. I looked into getting a passport and found I'd first have to become an Australian citizen. If ever anything got up my nose, the idea of having to apply to be a citizen of the country I'd lived in for over thirty years, this did.

Since my first day's work in Australia, I had felt Australian, the Halligans had taken me in and treated me as a fellow Australian. In no time at all, I felt that Australia was my home and I didn't want to live anywhere else. I paid my taxes – at least some of them – and I had taken very little from my adopted country, never stooping to draw on social security and here was my reward, I'd have to apply for Australian citizenship. I think the word 'apply' was what got up my nose. If I could have gone to some office in Perth and picked up a citizenship certificate, that would have been fine with me, but apply, no I'm still reeling.

Well, I had to go to that office in Perth to get the application form, and it felt like an interview, with a lady with a distinctly European accent. That felt like the last straw and withholding my feelings was very hard. I now had to get all my paperwork together to go in with the form, strangely, they didn't ask for my tax file number. Naturally, I exaggerate when I write 'all my paperwork,' as all I had was my Document of Identity that I got in England when I left, in place of a passport. There was probably my Marriage Certificate as the European-sounding lady thought I may have changed my name when I got married.

I'm not sure how long this lengthy process took but it came to a climax in June of 1999 in the City of Cockburn municipal offices. After being so frustrated by the process, I was so chuffed to be presented with my Certificate of Citizenship. Anne was so happy for me and Julie-Anne couldn't have cared less. Along with my certificate, I got a collection of tat, worthless coins and the like and a less than, cold beer. No Australians I know have to have a citizenship certificate, but I do. Even with my new certificate, I didn't feel any more Australian and I still get called a Pommie bastard from time to time.

I was now ready to apply for an Australian passport, but after the citizenship ordeal I was in no hurry and work was keeping me away from most things. Although I no longer had the work with Coles - it had faded away and their new deli idea hadn't worked as well as they'd hoped – I still had plenty of work.

Liquor stores were keeping me busy, most were signing up to 'buying groups' and had their specials signs repainted every month. This was good steady work and I shared this work with two other signwriters, they had been signwriting since Adam was doing apple tasting. I was the new boy on the block in what was a dying trade. The trade wasn't dying because there was no work but because no new boys were moving into it. Computers were being used where ever possible, but handpainted signs were still more economical when frequent changes were required.

The big news towards the end of 1999 was the Y2K bug, everything was going to come to a halt and aeroplanes were going to fall out of the sky when the clocks struck midnight on the 31st of December. I knew we'd be fine as we didn't have a clock with a striker, so it wouldn't affect us. My mind at this time was focused on what would be the end of the world as I knew it on the 30th June 2000. The Australian government in their wisdom was to introduce a Goods and Services Tax, on the 1st July 2000.

There was to be no more 'black economy' all invoices must be 'tax invoices' and my world was to end. Most of my waking hours were spent on how I could avoid this demon tax, there were to be tax inspectors on every corner and rorting of the system was impossible. All businesses must apply for an Australian Business Number (ABN.) and record all their business activity either monthly or quarterly.

I felt like handing back my newly minted Australian Citizenship Certificate, this was an invasion of my style of business. I think most small business people felt the same way, the scare campaign launched by the government was working a treat. The government, of course, called it something else but in my eyes, it was a scare campaign and we were all fearful of this new tax, I saw no benefit in this new system of taxation.

By the time June came around, I found this new tax system had an upside, I was being booked to change prices on blackboard menus everywhere. Of course, this work would have to be undertaken before 1st July and not subject to the new tax, I was onto a winner whichever way I looked. I was very busy and forgot to register for an ABN and just carried on. The thousands of tax inspectors never eventuated and life went on, it was very much like the Y2K bug.

When I did put my figures into Becksy for my tax return that year he registered me and I got an Australian Business Number and all my invoices became tax invoices. I soon discovered this new system was better than the old one, you paid your income tax in instalments and the GST you had to pay had been paid to you anyway. Another upside was the fact you were forced to see how your business was going every three months, as your Business Activity Statement was a brief profit and loss statement.

The Business Activity Statement or BAS soon became known as your Billy Bass and was simplified so that normal people could under-stand it. Yes, there were teething problems for some, but nothing that required a dentist. I can't comment on the 'black economy,' as I was never sure what it was.

86 A BOOKING

Now sleeping comfortably at night, it seemed like a good time to get our passports. I acquired the forms from the post office – I'm sure there's a good quid in passports for post office franchisees – my forms were handed over with a smile and post office franchisees never smile. For some time I'd taken a dislike to forms, for some reason they seemed to be more difficult than in former years. It wasn't so much answering the questions, it was understanding the questions. I fought my way through the minefield of these forms and got photographs identified the whole shebang, I thought.

Off to the post office with everything intact, I felt quite proud of myself. Today the post office franchisee wasn't smiling, (I call them franchisees because they are, the old Postmaster/mistress are long gone.) he said two words, "Blue pen."

"What's wrong with that?" I promptly replied.

"It's got to be filled out in black pen, it says so on the front page."

"You're taking the piss," I charm him.

Now, I think I mentioned that these franchisees are not into humour, and my retort was not treated as humour and the thought of filling out these forms again in black pen didn't augur well with me. I could now see that I'd have to grovel to get a couple of new forms, I got the new forms but won't confess to grovelling. What really, pissed me off was the fact that I used a black pen for most of my letter writing and invoice writing, why I'd picked up a blue pen for these forms remains a mystery. Why I didn't read the instructions on the first page? Must be obvious to any man, we never read instructions.

My second effort was accepted by the post office franchisee with, I suspect a wry smile, he'd pulled the blue pen trick before, I could see it in his eye. He took the forms and told me I'd have to make an appointment for an interview, with him. Perhaps I should mention now that most post office franchisees, have English as a second language, my man was no exception. This interview seemed to take a few seconds and consisted of some dumb question, it seemed pointless to me.

Sometime later we got a message from the post office to say we had some registered mail to pick up.

'What the hell can that be?' I thought, 'Maybe something valuable, that I've been sent.'

Well, it turns out it was valuable, it was the first of our passports and they don't come cheap. They must have known we were a bit short as the passports came in instalments, Anne's and then mine.

The trip to England was now looking like a reality, there would have to be months of planning and the decision on an airline was a major consideration, could we afford it? I assure you that there was no such planning or preparation.

One Monday morning when I was doing my quick change boards, I landed at Thornlie Square shopping centre where I did a travel agent's blackboard each week. The special that week was Singapore Airlines to England (It was probably to the U.K. but I never use that.) I finished the board and got my money and said to Lesley – the travel agent – "I'll have some of that, it's a good price isn't it?"

"Yes, it's a brilliant price." She tells me. I go out to the van and get my chequebook and the deal is done.

On my arrival home that night, I break the news to Anne. I'm sure the consultation process was mentioned, and would the dates I'd chosen fit in with anything that could be thought of, and what about Julie-Anne? In the end, Anne was happy and suitcases would need to be purchased and clothes arranged and what would the weather be like? Well, it's now I come in with my superior knowledge of the British climate.

"We're going in June, it's summer in England in June, we'll only need summer clothes." I brazenly put forth as I remember the English summers of my youth. Perhaps the memories of my youth were not as vivid as I thought they were. There was a degree of anxiety creeping into my mind about this trip, how would I be greeted by these people I hadn't seen for thirty-three years? Had I made the right decision? We got on well enough with Harry and Ivy Robinson, but in all honesty, I had never known them very well in England.

I had booked this holiday in February so had plenty of time to organise things. First I wrote to my older sister Marion, advising her of my intentions and hoping we could stay with her. Next, I informed Ivy, the letters, between Ivy and me, were the most regular letters I wrote, mostly because Ivy was a prolific letter writer. There was no need to inform anyone else as both Marion and Ivy belonged to the Women's Institute, an effective means of broadcasting news in Cumbria.

As seasoned travellers – we'd been to Broome for a week – Anne and I were well at sea. Our experience in Broome told me I'd have to organise money. I sent Marion a cheque in good time so she could get it cashed for when we arrived and ordered some English money from the bank. The English money we got was in fifty-pound notes, little did I know how much fun I could have with them.

'nearer and nearer draws the time, the time that surely be.' The words of Arthur Campbell Ainger ring in my ears as I write. My days as a choirboy may not have been, totally wasted. I prepared my regular clients for my impending absence from their lives and we were ready to go, seems they weren't going to miss me anyway.

87 UP, UP AND AWAY

As Anne and I sat on the plane waiting for take-off, our hands reached out and touched to calm our nerves for when this big bird would take off. My head was full of excitement and apprehension. Excitement because I knew the meals were going to be fantastic, I knew this as I'd read an article in the travel pages of the Sunday Times reporting that much had been done with the catering on Singapore Airlines. I was already hungry.

The apprehension related to how this Prodigal Son would be received on his return to the Promised Land. I seem to be getting religiously entwined, quoting from hymns and drawing on parables, when I'm not religiously inclined. This may have come about after I remember writing to Marion saying that I expected a veal roast, referring to, of course, the fatted calf in the said parable.

As lunch draws close we're given a menu, my excitement now starts to wane, not much I fancy, I'll go chicken, 'they can't stuff up chicken,' I thought. I was wrong, the first meal I was presented with on my flight to Australia was picked over by me because I didn't recognise any of the food, it was ten times better than the much-vaunted food on Singapore Airlines, thirty-three years later.

What a small pond I'd been living in, we landed in Singapore, to find that the airport is massive and we have to change planes and negotiate a proper airport. Our eyes were opened but rapidly closing as tiredness was starting to set in. I'm sure our next stop was Amsterdam, a long haul but we could look down on Europe as we travelled, barely a square inch of land uncultivated.

The final leg, Amsterdam to Manchester, if it was a long haul from Singapore to Amsterdam, I'll swear this was longer. Anne was bored and I was running on emotion, I was almost home. Across the North Sea and flying over, 'That green and pleasant land.' Nostalgia is flowing over me as I quote William Blake, a hymn from my childhood, will it run true, from the plane it appeared to.

We land at Manchester Aiport and get through customs with so much ease I realise I should have brought some drugs with me. Marion has me organised here, I'm to go to the railway station - there's one in the airport – and buy two return tickets to Penrith as they're cheaper than one-way tickets to Oxenholme, our destination. This sounds complex but I trust my sister and we, literally walk onto the train waiting at the station.

This has all been far too easy, I now feel we're travelling in the wrong direction. This is my third train journey in England so I'm something of a veteran of British train travel. Since my first journey, they seem to have moved from steam to electric and that green and pleasant land I'd seen from the plane has turned to a dirty grey and unpleasant land. We travel through every dirty grey town and city in England before I see to my right, more grey, the grey of Farelton Knott. I now know that the train was heading in the right direction, Milnthorpe and then Oxenholme.

The train draws to a halt and there's an announcement telling us there'd be a slight delay. A slight delay? From where we are stopped I can see my sister's house – I presume I can, I've never seen it before – Natland Church is down there. I could get off this train and walk across the fields to Marion's house. The slight delay seemed to last around two hours and we finally pull into Oxenholme station, a mile further along the line.

I'm supposedly a native of this green and pleasant land, yet I had never set foot on the side of Oxenholme station we find ourselves on. My travel director (Sister Marion.) has me covered, she has sent me a telephone card that I can use to ring brother-in-law Fred, she realises I won't have any small change. Fred promptly picks us up and takes us home, Fred has lost weight and some of his hair. "Sit down." Says Fred as soon as we enter the house. We are served sandwiches made with homemade bread and a pleasant cup of tea.

Marion has an accountancy practice in Kendal and is still working, Fred has taken 'early retirement,' something I don't understand but don't question. Fred is the perfect host and shows us our room and makes small talk. It's very nice, but lonely without the sister I haven't seen for thirty-three years. When Marion arrives home there are no big hugs and kisses, just a hello and we start to talk as if I'd last seen her the day before, strange some may think, but for us, it was all we needed to reunite.

After a day in her office, Marion makes tea, not a veal roast but something good and hearty and dessert to die for. No sooner was tea out of the way than I'm starting to realise that it doesn't get dark here at seven o'clock. Marion has washed up with - I'm guessing - Anne's help (She rarely misses an opportunity to wash up.) and comes into the loungeroom and asks me, "Do you want to come for a drive?"

"Yes." I joyfully reply.

There was no discussion as to where I'd like to go, we just got in the car and Marion drove, giving a running commentary as we travelled, it was Japanese to the rapidly tiring Anne. It was music to me, hearing my sister's voice again and she just drove where I wanted to go. The first stop was Ivy Garth, the home I'd left behind thirty-three years earlier, it looked much the same. The current owners were outside and spoke to us, mostly Marion, they were having a coffee morning for the Church on Saturday, and I was cordially invited. Coffee mornings were one of my favourite pursuits and was quickly forgotten.

We continued on, through Millness, Milton and passed the Greenhouses that were no more, we must have backtracked somewhere and we took the old school route to Endmoor. Just as we approached Tommy Fletcher Field, (Yes, they'd named the bowling green after my childhood hero.) a white Toyota ute flew passed heading down to Low Cottages.

"I think that was Linda Beck." Said Marion, "Do you want to see her? She lives down at Low Cottages somewhere I think."

"Bloody oath," I reply.

I'm not sure Marion was familiar with 'bloody oath,' but she stopped and I got out of the car and ran down to Low Cottages and approach the house with the white Toyota parked outside.

"Get off my stones, you bloody idiot."

"You don't remember me, do you? You cried when I left for Australia."

"I bloody didn't." Is the swift retort, "Who are you anyway?"

"I'm Thomas Watson, I worked for your dad at Cox Bank."

"Bugger me, Thomas Watson, my dad reckoned you were the hardest worker he ever knew, come in and I'll ring him before he gets too pissed. He won't believe this."

Linda duly rings Jack and we have difficulty communicating as Jack can't understand my Australian accent. He puts his wife Ann on and we agree to catch up on their day back in the area, they now live in Ulverston. Linda and I are instant best friends, but I have to explain that Marion is waiting for me and I must get back to the car.

I not only had to get back to the car, I had to get back to bed, that was nothing, Anne must also have been bamboozled and tired beyond belief and she had been given little or no consideration by me. This had suddenly become my trip and no one else mattered.

We go to bed on our return to Fred and Marion's house and sleep, in my case to quote Harry Chapin, 'Till the daybreak comes around.' I don't disturb Anne and step outside. On the doorstep are two cans of Foster's lager, I immediately thought someone had been thinking of me. I later discovered it was Fred's way of keeping his beer cold, refrigeration will be exposed to these people in time.

It's fair to say, I was champing at the bit by the time Marion and later Anne rose from their slumber and breakfast was partaken of. I had plans, we'd catch the bus to Gatebeck Lane End and walk down to Ivy Garth and on to the Church and drop in and see Dennis Atkinson and Stephen Hunter who both had petrol-related businesses in Crooklands.

Anne was expected to go along with my plans and, of course, willingly did.

As we head out for the bus, a white Ford Transit van stopped in the middle of the lane to the bus stop. I should point out that finding the middle of the lane isn't difficult as it's only one vehicle wide at the widest point. A brown uniformed, balding Richard Berrie jumps out and spreads his arms and says, "Bloody look at you, in your shorts in this weather, you haven't got much smarter in Australia have you?"

"What happened to you, you fat bastard, you've whittled down to nothing?" Was my rapid reply.

"I can't bloody believe it, Thomas Watson wandering around Natland in shorts, what's wrong with you, man?"

"There's bugger all wrong with me."

"Where are you going?" Asks Richard.

I explain my plan and he tells me he'll give us a lift, I introduce Anne and she gets a hug and we just talk. "Sorry I can't make your do on Saturday but I've got to work," Richard tells me. I think Marion had shown me a letter from Richard explaining he couldn't attend something on Saturday, but my head was a blur. 'What's this do on Saturday?' I think as we drive.

"Want to do lunch? We'll be at the Crooklands Inn about lunchtime." I advise Richard as we draw to a halt. He rings his wife and we're all set for lunch, he has work to do and we part and take the walk I'd planned. No sooner had Richard dropped us off than the white Toyota ute of Linda Beck fame pulls up and offers us a lift, I decline as I want to soak up this land of my birth.

We wander through Goose Green, passed Aunty Bell's house and on to Kaker Mill and then to Church and the Churchyard full of dead people I once knew, Anne is lost in all my nostalgia. We go down to Dennis Atkinson's garage and caravan park. This was once Steve's home, Crooklands Garage, but things change it seems. We enter the once-upon-a-time shop and meet Dennis' front-of-house lady with her one tooth and I'm directed to his workshop come office, there's a, "Look at thi." And years drift away.

I'm sent to surprise Dennis' wife Sandra, Harry and Ivy's daughter, she's front-of-house at the adjoining caravan park. She's a little slow to answer my call and I tear strips off her for bad service, she hasn't recognised me and starts to get all apologetic. I identify myself and get an "Aw, you bugger," and a hug, laughs all around, except Anne who feels I'm embarrassing.

The next stop is Bobbin Mill Garage, Stephen Hunter's petrol-related enterprise. Steve is oiled up and overalled, a big handshake and apology as his hands aren't the cleanest. No apology is required from this lanky bespectacled old friend, "When did you arrive? Have you seen Dennis yet? Fuck, it's good to see you, is this your wife? Sorry about that."

Had I been on my best form I would have told him Anne was some shelia I picked up on the plane, but obviously, I wasn't on my best form. After too little banter, I look at my watch and explain we're meeting Richard for lunch at the Crooklands Hotel, a hundred yards away.

"Richard, I haven't seen him since – it must be since you left for Australia – you kept that quiet didn't you? We all wondered where you'd gone, we must catch up one night. Give my regards to Richard, it'll be good to see him again."

Anne and I descended on the pub, I hadn't been in this pub for over thirty-three years, and I didn't remember it. Thankfully Richard had just pulled up in the carpark and knew his way around, we get to meet his wife, luckily it wasn't the one I'd met before as I wouldn't have remembered her name. We meet Gill, a rather attractive woman, who is, obviously, younger than Richard and short-sighted, she could have done much better.

Our lunch becomes a huge question-and-answer session as you can expect when two best friends catch up after losing contact over thirty years earlier. It was mainly aimed at my life as Richard had been divorced and remarried and surely there would be some sensitivity involved. Nevertheless, we heard Richard and Gill's love story and were the richer for it.

What a morning I'd had, I'd caught up with three old friends and nothing much had changed as far as our relationship went, we were still good friends and we spoke the same language, in that we were all self-employed. Dennis and Steve had done apprenticeships so had a trade, Richard and I had been lowly labourers and here we were just as good as the grammar school boys.

I don't remember our return to Natland, but I had had a call from Jack Beck, they'd be over this way tomorrow and would take us out for the day. I had to return the call and confirm, again I got Jack and he had accent troubles but I got through to Ann. They were to pick us up in the morning, I couldn't wait, Jack and Ann were two of the last people I said goodbye to all those years ago, sadly they were no longer at Cox Bank, the farm where I'd been born.

It was the night before I'd discovered I was born at Cox Bank as Marion had given me my Birth Certificate, the first time I'd seen it. She gave me some other stuff too, probably things that she found when Dad died, nothing meant more than my Birth Certificate and finding I was born at Cox Bank.

Sleep wasn't hard that night, perhaps going to bed before it got dark seemed a little unusual, this country was strange in that regard. And cooling beer on the back step, that was weird.

88 A REUNION OF SORTS

The next morning I rose early and ventured out alone, I would have loved to have climbed up the Helm, a hill of bracken that overlooks Natland and has views forever. Sadly Britain was just recovering from a Foot and Mouth Disease epidemic and wandering over farmland was prohibited. My only other choice for a walk was the lanes of Natland, abit flat and boring but sang out 'green and pleasant land.' My walk took me to the Lancaster-Kendal canal, a playground of my childhood a few miles to the south.

I'd wandered miles of this kind of lane in my youth and never seen a wild rabbit. On this stroll, I saw dozens of the little bastards and they showed no fear of me, God this land had changed, and not for the better. I returned to Fred and Marion's and hadn't seen a soul, it seem they don't get up early enough to see the rabbits or breath the air. I'm in time for breakfast with Marion, Anne and Fred are still in bed.

Once we're organised for our day with Jack and Ann, we get a call from Jack Beck, he can't find Marion's house, I think Fred gave him directions. Seeing Jack and Ann again after thirty-three years was great, but they weren't the young couple I'd left behind. Jack drove us to all the right places and Ann and Anne got on like a house on fire, we lunched at the Crooklands Inn and were duly driven back to camp. A lot was talked about and we had visited their youngest daughter, who was merely a bump in Ann's belly when I'd left.

Things were happening in the Thornton household that Friday afternoon to which I wasn't privy. The first thing was the arrival of my sister Barbara and husband David from Northern Ireland, familiar faces for Anne as they'd visited us. I now had two sisters on my case and they had plans for me, whether I liked it or not.

In the evening, I meet for the first time my two English nieces, Anna-Marie and Alison. These girls are Fred and Marion's daughters and look at me as if I'm an exhibit in a zoo, or it was how it felt. I had been writing to Anna-Marie since she was fifteen and she was now all grown up with a husband. We circled each other a couple of times before we spoke, we knew each other so well from our letters but had never seen each other in the flesh. It was a strange but beautiful experience.

I hadn't yet experienced jetlag, as one is expected to after a long air journey but I was on a high and couldn't get down. My sisters had had their heads together and it is obvious that the coffee morning at Ivy Garth had been discussed. If ever something could bring me down from a high, it would be the idea of a coffee morning for the Church, but it didn't. I wasn't keen, but I went along with Barbara, David and Anne to be bored out of my brain at a Church coffee morning.

On our arrival at Ivy Garth, I noticed a red carpet had been laid from the front gate to the front door - I may have exaggerated there - it seemed that way. I was, after all, a Prodigal Son from the Church, of some long-standing. My fame flew through people I couldn't remember and some I could. This was another time for Anne to be at sea, even though a Church coffee morning was more her thing than mine.

As I flitted through the few I remembered and was remembered by the few I didn't remember, Anne had been drawn aside by an older lady and was off my radar, I hoped she was alright. As my fans dispersed, Anne brought her newfound friend to meet me, it was none other than my Aunty Bell, from whom we'd – the Watsons – been estranged for over forty years. If I wasn't a Prodigal Son, there was little doubt that I was a prodigal nephew, a light in the life of a lovely old lady, it was love at first sight.

"It was a long time ago and best forgotten." They were the words that summed up the long estrangement and were softly spoken as I walked Aunty Bell home arm in arm. The others would pick me up later and marvel at my charm, few have ever marvelled at my charm!

By now I'm aware that Marion has plans for Saturday afternoon, a reunion of sorts I'd been told. I hadn't been consulted about the guest list, but it is obvious that Marion had put in a lot of work assembling a wide array of my old friends and acquaintances, I'm sure writing longhand to many, if not all.

As I nervously await the arrival of my guests, Marion tells me that Percy Bryers visits the people over the road every Saturday afternoon.

"You wanted to see Mrs Bryers didn't you?" she asks, "Percy just pulled up now, you can catch him now if you want."

I did want to see Mrs Bryers and dashed over the road to see Percy. In brash Aussie style, I approached Percy and told him I was a student of Mrs Bryers and wanted to see her. Percy didn't know me from a bar of Burford's and was a little taken aback, I was probably the only student of Mrs Bryers who ever wanted to see her again. Percy told me she was in care and the name of the place and thanked me for my interest.

As I leave Percy I see my two old friends from school striding across the road to Marion's house, Stephen Hunter and Dennis Atkinson, Dennis has his wife Sandra in tow, and Steve is alone.

"We meet again tha old bugger." Is Dennis' greeting.

I can see this is going to be a good afternoon as we four walk into the house. 'Marion has been magic from the moment I arrived and has invited all the right people.' I think as we settle in. The conversation is boisterous and other guests start to arrive, the tone lowers as these guests were probably people I wouldn't have invited. Even so, it's a reunion for them as they haven't seen each other for a while, this is good as I have nothing in common with these other people and they're entertaining each other.

"Where's Richard?" Asks Steve as he notices the obvious absentee. I explain he's working and puts work before pleasure.

Anne has latched on to Sandra and they talk about her mum, I'm approached by a woman I'd never seen before. This is difficult as she knows me, Marion elbows her way in and advises me that it's Jennifer Robinson from Dove House. I have my doubts as this woman is a vivacious being and the Jennifer Robinson I knew was rather dowdy and had thick reddish plaits, at least one guest I wouldn't have invited had changed for the better, she was a delight.

I could probably quote from Robbie Burns, but won't. Marion had indeed been a caring and thoughtful sister concerning my visit to the country of my birth, but this reunion wasn't the best idea. It went alright but some there hardly remembered me and if they did we had grown very much apart, never mind she could handball me to sister Barbara for a couple of days. At least Barbara didn't have plans for me.

89 THE SABBATH

Sister Barbara may not have had plans for me but she wanted requests from me, what did I want to do? Well, with Sunday on the horizon, I had the strongest desire to go to Church, I hadn't been to Church since Julie-Anne's First Communion and that didn't count as Church in my book. I had the strongest desire to attend Preston Patrick Church, where I'd served as a choirboy all those years ago. Barbara and David had been married there and also had a desire to return to the Church of their vows.

I think we were running a little late and all was still in the Churchyard, as we entered the Church, they'd been tipped off that the Prodigal Son was to be there. I was welcomed by the Churchwardens, Jean Clark (I'd known her as Wilson.) and Tony Mason my fellow choirboy and conspirator on matters sexual in primary school. Jean had grown richer by marriage, and Tony had grown a beard and more serious. Handshakes and hugs were in order.

We found a pew that wasn't taken and made all the right moves, we saw Ivy Robinson and waved as you do in Church. I opened my hymn book and found it void of all the hymns I'd mouthed as a child, 'What the fuck have they done in my absence?' I thought.

This was not the Church service I was expecting, and the Vicar used a microphone, it was all foreign to me, but I was in my Church. Barbara, David and I were welcomed in an announcement by the Vicar and stared at, that zoo exhibit feeling again came to mind. It was now time to start crying, the emotion had welled up and now it started to pour from my eyes. My eyes dried by the end of the service but only because I was dehydrated.

At the end of the service, Aunty Bell took possession of me and took great joy in showing off her prodigal nephew to the Vicar and all who had any degree of importance. Anne had found Ivy and was thrilled to have someone she knew to talk to, they both excelled in the field of talk. It seemed we didn't have time to dally, more plans had been made for us in the shape of a family lunch.

This family lunch would be the first time the Watson children had had a meal together in a very long time, and it was a first for the spouses. Marion was hosting this event and had put on the veal roast for the prodigal brother, she was simply marvellous and spared nothing for her brother. I now wept every time I spoke her name, she couldn't do enough for me, I felt a little embarrassed by her kindness because I knew I could never repay it.

Barbara and David were keen to take us back to Northern Ireland, but they had had a flat no from me, I'd come to see the country of my birth, not a foreign land. Anne was more forthcoming and had given a feeble nod to acceptance, she, after all, would be with people she knew.

"What do you want to do tomorrow?" Barbara asks as they leave for their hotel.

"I'd like to go on the Ravenglass and Eskdale railway," I advise Barbara.

"O.K. then."

The deal is done and we part, why I'd gone for the miniature railway is now beyond me but I did, we'd had a school excursion there with Mrs Bryers and I'd never worked out why, as Mrs Bryers' excursions always had an educational angle to them. I couldn't for the life of me find the educational angle to that excursion.

Monday brings with it misery, in the shape of English weather. English weather is not like Australian weather, it's not black and white, it's grey and the most miserable shade of grey imaginable. It doesn't rain, it half rains and it's reliably cold for someone who wears shorts in summer. It is not the kind of weather for visiting the Ravenglass and Eskdale railway. The day was a disaster, and I still don't know why anyone would want to go on the Ravenglass and Eskdale railway. There was one positive, could I call it a glimmer of sunlight on a grey day? It brightened my day at least, there was a pallet of jarrah sleepers from Western Australia waiting to be laid during winter maintenance, which gave me a touch of homesickness.

Barbara and David have now kidnapped my wife and left me to my own devices, this should be a release for Anne as she doesn't have to be dragged around to boring places by me. I on the other hand am free to do the stuff I want to do on my own.

My first move is to catch the bus to Endmoor and retrace the steps of my youth, I now learn that the bus service isn't what it used to be. The steps of my youth are different too, the M6 motorway has carved a divide through the fields and lanes of my youth. You can go under or over the motorway, but the divide is still the divide. There is a constant drone in the stillness that wasn't there in my youth, the constant drone of motorway traffic.

I take the lane to Camsgill the farm I worked on for a couple of years of my life and discover it's no longer a working farm. It's a sad shadow with buildings demolished and an empty house to one day be the holiday home of some rich town dweller. I feel a twinge as there is a tug on my heartstrings.

On I go to Cox Bank, my birthplace and when I left, the home of the Becks, again this is no longer a working farm and a sad sight. The outbuildings have become homes to people who don't know I'm looking at their homes because they're not there. Some buildings that have been added by the Becks since my time, now lie empty and deserted. This is not what I came to see, this is not what I left behind, these places were alive when I left.

I spend the day just wandering around my old haunts and finding nothing, there is so little that hasn't been neglected or forgotten, and there's the drone of the motorway. Ivy Garth has changed, the whole of Goose Green has changed and the chestnut tree that shaded the letterbox where I posted my emigration papers has gone. Aunty Bell's bungalow has stayed the same and is, as always immaculate, she makes me feel proud.

My day hadn't exhausted me, but it had depressed me a little, I ponder in my head and wait patiently for the bus at the clearly marked bus stop, it's in huge letters on the road. I watch as a bus goes down Gatebeck Road and wonder why it's going that way when I'm at the bus stop it has bypassed. It's getting late, well five thirty and I don't want to be late for tea at Marion's, it would be ungracious as she has been so kind. I'd better give her a call, there's a phone box over the road, I get to the phone box and realise I've forgotten her number.

I now realise that I wasn't going to catch a bus and I'm going to have to walk back to Natland and make good time if I'm not to be late. I managed to get back to Marion's place in time for tea, I'm now knackered, the five-mile high-paced walk has taken its toll.

I had never seen Mum and Dad's last house in Ackenthwaite, Greycote they had named it and I felt sure it was – it seems strange to say this – their home, a house they had bought straight out without any encumbrances. It was a house that they chose to live in, unlike Ivy Garth which had been thrust upon them, it had been their house to live out their years in, and they did.

After over-exerting the previous day I determined to visit the house Mum and Dad had called home for their latter years. A bus to Kendal and then one to Milnthorpe, was by no means exertion and a stroll to Ackenthwaite eased muscles a little. I had no idea where this house was, other than Ackenthwaite, which in my day had been home to half a dozen houses, wouldn't be hard, surely. Since 'my day,' Ackenthwaite had grown somewhat, what in the sixties, had been a field was now all houses and Greycote was one of them.

I found the house without much difficulty and just stood and looked and could almost see Dad in the garden with one foot on his spade ready to turn the soil. I must have looked noticeably weird as the new owner asked if he could help me. With tears in my eyes, I blurted out, "This used to be my parent's house, I've never seen it before."

"Would you like to look over the garden and around the house?"

The new owner asked me, I think my moist eyes and slight Aussie twang got me in. We sat on a seat in the garden and the new owner droned on as tears poured from my eyes, I think he was a little embarrassed, I wasn't the least. I could see Dad's hand in this garden and knew, that when he was alive it would have been brimming with produce.

As I'd seen on my visits to Camsgill and Cox Bank, things weren't as they once had been, the world had moved on, and everything was different now. I should grin and bare it, after all, I'd moved on thirty-three years earlier and I was different too.

90 JOYCE AND OTHER THINGS

I had kept in touch with Richard and he, like me enjoyed a drink with friends on Friday nights. My Friday night drinks were in the back of the butcher's shop, and Richard's were at the Duke of Cumberland - a pub at the intersection of Shap and Appleby Roads. Fred had been elected to drive me into Kendal and pick me up, I think, again this was sister Marion in charge.

I entered a more than rowdy pub and found the noisiest group of drinkers and found my old friend in their midst. All these guys were drinking pints of beer – we in Australia had not yet graduated to pints – so I had to join in the merriment with a pint of lager. It was loud and raucous pretty much the same as our Friday night drinks at the butcher's but in a foreign language and in pints rather than our cans and stubbies. I had to call stumps before acceptances as I was full of lager and couldn't drink anymore. Richard called Gill and she drove me home, I'd had a good night and had had the chance to talk to Richard in a man-to-man manner, warts and all.

Saturday, again Fred was drawn in as my chauffeur, he was to drop me off at Mrs Bryers' nursing home. "Don't know why you want to go and see that old bitch," Fred said as we pulled up outside.

"She was the best teacher I ever had," I told Fred.

"It's not what I've heard," answers Fred, "I'll pick you up about half eleven, OK?"

"That'll be fine, thanks, Fred."

I enter the very nice nursing home and ask for Mrs Bryers, "Oh, Joyce, she doesn't get many visitors, are you a relation?" asks the nice lady. I explain I'm just an ex-student of hers as I'm taken to see Joyce in the common room.

I had seen Joyce a few times since my primary school days, as she used to buy flowers at Woodlands Nursery when I worked there. She was always very pleasant and not the ogress we thought her to be as a teacher. It had only been in later years that I discovered what a wonderful teacher she had been, she had been the last true teacher I had had at school, as I'd learnt nothing at secondary school of any consequence. What am I going to say? I've come here and I don't know what I'm going to say.

I'm directed to Mrs Bryers and she looks up and smiles. "Hello, Mrs Bryers."

"Hello, Thomas, it's so nice to see you, you wrote me a letter from Australia didn't you? You've done so well. Are you staying with Marion?"

We talked and remembered and we talked and I wondered, what this woman was doing in this place she didn't belong in here with all these brain-dead old women. The nurse happened to walk past as I was talking with Joyce and Joyce asked, "When's Percy coming?"

"He'll be here shortly Joyce." Comes the well-practised reply.

Another old lady pipes up, "He'll be here shortly Joyce."

I've had the best time with Joyce, and yes, she's now Joyce to me and she's so lovely and I have to leave as Fred is picking me up. As I leave, I'm thanked by the lady who directed me to Joyce and I hear in the background a feeble voice, "When's Percy coming?" Had what I'd just experienced been an apparition?

On Sunday morning I'm bundled into Fred's car with Marion, Anna-Marie and her husband Matt and off we go, I've no idea where we're going I just know we're going. Fred's into trains and stuff so when we spot a steam train travelling over a viaduct, photographs are taken and I think the day's over. It seems I'm wrong, we travel on and arrive in a Yorkshire Dales town full of cars. We have lunch in the Wensleydale cheese restaurant, where everything on the menu has cheese in it or on it, it's not unpleasant.

The town we're in, I discover it's Hawes, is full of cars because it's holding some kind of show, not an agricultural show, but a sort of fair with an agricultural flavour, it's brilliant. Where's Anne when you want her? I think this fair with an agricultural flavour is special because of the atmosphere, the country people have just been through the Foot and Mouth epidemic and this seems to be the time to let their hair down. I had my photograph taken with David from Heartbeat, a television show both Anne and I were fans of in Australia.

I knew I'd never be forgiven for going through the ordeal of this day without Anne. Although I'd had the best day, it broke my heart that I'd been unable to share it with Anne, I knew she would have loved it. I'm not sure whether this day had been organised by Marion for my entertainment or had just been a day of good fortune, one of those times when you're in the right place at the right time, it was a magic day.

On our return to camp, there is a message on the phone, that Anne would be returning from Northern Ireland earlier than planned as she was missing me. It would be fair to say, that I was missing Anne, and even more so after having a day out, she would have loved. Fred and I picked Anne up at Heysham on Monday evening, she had become desperately homesick and needed to ring her father. We had to organise that the next day, it would have been too much to expect to use Marion and Fred's phone.

91 MORE CATCHING UP

It was now time for me to do some organisation, not that I didn't appreciate the organisation Marion had done for me, but there were things that I wanted to do. The first cab off the rank was a catch-up with Steve, Dennis and Richard. It's amazing how easy it is to organise a men's do when alcohol is involved, three phone calls had us at the Crooklands Hotel with pint glasses waiting for our table in the dining room. What a night, Richard hadn't seen these two since I'd left for Australia and it seemed like it was only yesterday.

With that successful venture out of the way, it was agreed that we should repeat the process with our brides in tow. For this meeting, Dennis chose the venue, this was a little trickier as Gill and Anne had never met Steve's wife Pat or Dennis' wife Sandra - Anne had met Sandra once – would these ladies get on? Yet again, I'd pulled off a social coup and we blokes were cast aside to have gentle, quiet conversations while the ladies maintained their volume. A good time was had by all!

Enter the lady who got us to England, Ivy Robinson, Ivy had, to my surprise kept off our radar, we'd seen her at Church but not had much contact other than that. We knew we would be having a day out with Harry and Ivy but didn't know when. It was soon arranged as our social calendar by now, was full of vacancies. Anne had been looking forward to this day since the moment we landed and I wasn't averse to the idea of spending a day in the company of Harry and Ivy as we had done so many times at home, they were great company.

The day arrived for that much anticipated day out with Harry and

Ivy, Ivy picks us up in the Range Rover and we head back to Owert Field, Harry and Ivy's home. Harry had been completing his jobs on the farm. Harry asks if he can drive, I find this a little strange, but evidently, his eyesight wasn't the best. We are driven through the Yorkshire Dales and I relate my day in Hawes, and I think we visited there.

On returning to Owert Field we had to stop and disinfect the Range Rover, a reminder of the Foot and Mouth Disease that still hung over the farmers. I trailed after Harry as he did his 'jobs' and we returned to the house for tea. This meal was amazing, it was just like something my mother would have cooked, I can't remember what it was, but the flavours were just like my mother's cooking. We had, had the best day and Ivy's cooking brought back memories, what a wonderful gift these people had given me.

Ivy drove us back to Marion's place and the weather was sort of strange when we got back, this didn't feel like the weather we had slowly been coming to acclimatise to.

Heaven help us, the next morning we awoke to an English heatwave, we didn't realise it at the time and shipped ourselves off to Kendal. It was early afternoon when we wandered into the Westmorland Gazette shop – the Westmorland Gazette was the local newspaper – it seems strange that the local newspaper should have a shop, but they did. It was here we heard for the first time, people complaining about the heat, brows being mopped, clothes being shed and predictions of the end of the world. I will confess it was a little oppressive, but nothing special, at least to us, I think the temperature soared to the high twenties.

We had gone into the Westmorland Gazette shop to look for a present for Julie-Anne, we wanted something different. The heat of the day must have inspired us, we bought her a bag of Herdwick wool and a jumper pattern, Julie-Anne had inherited her Aunty Marion's knitting skills. We had come from the world's largest wool-producing country and here we are returning with a bag of wool as a gift. You couldn't get wool like this in Australia, in my wool handling days I would have called it 'fencing wire.'

There were two guests who couldn't make the reunion Marion had organised on our first Saturday - both due to work commitments – Richard Berrie and Frank Robinson. As you've read I caught up with Richard, but Frank had proved a little elusive, but Marion had kept in contact with him as he was one of her accountancy clients. I'd liked Frank, he was a simple bloke, a farmer who had disliked school a degree or two more than me, something I felt was impossible.

Frank invited us to lunch towards the end of our visit, as I'd had no contact with Frank and never met his wife I had no idea what to expect. Well, that's hardly true, as I knew exactly what to expect, an honest meal, honest company and a man who hadn't changed a lot, it's what we got. It was fantastic to see Frank, he was a constant, he was like Aunty Bell's garden and bungalow, he was like Kaker Mill, he was like the Church and yet his life was a work in progress. Frank didn't have a boring old farm, he had a farm, but he also had a fishing lake and tea rooms and an embryo of a garden centre. It was a joy to catch up with Frank, the last catch-up before we were to head home.

92 MY SECOND FLIGHT TO AUSTRALIA

As our return journey to Australia loomed large, I sought Marion's counsel as to the best way to get to Manchester airport. I got nowhere, I was told that Fred would drive us all down and I wasn't to worry about anything.

We went through all the procedures at the airport and it was time for us to leave for the departure lounge, time for farewells. The formal handshake with Fred, and the "Thanks, mate."

For Marion there was a hug, a real hug, Marion doesn't do emotion well, but there was a tear in both our eyes, "Look after yourself," she said. "Thank you, Sis, you've been the best, we'll be back." Anne and I wandered off to the departure lounge and the plane for our journey home.

This was the second time I would board a plane to Australia, the first time I had no idea what to expect when I landed. The land I was leaving was, in my eyes, changing. I'd now seen how it had changed and didn't much like it, all it held for me now was nostalgia and it was home to a few friends and relatives. This time I was boarding a plane and knew I was flying home to Australia!

www.ingramcontent.com/pod-product-compliance
Lightning Source LLC
Chambersburg PA
CBHW031220090426
42740CB00038B/209